CDT

PROJECTS AND APPROACHES

David Barlex
and
Richard Kimbell

MACMILLAN EDUCATION

First published 1986

Published by
MACMILLAN EDUCATION LTD
Houndmills, Basingstoke, Hampshire RG21 2XS
and London
Companies and representatives throughout the world

Printed in Hong Kong

British Library Cataloguing in Publication Data

Barlex, David
Craft design technology: projects and
approaches.
1. Design
I. Title   II. Kimbell, Richard
745.4   NK1510
ISBN 0-333-36620-4

CONTENTS

ACKNOWLEDGEMENTS

The authors and publishers would like to thank the following people who have helped in the preparation of this book:

Tony Gibbs of Helix Associates for information and most of the illustrations of the new post box
The Post Office for their cooperation in the post box project
The Ford Motor Company for information and illustrations of the Ford Sierra
Malcolm Johnston of Zygotec for information and illustrations of the Flexistand
The Design Council for much useful advice and for permission to reproduce the letters on pages 49 and 72
The University of Oxford Delegacy of Local Examinations for assistance with chapter 5.

The following examination boards have given permission for the use of questions from past examination papers:

Associated Examining Board (AEB)
Northern Examining Association for questions from the North Regional Examination Board (NREB)
The University of Oxford Delegacy of Local Examinations
Southern Universities Joint Board (SUJB)
University of Cambridge Local Examinations Syndicate

The authors and publishers wish to acknowledge the following photograph sources:

David Barlex pp. 71, 72, 73 (right), 76, 78, 79, 85, 86
British Steel Corporation p. 106
British Telecom p. 133
The Design Council p. 131 (right)
Directel Ltd p. 89
Ford Motor Company pp. 26–29, 97 (right)
Griffin and George p. 103
Alan Hutchison Library p. 73 (left)
Richard Kimbell pp. 34, 35 (left), 36, 37 (right), 38, 39, 63, 75, 80, 82, 96, 112, 116, 117, 118, 119, 128
LAT Photographic p. 13
Lego UK Ltd p. 97 (bottom left)
Lotus Cars Ltd p. 109

Meccano International p. 97 (top left)
National Trust p. 131 (left)
Neill Tools Ltd p. 115
The Pre-school Playgroup Association p. 47
Valerie Randall p. 108
Spear and Jackson Tools Ltd p. 114
Jim Turner pp. 6, 24, 25, 35 (right), 37 (left), 101, 124

The publishers have made every effort to trace the copyright holders, but where they have failed to do so they will be pleased to make the necessary arrangements at the first opportunity.

Designer: Nigel Partridge
Illustrations by Andrew Miller, Malcolm Stokes and Nigel Partridge
Cover design: Nigel Partridge

INTRODUCTION

This book is a guide to the design process. Chapter 1 describes how the process is used in industry. Chapters 2 and 3 show *you* how to use this process in your CDT project work. There are lots of examples of school projects carried out by students aged between 15 and 16 years. Chapter 4 gives information about the skills you need in using the design process.

Chapter 5 contains examples of examination answers. It will show you how to use the design process during CDT examinations. There is a large section of questions taken from recent CDT examinations. Your teacher will tell you which ones to tackle.

There are lots of other questions throughout the book. Answering these will focus your attention and help you towards greater understanding. You will need to use this book to answer those questions marked '**c**'. Those questions marked '**x**' require the use of extra materials. You will need to carry out outside observation to answer the questions marked '**o**'.

This book is not a textbook. It is a guide to the design process that will help you not only with your CDT project work, but with many other problems as well.

ONE

THE DESIGNER AT WORK

THE POST BOX

Have you ever wondered why post boxes in Britain look like this? You can see that the post boxes in France and America are quite different. The most common type of British post box is a large, heavy, cast-iron unit set into the pavement. It stands about head high and is painted bright red. In most countries post boxes are much smaller, usually fixed onto a wall and often painted yellow. They are also usually made of pressed metal sheet which makes them lighter and cheaper than the British box but also easier to damage and break into. Why do you think the British one is so different? Think carefully about how we use the present postal delivery system.

►Fig. 1 A typical British post box

▼Fig. 2 A French post box

◄Fig. 3 An American post box

1. The *customer* uses a post box to 'deliver' a letter or small parcel into the postal system.

2. The *post office* uses post boxes as collection points for these letters and parcels. They are collected in vans and taken to a central post office that covers the area in which the letter was posted.

3. The letters are sorted at the post office and sent by road or rail to the appropriate main post office of the town to which the letter is addressed.

4. Once in the right town a more detailed sorting divides the letters into the various streets and house numbers.

5. The individual postman takes a batch of streets and works his or her way round every house delivering all the letters to the right address. The postman's 'round' may take several hours.

Think about this procedure for the delivery of letters and small parcels and see if you can think of a way to eliminate the need for post boxes altogether. Any alternative system would have to work as well in country areas with a small, thinly spread population.

The Post Office in Britain has many thousands of post boxes spread all over the country. They require only a few new ones each year. In 1982 they installed 200 new boxes. Until very recently the boxes being installed were those designed in the 1950s and they are looking more and more outdated.

Towards the end of the 1970s the Post Office decided to commission a new design for the post box. The postal/delivery system was to stay exactly the same, but the post box was to be updated and improved.

The Post Office do not make their own post boxes; they are produced and assembled in Scotland by the Lion Foundry in Kirkintilloch. The manufacturers are not responsible for the DESIGN of the box, though. They merely produce it to the drawings they are given. The design of the box is the job of an INDUSTRIAL DESIGNER. On this occasion the Post Office chose Tony Gibbs of Helix Associates to do the design work.

Having chosen their designer, the Post Office contract manager spent a considerable amount of time talking to him so that they were both quite clear about what was required of the box and what exactly the designer's job involved. If the designer is not

◄Fig. 4

correctly directed (BRIEFED) by the client, problems will inevitably arise later on. It was made clear at the briefings that the basic nature of the post box (a large, free-standing structure set into the pavement) was to remain unchanged. The designer was to work within tightly defined limits.

▲Fig. 5 The first design briefing

Questions

1 Why doesn't the Post Office have its own team of designers and its own workshops for producing its products?

2 How many different post boxes can you find in your town? Draw them and identify the differences. Why do you think the changes were made? o

3 How many Industrial Designers can you find in your town? You can find them through *Yellow Pages*, the Design Council, or your local Chamber of Commerce. x

4 What other sorts of designers are there? Try to arrange to visit some to see what they do. o

RESEARCHING THE POST BOX

One starting point for the designer is to examine the existing post box in detail in order to identify any problems that it might have. Any problems that are identified can be noted and avoided in the new design. Some of the problems that were noted with the old design were:

1. The system for informing the public about the next collection is very poor. Loose numbers are slotted into a frame beside the word 'collection' which is cast into the body of the box. The postman has to have the right number available (in his pocket!) for each box that he visits. Also it is easy for vandals to break the numbers loose.

2. Whilst the size of the posting slot is just right for normal letters and packets, it is not possible to blank it off so that only slim letters can be posted. This might be necessary in the event of a letter bomb campaign. Also it is not possible to close off the slot completely. In some circumstances this is a great drawback.

3. The easiest way to move the boxes in the foundry where they are made and the warehouse where they are stored is by rolling them. The existing design rolls round in circles! It would be helpful if it could roll in a straight line.

4. The present box looks very dated. It does not give the impression of a modern, up-to-date postal service.

5. In a heavy storm, or in a high wind, rain can drip over the lower lip of the posting slot. This can result in letters getting wet as they are posted.

You can see that we have identified five problems. How many others can you think of? (For example what do you think of the layout of the information display panel?)

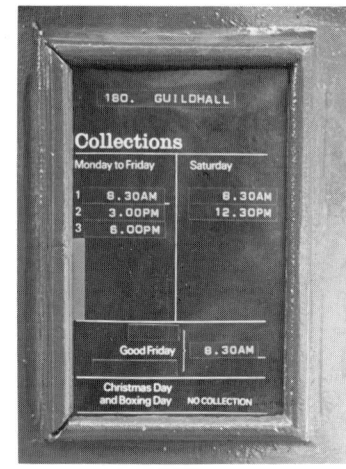

▶Fig. 8 Rain can easily wet the posting slot

▲Fig. 7 The collection number tells us when the box will next be emptied

◀Fig. 6 The collection number may be different in many boxes

Questions

1 Under what circumstances would it be useful or necessary to blank off a post box slot entirely?

2 How many times is a post box usually emptied in a day? Which days have most collections, which have least, and why? Why do some boxes get emptied more than others? ○

3 Why do post boxes always display the crown of the royal family?

4 Why does the existing post box roll round in circles when it is on its side? Measure a box and calculate how big the circle would be (i.e. what is the diameter of the rolled circle)? It might help you to make a scale model. **x**

5 What do you think is the purpose of the 'cap' on top of the existing box?

6 Watch a post box being emptied. Observe closely and note exactly how it is done. What problems does the postman have? Do you think it makes a difference if the postman is right or left handed? ○

7 What problems would result from a letter getting wet?

8 How does the design prevent anyone but the postman from removing the collection number?

DEFINING THE DESIGN BRIEF

After this careful observation of the existing box in use, and after further detailed discussion with the Post Office, Tony Gibbs prepared a fully worked out DESIGN BRIEF. This was a long and detailed document setting out all the identified problems that the designer had to solve. It covered all the points below and many more besides.

1. The posting slot has to be the right size and the right height above the ground.
2. The box has to be big enough to hold a specified number of letters and parcels.
3. The box must open and close correctly, be lockable and secure (i.e. no exposed hinges).
4. The box must be weather-proof, especially against the rain.
5. The information about collection times must be clearly displayed. The collection number must be easy to change by the postman (but not by anyone else).
6. The box must be easy to empty.
7. It must not be possible to 'fish' out letters from inside the box. Also they must not blow out in a very high wind.
8. The box must be vandal-proof (i.e. no easily breakable or removable parts).
9. It must be possible to seal off the box from large packages (letter bombs!) or from all packages.
10. The box must reflect the image of an up-to-date and modern post office. It must be attractive to look at, but at the same time must be immediately recognisable to the general public as a post box.
11. The box must display the heraldry of the royal family.

Questions

1 List the research that the designer would need to do in order to establish the important sizes (critical dimensions) for (1) in the brief. **c**

2 Design a simple questionnaire that you could use to find out this information. How many copies of the questionnaire would you need? Who would you give them to?

3 If you do not have the time to do your own research for these dimensions, where could you get all the information from? You could start by looking at the Design Council book list, or by writing to the Post Office. **x**

4 List some products other than the post box that have to be designed to reduce the effects of vandalism. Examine a specific product and describe how effective the design is against vandal attack. One example is a bank automatic cash dispenser. **o**

▲Fig. 9 The height of the posting slot has to be thought about carefully

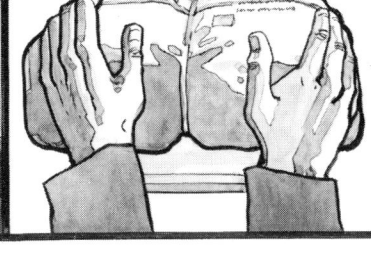

▲Fig. 10 How big must the slot be?

▲Fig. 11 How many letters should the post box hold?

▲Fig. 12 The letters must be secure

▲Fig. 13 How can you stop letter bombs being posted?

THE EARLY DESIGN SKETCHES

All the points in the design brief have to be tackled by the designer. However, in the early stages of designing it is the overall form of the product that is the first priority. The designer works on a sketch pad, using pens and pencils, trying to find an overall form that suits all the main requirements. One of the big decisions the designer had to make at this stage was whether or not to develop the 'beret' top of the old style box. Eventually he decided to leave it off altogether in favour of a clean, straight cylindrical form.

►Fig. 14B

▼Fig. 14A

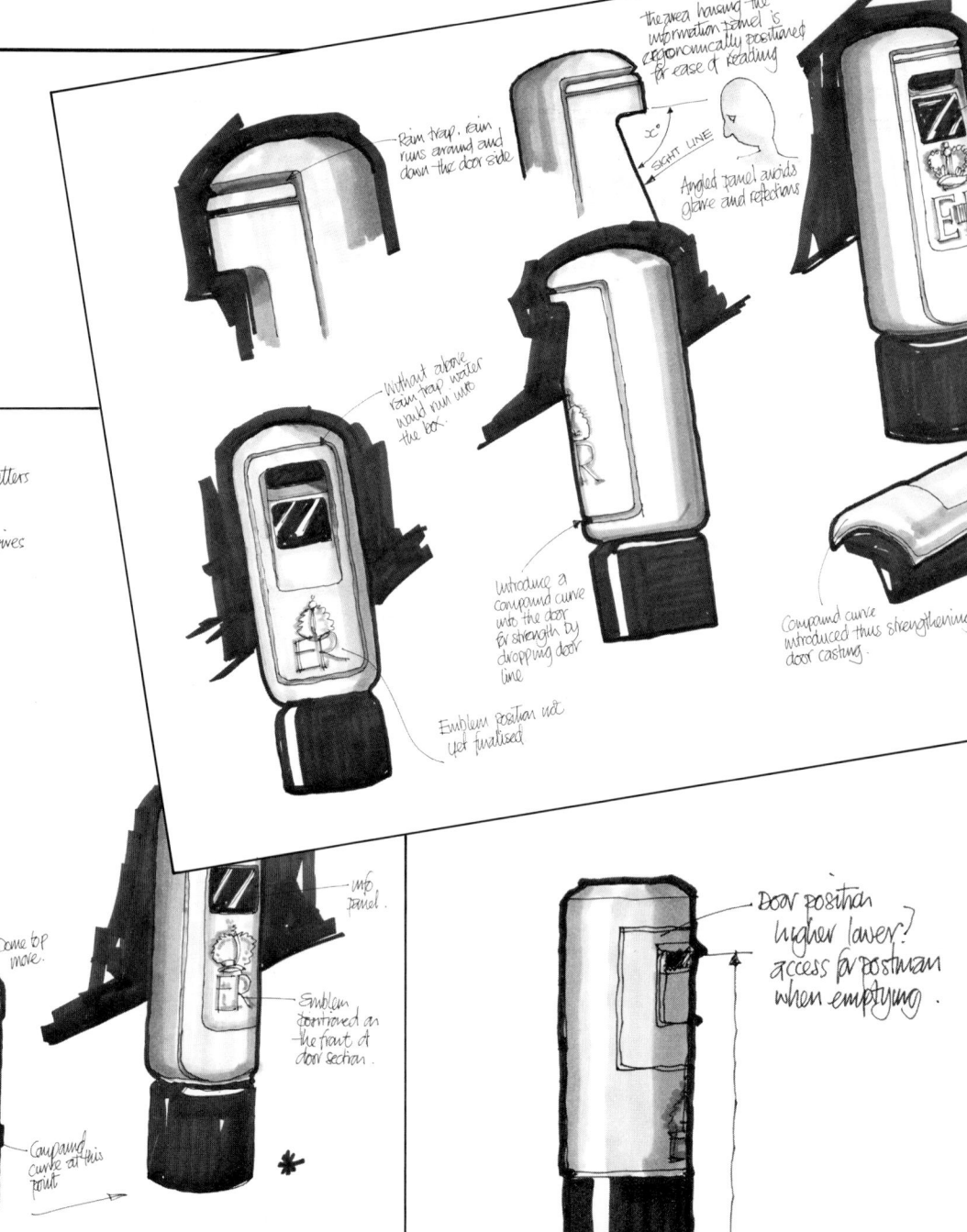

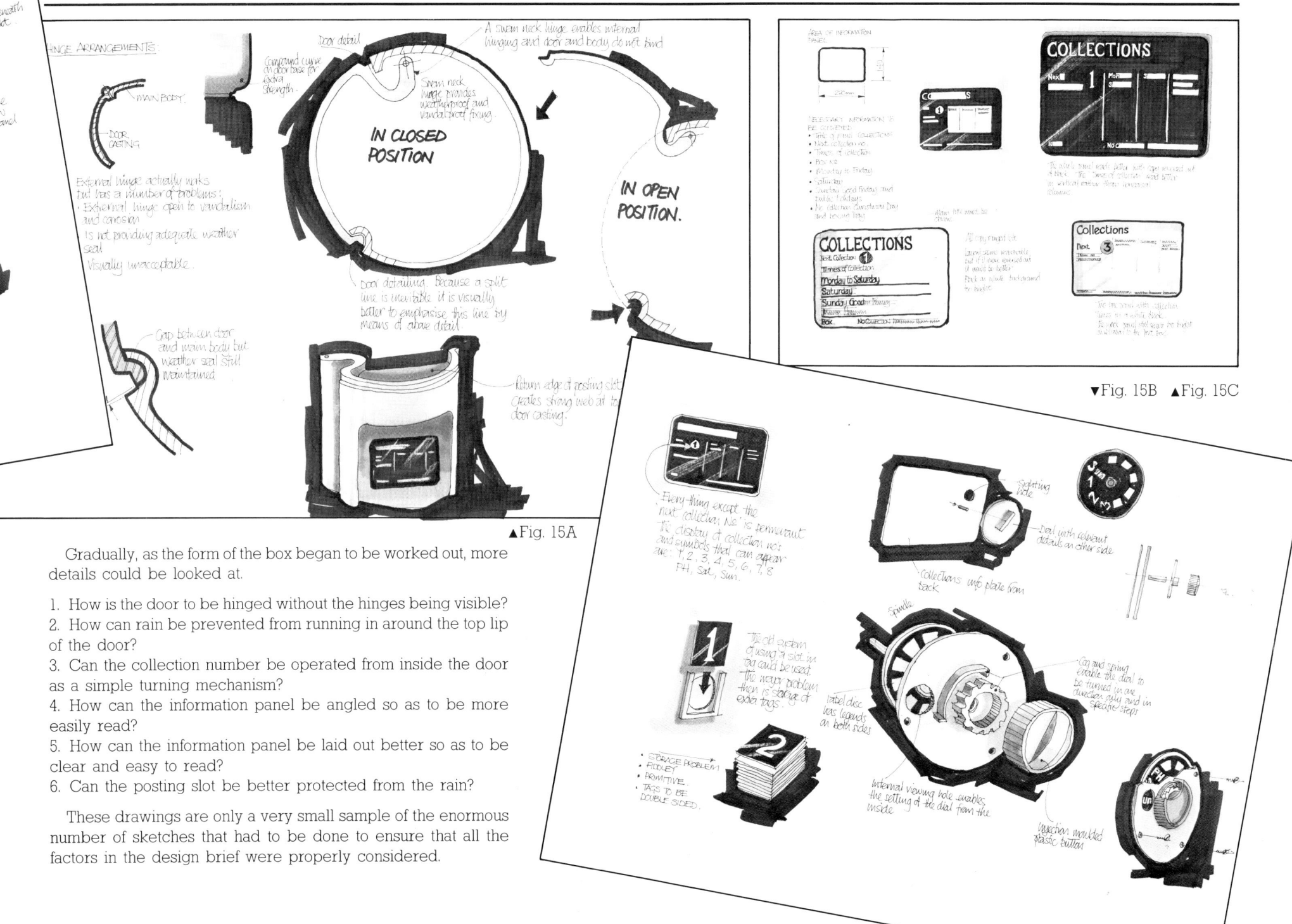

▲Fig. 15A

Gradually, as the form of the box began to be worked out, more details could be looked at.

1. How is the door to be hinged without the hinges being visible?
2. How can rain be prevented from running in around the top lip of the door?
3. Can the collection number be operated from inside the door as a simple turning mechanism?
4. How can the information panel be angled so as to be more easily read?
5. How can the information panel be laid out better so as to be clear and easy to read?
6. Can the posting slot be better protected from the rain?

These drawings are only a very small sample of the enormous number of sketches that had to be done to ensure that all the factors in the design brief were properly considered.

MATERIALS AND PROCESSES

As the designer got to the point of deciding upon the overall form of the post box, he had to think about the materials he might use. Also, he needed to think of the processes that were involved. In this case the basic body shell of the box *could* have been produced in a number of different materials, using several different processes. However, from his previous experience the designer selected four materials and processes which he thought might be the most suitable for this job. He examined these options carefully before deciding which to choose.

In making the choice between these processes and materials the designer must consider two important factors:

1. Will the finished product stand up to the wear and tear that it might receive and continue to do the job for which it was designed?

2. Will the production process be economic – or will the box be very expensive to produce? To answer this question you need to know about the SCALE OF PRODUCTION (i.e. how many boxes are needed). When talking about the cost of a manufacturing process, it is necessary to distinguish between OVERALL COST and UNIT COST. For example, the die for die casting aluminium costs a lot of money to produce and therefore the overall costs are high. The unit cost of the casting will depend on the number of units (or castings) made. If a die costs £10 000 to make and 10 000 castings are taken from it, then the unit cost of the castings is only £1. The more you make the cheaper they get!

This chart illustrates the many reasons for *not* using reinforced plastics for the box. Whilst it is reasonably cheap to make and eay to handle, it is not sufficiently durable. The dies for die casting aluminium would be so costly to make that it would only be economic if an enormous number of boxes were needed. (See page 7 for the number needed each year.) Also, aluminium may well not be strong enough to prevent serious damage in some circumstances. Whilst the reinforced concrete box would be reasonably cheap to produce, its ability to withstand the weather and other sources of wear and tear is doubtful. A post box has to continue to look clean and smart for 50 or even 100 years. The surface finish on old concrete can seriously deteriorate.

MAKING THE CHOICE OF MATERIAL

	CAST IRON	REINFORCED CONCRETE
Effects of heat (e.g. internal fire)	paintwork may blister but box undamaged	with very intense fire it may crack, otherwise no effect
Vandal attack (e.g. with a hammer)	surface scratching only	pieces may chip off
Effects of weathering		
1. Abrasion from dusty winds	minimal effect	surface finish may become pitted
2. Chemical corrosion from urban (acid) rain	minimal effect on C.I. but may rust non C.I. components.	possible staining of surface from rain penetration
3. Hot sunshine	minimal effect	minimal effect
Length of life (normal circumstances)	unlimited	unlimited – except surface may require cleaning and protecting.
Ease of handling (during installation)	very heavy and cumbersome	very heavy and cumbersome

MANUFACTURING COSTS

	CAST IRON	REINFORCED CONCRETE
1. Material cost	readily available and fairly cheap – but high energy cost to melt it	very cheap and available
2. Mould costs	once the wooden pattern is made, sand moulds are cheap but take time and skill	the metal or plastic moulds would be moderately costly to produce
3. Production costs		
(i) speed of production	slow – because of repeated mould making	slow because of curing time (5–6 days) unless very many moulds are made
(ii) for small number (10 per week)	moderate cost – for mould making and energy cost	low cost once moulds are made
(iii) for large number (100 per week)	same unit cost but constant mould making is required	low cost once moulds are made but *very* many moulds are required

REINFORCED PLASTICS	DIE CAST ALUMINIUM
can burn violently giving off poisonous fumes	paintwork may blister, otherwise no effect up to 500°C
could be completely broken open	easily scratched, could be badly dented and deformed
surface will lose its high gloss finish	minimal effect – some surface scouring.
minimal effect	no effect on Al but the non Al components may rust
may break down	minimal effect
less predictable as there are several sources of possible breakdown	unlimited, given some surface protection
relatively light and easy to handle	moderately heavy but much less so than C.I. or concrete
moderate cost but rising rapidly with cost of crude oil	expensive material to produce and high energy cost to melt it
metal or plastic moulds would be moderately costly to produce	very costly moulds made from tool steel or other high-carbon steel
moderately slow because of curing time (5–6 hours) unless many moulds are made	fast – a casting every 5 mins once mould and machinery is set up
moderate costs once moulds are made	machinery/energy/material/ costs are all high
moderate costs but several moulds would be required	cost per unit goes down as production goes up – process is fast

Overall therefore, whilst cast iron has some serious drawbacks (such as its great weight and the consequent difficulty of handling the boxes), it has all the strength and durability that is required and it is also reasonably economic.

Questions

1 Look at the photographs, fig. 16. Why has the designer chosen the particular material used in each case?

◀▲Fig. 16 Materials for different purposes: a GRP crash helmet, cast iron drain covers, a reinforced concrete lamp post

2 We have seen that the *overall cost* and the *unit cost* of a manufacturing process are very different things. Imagine that you have to make a choice between a die casting process and a sand casting process (using the same material) for the production of a component. Using the following figures find out how many units have to be produced before the die casting process becomes cheaper *per item* than the sand moulding process.   **c**

	DIE CASTING	SAND MOULDING
Mould/pattern cost (once only expenditure)	£10 000	£2000
Cost per casting for materials, energy, labour, mould etc. (recurring expenditure	£25	£45

The cost of the production of 100 die cast units can be calculated as follows:

Cost for 100 items = once only   + recurring   × number of
             expenditure   expenditure per item   items produced
             = £10 000   + £25   × 100
             = £10 000   + £2500
             = £12 500.
Cost of one item in a 100 long production run
             = £12 500/100
             = £125.

The cost for the production of 200 units can be worked out in a similar way:

Cost for 200 items = £10 000 + £25 × 200
             = £10 000 + £5000
             = £15 000.
Cost of one item in a 200 long production run
             = £15 000/200
             = £75.

Notice how this is much lower than the cost of a unit from a 100 long production run.

Carry out this type of calculation to work out the cost of one unit

for 300, 400, 500, 600 and 700 long production runs. Present your answers in table form.

In the same way we can work out the cost of 100 sand moulded units:

Cost for 100 items = £2000 + £45 × 100
             = £6500.
Cost of one item in a 100 long production run
             = £6500/100
             = £65.

Carry out this type of calculation to work out the cost of one sand moulded unit for production runs of 200, 300, 400, 500, 600 and 700. Present your answers in table form.

You can now use the information from your calculations to find out what length of production run is required for the die cast units to be cheaper than the sand moulded units. The cost per item has to be plotted against the length of production run, on axes like those shown in fig. 17. The first two points for the die cast process have been plotted.

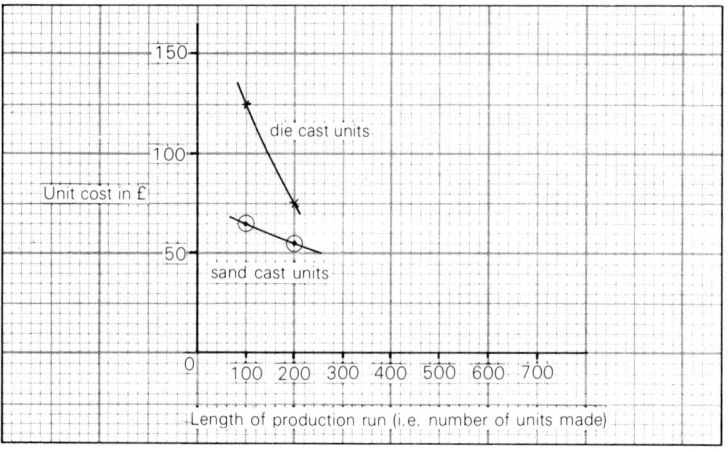

▶Fig. 17

On a neat copy of the axes plot the points for both processes. Be careful not to get the two sets of points mixed up. Join each set of points with a smooth line and label the resulting curves clearly. Where they cross is the break-even point. Use your graphs to find out the run length necessary for the sand casting and the die casting to result in the same unit cost.

3 It is important to be able to work out how much cast iron will be needed for a post box so that enough can be melted. If not enough is melted, the entire casting has to be scrapped; if too much is melted it is a waste of precious high cost energy. It is possible for our purposes to use approximations that will allow us to do the sums quickly.

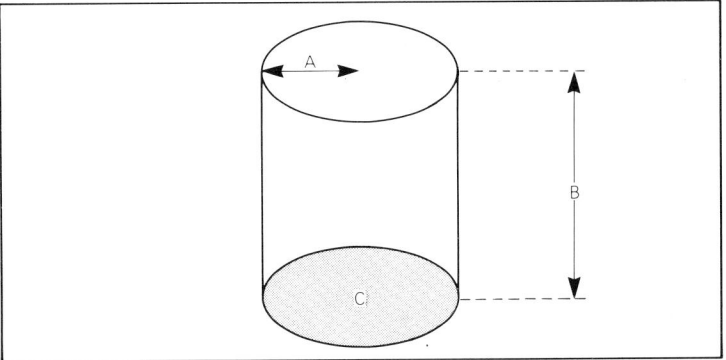

First, imagine that the pillar box is a simple solid cylinder:

height = 1.8 m
diameter of base = 0.5 m.

The total volume of the cylinder is worked out from:

height × area of base

where the area of the base is given by

$\pi \times r^2$ where r = radius of base
i.e. $3.14 \times 0.25^2 = 0.19\,\text{m}^2$
Total volume of cylinder = area of base × height
= 0.19 × 1.8
= 0.35 m³.

This is the *total volume* of the post box.

However, the box is not solid, it is hollow. So we now have to estimate the amount of space inside the box. We can imagine our cylindrical box looking like fig. 19.

►Fig. 19 A hollow cylinder
A = wall thickness = 0.02 m

◄Fig. 18 A simple cylinder
A = radius of cylinder
B = height
C = area of base

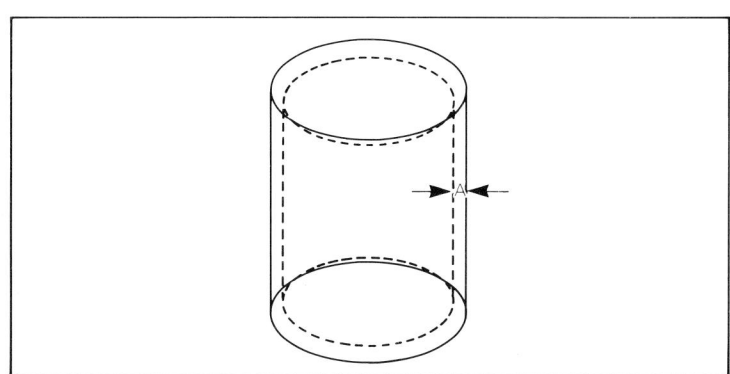

The dotted lines show the space inside the box.
If we know the average wall thickness, we can work out the volume of this space.

The average wall thickness = 20 mm = 0.02 m.
You can now work out the height of the inside cylinder and the diameter of the inside cylinder, which makes it possible to work out the volume of the inside cylinder.
A rough estimate of the volume of cast iron in a post box is given by

volume of overall cylinder − volume of internal space.

Given that the density of cast iron is 7100 kg/m³, work out the approximate mass of a cast iron post box.

Remember, $\dfrac{\text{mass}}{\text{volume}}$ = density,

so, mass = density × volume.

Given that a concrete post box will need to be three times as thick as a cast iron one, calculate the approximate volume of concrete needed to make one.
Given that the density of concrete is 2240 kg/m³, work out the approximate mass of a concrete post box.
Given that an aluminium alloy post box would be the same size as a concrete post box and that the density of aluminium alloy is 2800 kg/m³, work out the approximate mass of an aluminium alloy post box.

MODELS AND PROTOTYPES

As the early ideas are gradually refined, and the decision about which material to use is made, the designer will use a model to get a better impression of what the finished box might look like. This is not just for his own benefit but also for his client (the Post Office). They need to be convinced that the overall appearance is right.

Once this is agreed however, another much more detailed modelling stage is carried through. A real size model or PROTOTYPE is made to check the workings of all the major features of the box. In this case the full size model was made in Glass Reinforced Plastic (GRP). It was delivered to the design studio and examined very thoroughly by the designer to make sure everything worked as he had planned. Making a model as complicated as this is a very skilled job. The designer uses a professional model maker to make the model exactly to the drawings he provides.

▲Fig. 20 Models are used to show the client the design

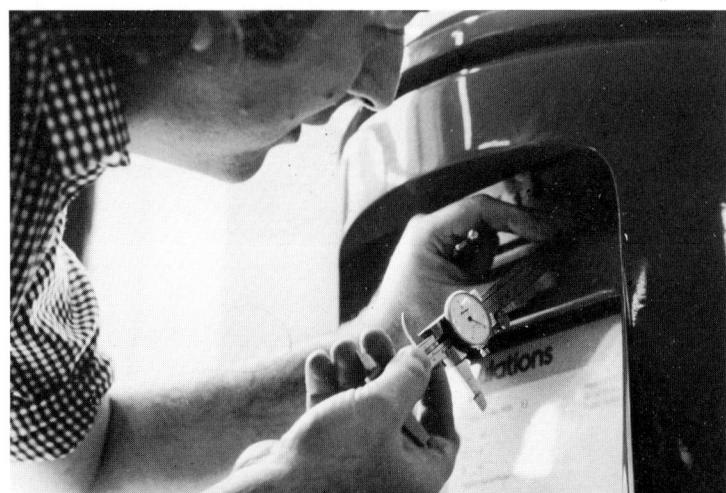

▶Fig. 21 Checking the working model for size

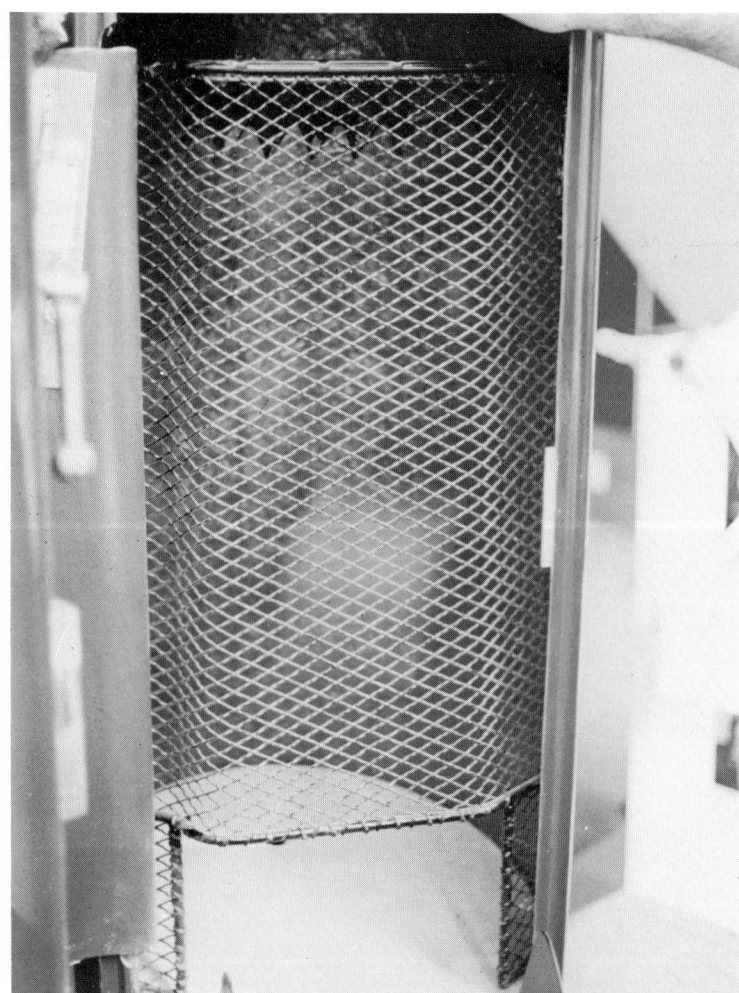

▶Fig. 22 Checking the letter basket

Several problems emerged at this stage. Most of them were problems that it was very difficult to foresee when drawing ideas on flat paper. For example, the lettering and crown of the royal family presented a great problem as it was mounted on the inset plate at the front of the box. This plate is not flat. It is rounded at the bottom where it merges into the box, but flat at the top where it leads into the information panel and posting slot. So the letters E R were not only wrapped around a curve but also the curve

was not regular and by the top of the crown had become almost flat. This led to visual distortion in the lettering and crown and they had to be changed several times to get them to look right.

► Fig. 23 Several changes had to be made to make the emblem look right

Questions

1 What materials could have been used to make the first (small) discussion model of the post box. How could it have been made?
2 Describe in notes and sketches the procedure for making the main body of the post box in glass reinforced plastic (GRP). The form of the main body can be seen in fig. 42 (page 24). Think particularly about how and where the mould is split to remove the finished box. Explain what materials you would use for each stage. (Look at the section about choosing materials in chapter 4, pages 102–105.)   **c**
3 Why did the model maker use GRP for this full size model? What other choices were possible? (Look at the section on modelling in chapter 4, pages 96–7.)   **c**
4 Designers use several sorts of models and prototypes, from the simple small models used to see if the product looks right, up to full size working prototypes like the prototype APT (Advanced Passenger Train) or the prototypes of Concorde. Look at some of the designed objects around you (e.g. cars, felt-tip pens, table lamps etc.). Think about the sort of model or prototype that would have been needed to work out the final design details for these objects.

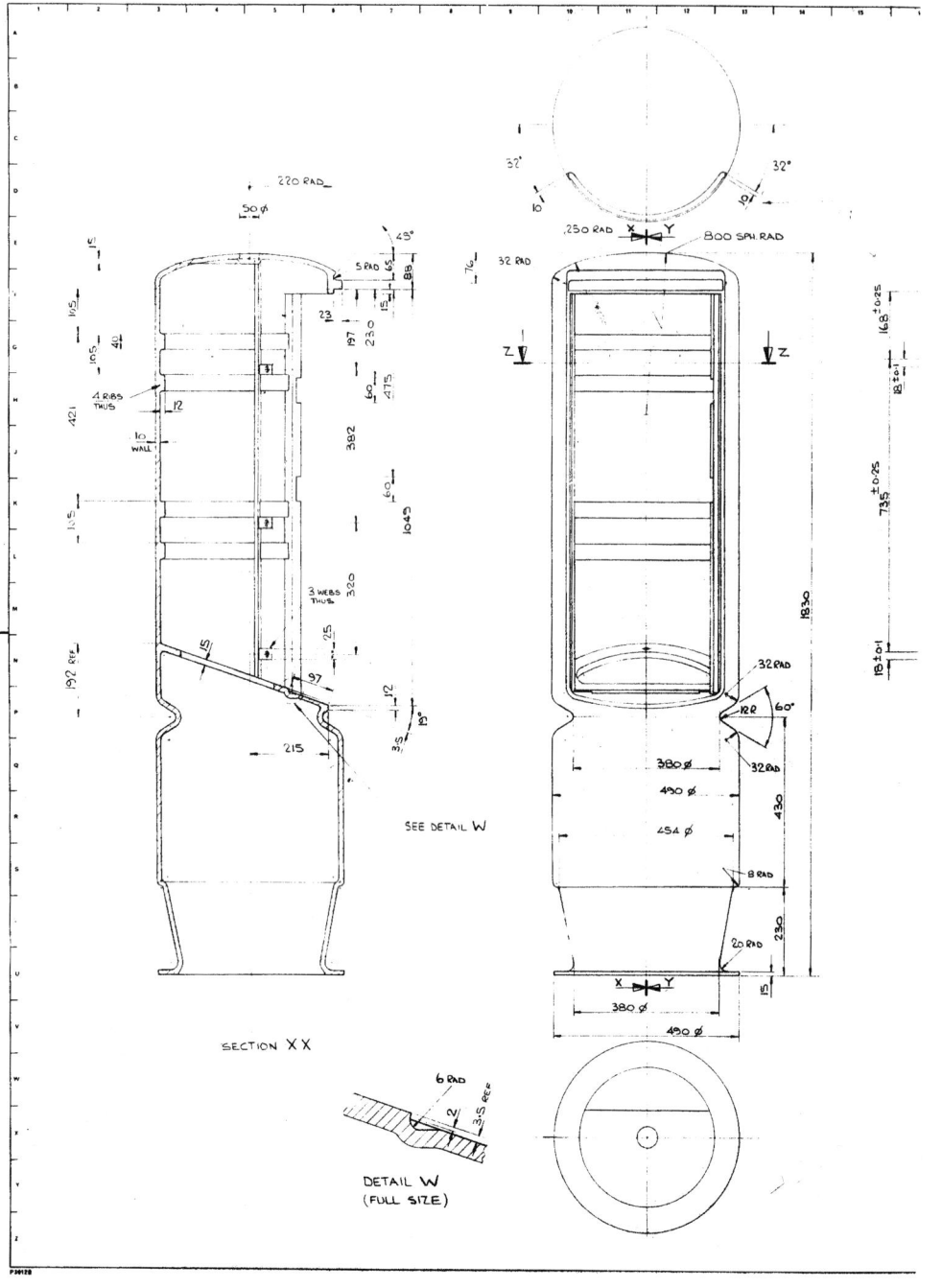

WORKING DRAWINGS

In order to produce a full size working model of the post box, the designer needs to provide very detailed drawings of every aspect and component of the box. These drawings would not need to be full size but would be SCALED so that they would fit onto a large sheet of paper. A working drawing must show *all* the information that is required to make the item. So it will specify in detail all the materials, sizes, shapes and constructions that a manufacturer would need to know to construct the model.

The working drawing is drawn in ORTHOGRAPHIC PROJECTION which shows front, side and top views of the unit. Often this alone is not sufficient and additional views are taken from different angles so that the designer can show more detail. These extra views are called AUXILIARY views and the designer can put in as many as he or she thinks are necessary to explain the design. Sometimes it is useful to show parts of the unit cut away so as to show what is inside or behind it. These are called SECTIONAL views and they are always shaded. The drawings can become very complicated indeed and therefore they have to be laid out very carefully so that it is quite clear how and where each part fits.

◀Fig. 24 Detailed working drawing of the post box body

▶Fig. 25 Drawing detail of the door

Questions

You will need to use chapter 4, pages 98–101, to help you answer these questions.

1 What scale is the drawing of the door drawn to?   **C**

2 Look at the side view of the body. Why is the bottom of the letter compartment sloping?   **C**

3 The drawing of the door has ordinary orthographic views, some auxiliary views and some sectional views. Find an example of each. What do you think the designer was trying to show by using the auxiliary and sectional views?   **C**

4 Examine the sectional side view of the door and work out at what angle the rain would need to fall in order to blow through the slot into the box. **c**

5 Trace the ordinary front and side views of the door into your sketchbook. On both views draw in the E R and crown. **c**

6 On the sectional side view of the body identify the stiffening ribs that run round the inside of the box. **c**

7 The three drawings above each other on the right hand side of fig. 25 are all sections through the door. Can you see where the sections were taken from, and why so many were necessary? **c**

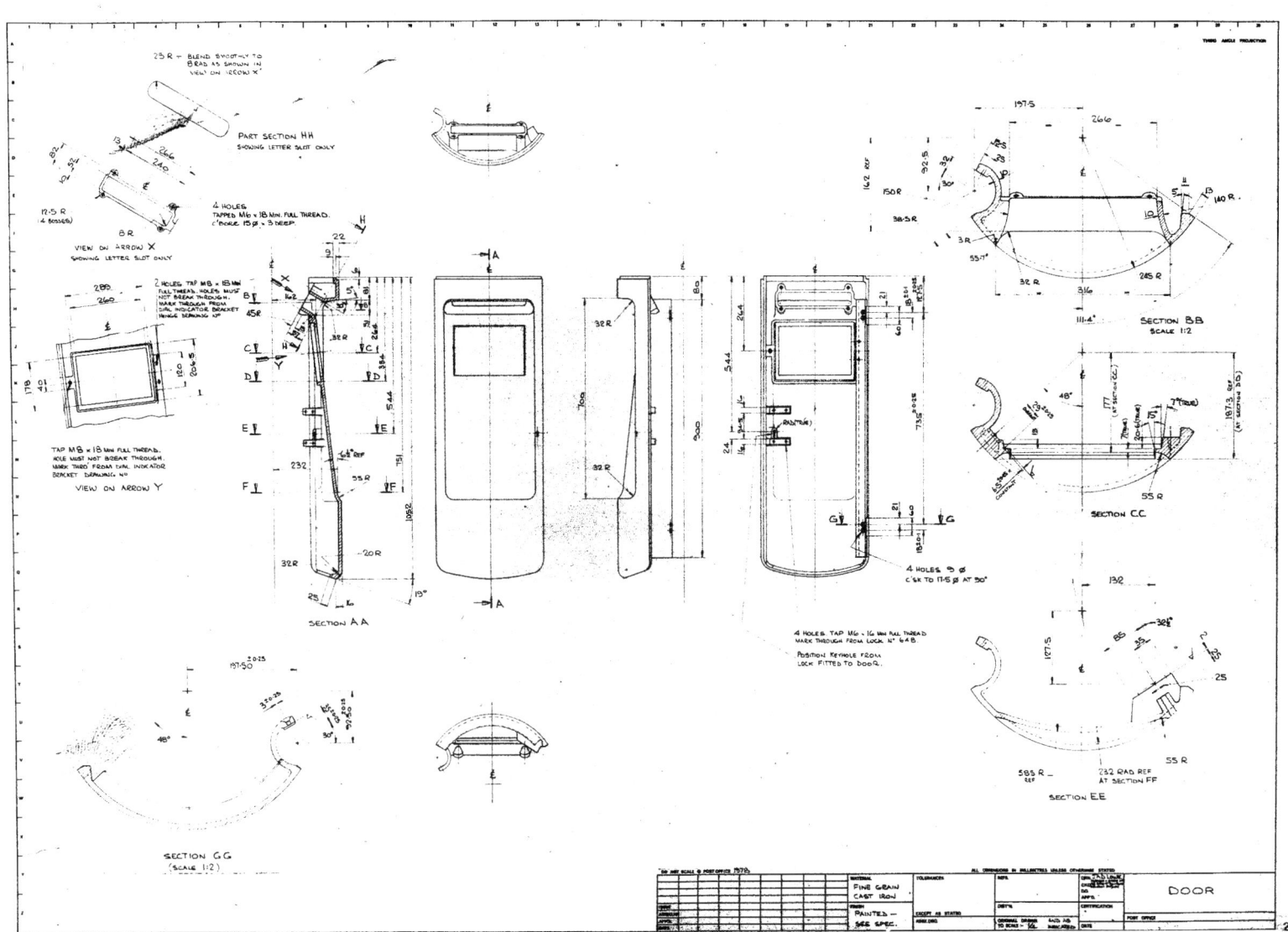

PATTERN MAKING

Once the details of the design are finalised and recorded on the further modified working drawings, the first real post boxes can be made. The decision to use cast iron for the box means that the manufacturing procedure has to start with pattern making. The patterns are then used to make the sand moulds for casting the cast iron.

The pattern is made to the shape of the real post box except that it is solid and made of wood. Absolutely every detail and blemish that appears on the pattern will be reproduced exactly on the final casting, so it is very important to make the patterns extremely accurately. Pattern making is the most skilled part of the whole manufacturing process.

Because of the casting process, the post box has to be moulded in two halves with the split line down the middle. This means that the patterns have to be split exactly in this way. Figure 27 shows the pattern for the front half on the trestle and the pattern for the back half on the floor beside it. The two halves have to fit together exactly.

The major patterns for the box are made from an ordinary, stable timber – possibly jelutong. The lettering and crown, however, need a far more detailed treatment and are carved in lime wood which has an extremely fine grain. The carvings are then used to cast identical plastic letters and crowns and these can be heat formed around the curve of the box to fit neatly on the front panel. This is a skilled and delicate operation.

As the metal cools (after the casting process) it will also contract. Therefore, for the final cast iron box to be the right size, the patterns have to be slightly bigger than the real size. The amount that the metal contracts varies according to what material is being cast. Pattern makers have special rulers that measure oversize by the right amount. The contraction rate for cast iron is usually 1 per cent.

▲Fig. 28 The crown is carved by hand in wood

▼Fig. 29 The crown and letters have to be formed to the curve of the box

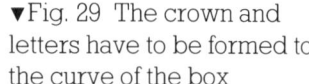

◄Fig. 26 Pattern making is a highly skilled job

◄Fig. 27 The pattern is an almost exact replica of the final post box

Question

1 If the post box has to end up at an overall height of 1.8 metres, what is the overall height of the pattern?   c

2 If you had to arrange for two pieces of wood to fit together accurately, like the two sides of a split pattern, how could you do it? Remember the outside surface must be untouched and the two pieces may have to be taken apart and reassembled many times. Explain your system with notes and sketches. (See chapter 4, pages 106–9.)   c

3 Look carefully at all the patterns illustrated. All the sides and edges slope inwards towards the middle – never outwards. Why is this?   c

MAKING THE MOULD

Making the mould for the main body of the post box is a very tricky job because of its complex shape. To cast a flat shape is quite simple. Even casting a solid cylinder is fairly straightforward. Casting a hollow cylinder (like the post box) is much more difficult.

To make the sections of the mould, a moulding box is used to surround the pattern and fine sand is sifted over the surface and rammed in hard. In order to take up and retain the shape of the pattern, the sand must either be moist (as when building sand castles on the beach) or it must be a special sand which is impregnated with oil. Once 'ramming up' is complete (i.e. when the box is full) this half of the mould is turned over and the other half of the pattern fixed in place over the first half. This is then rammed up in exactly the same way. The mould can now be split and the pattern removed. (See Chapter 4, page 106, for full details of the sand casting process.)

In this form the mould would produce a solid cylinder of cast iron. To make a hollow cylinder, as well as a top box (cope) and bottom box (drag), you need a central core of sand. This core must be fixed accurately into the moulding boxes so that the liquid cast iron flows around it leaving an even wall thickness all round. The stiffening ribs shown in the working drawing on page 18 are cut into the surface of the core. Once the casting is solidified the whole core has to be broken up and removed. The final

▲Fig. 31 The bottom half of the sand mould of the post box body

▶Fig. 32 Sand mould of post box door – note that the letters are reversed

◀Fig. 30 Sand mould for casting the cylindrical body of the post box

▶Fig. 34 Which arrangement is best for removing the triangular or the square casting?

stage of the process is to make sure that the molten cast iron can get into the cavity in the middle of the mould and special holes (called runners) have to be made in the sand for this purpose. In a complex mould, several runners may be used to ensure that the metal reaches all parts of the cavity.

Questions

1 Why does the sand have to be *sifted* onto the pattern when ramming up the moulding box?

2 This casting has a circular cross section and can therefore be split through the middle and the pattern removed.

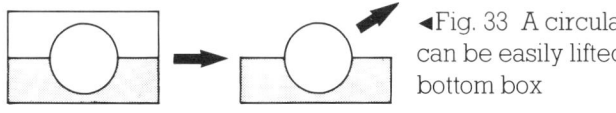

◀Fig. 33 A circular casting can be easily lifted out of the bottom box

How would you arrange a square pattern in a split mould? Or a triangular pattern? Why would you use the arrangement you have chosen?　**c**

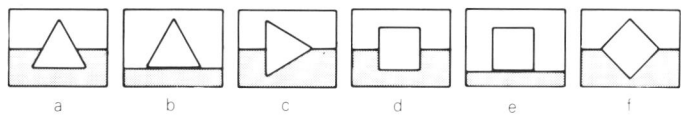

3 The pattern in fig. 27 has produced the half mould in fig. 31. What do you think is the purpose of the large rectangular block protruding from the front of the pattern?　**c**

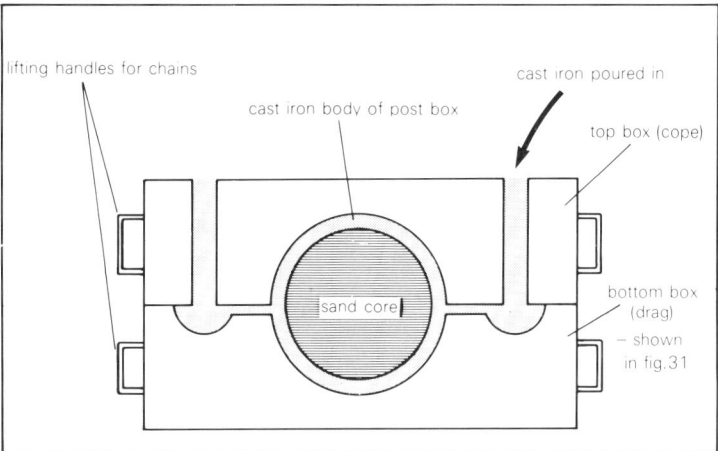

THE FIRST CASTINGS

When the mould is finally assembled and ready for pouring, a furnace has to be used to melt the ingots of cast iron. Because of the energy used to melt the iron it is an expensive process, and so it is best if all the contents of the furnace can be used up in one go rather than keeping some of the iron to be remelted another day. Several moulds are therefore prepared for pouring at the same time.

The metal is carried from the furnace to the mould in a ladle which is hung on steel cables from an overhead crane. When it is in position over the runner, the ladle can be titled to pour the cast iron. It is poured at a temperature of approximately 1600°C. Many safety precautions have to be enforced.

The first moulding to be produced was the door shown in fig. 36. It was a failure. Above the crown is the space where the information panel was to be fitted. Just above that is the posting slot. You will see that the top rim of the door has a great hole where the metal failed to flow. This probably resulted from the metal cooling (chilling) as it ran through the mould so that by the time it reached the far end it was solidifying. There was nothing wrong with the mould itself, but the runners that feed in the liquid metal had to be redesigned.

When that problem was solved the moulds were very successful and regularly produced good mouldings.

If you look carefully at the first moulding you will see that all

▼Fig. 36 The first door casting has a big hole in the top rim

◄Fig. 35 A crane holds the ladle in position for pouring

▼Fig. 37 The first good casting

around the edges, and in the information panel hole, excess metal is sticking out. This FLASH is created where the two halves of the mould come together and some of the edges of sand crumble away leaving holes for the metal to fill. This flash has to be removed by hand using a file or a hand grinding tool (the process is called FETTLING). You will also see that the casting retains some sand on the surface, particularly in the details of the lettering and crown and this too has to be removed. Once the whole door is cleaned up it is surprising what a good quality finish can be achieved.

▼Fig. 38 The cleaned cast iron surface is very good quality

Questions

1 If the mould is made of moist sand and the iron is poured into it at 1600°C, what will happen to the moisture in the sand? Look at fig. 35 to see it happening.　　　　　　　　　　　　　　c

2 What material is the ladle that carried the liquid cast iron from the furnace to the moulding made from?

3 List the major risks that result from casting metals in a school workshop. What safety precautions would you take to minimise the risk of injury?

4 A flash line will almost always result from a split moulding process and often it is possible to tell how a product was moulded by looking at the fine flash lines that remain on it. This is the same for casting metals and moulding plastics. Look carefully at a moulded metal or plastic component – find the flash lines and work out how the mould was split.　　　　　　　　　　　o

FINAL ASSEMBLY

The casting is by far the biggest and most difficult part of the whole manufacturing process. Once a casting is complete the other components can be fitted onto it: the hinges, the lock, the bullet proof glass panel over the information display, the mechanism for changing the collection number and the wire cage that fits inside the box and holds the letters. All these must be supplied and assembled into a complete post box. Of course the box must also be painted post office red. At this stage all the final details are carefully checked and the box is then ready for installation.

The finished box weighs 305 kg, or approximately 6 cwt which is nearly a third of a ton, so manhandling it into position on a pavement would be a very difficult exercise. The designer anticipated that problem and designed the top so that an eye bolt could be fitted. This makes it possible for the installation to be done from a lorry with a built-in hydraulic crane. The box can be dangled into position in the prepared hole in the pavement and then concreted in. Once the crane is unhitched the eye bolt can be removed and an insert fitted to fill the hole.

▼Fig. 39 Checking the first boxes

◄Fig. 40 Post boxes ready for installation

Questions

1 Do you think that all the components of the box are made by the foundry in Kirkintilloch, and if not why not?

2 If you needed a lock for a project of your own, where would you go to find one?

3 With this box the final assembly is fairly simple, but with some products the assembly is the most difficult part. Think of a television, for example, or a car. To make sure that the assembly is always accurate we sometimes use jigs to hold the work during an operation, so that as far as possible we eliminate human error and speed up the process. Design a simple jig so that the holes can be drilled quickly and accurately in the corners of the plate shown in fig. 41 using an ordinary pillar drill.   **c**

▼Fig. 41 Repetitive tasks should be 'jigged up' for quick production

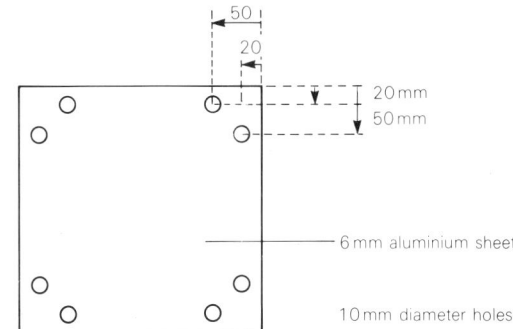

4 Design a simple system that makes it possible to fit an eye bolt into the top of the post box, remove it afterwards and fill the resulting hole so that the outside appears not to have a hole in it. Remember it might be necessary to refit the eye bolt at a later stage in order to remove the post box.

5 You can see in fig. 40 that there are two quite different emblems on the front of the two boxes. One is for use in England and the other in Scotland. Why did the designer produce two different crown designs?   **c**

EVALUATION

All through the process of designing and making the post box the designer has been evaluating his ideas and decisions, constantly trying to spot errors and difficulties so as to design them out. By this stage most of the problems should have been spotted and solved. It is, therefore, time to do a final evaluation, to see whether all the problems identified in the design brief have been successfully tackled.

The final real test of any product is to put it to use and ask the people who use it what they think of it and how it could be improved. We all use post boxes, so we can all say how good we think they are and what we like and dislike about them. A post box is going to be a part of our environment for very many years so we have a right and a responsibility to tell the Post Office what we think about it. However, whilst we all use post boxes, our use of them is very slight compared to that of the postmen, who have to open, empty and close them all day. The opinion of postmen about how good the box is and how well it works will be very important. The final evaluation, therefore, can be divided into three parts.

▲Fig. 42 The new post box in a classical setting

(a) How does the box look in the street? Is it an eye-sore or is it an elegant addition to the environment? This question can be asked of anybody.

(b) How easy is it to use the box for posting letters and for finding out when the letters will next be collected? Again, anybody who uses the post box will have something useful to say about this.

(c) How easy is it for the postman to open, empty and close the box and also to change the collection number? Is it easier and more convenient than the old box or is it more fiddly and troublesome? These questions can only be answered by postmen.

◄▲►Fig. 43 How easy is it to use?

It is important not just to get people's instant opinions about the box. As we know, any new design will be disliked by some people simply because it is new and they have not got used to it. So as well as asking for opinions we also have to ask for the *reasons* why a person has that opinion. If changes have to be made to the design it must be for good reasons.

▲Fig. 44 What's your opinion of the new design?

Questions

1 Where is the handle on the door of the post box? Compare this handle to the one in fig. 1. Why do you think the change was made? **c**

2 Our final evaluation has dealt with the general public (the users) and the postmen (the operators). What other groups of people might it be helpful to seek comments from? (e.g. the police might have something useful to say about post box theft and vandalism).

3 If you want to get the opinion of the general public on any particular issue, what different methods could you use?

4 Part (a) of the post box survey would probably have required at least five questions to get any useful results:

    1. Do you like the look of the new post box?

    2. Can you explain why/why not?

    3. Do you think it fits equally well into a modern environment and an older one?

    4. Is the new box immediately recognisable as a post box?

    5. If so, what is it about the box that makes it so recognisable? **c**

Make a list of the questions that would need to be asked for parts (b) and (c) of the survey.

5 Some 'market research' firms specialise in finding out about public opinion on consumer products or on public issues. (Think of all the opinion polls before a general election.) The Consumers' Association in Britain produce a magazine called *Which* that surveys and evaluates many consumer products. Read a *Which* survey and see how informative it is. Note how the results of the survey are displayed. **x**

6 Design your own survey of a product or range of similar products. Conduct the survey and display the results in a way that will be clear for the general public.

THE FORD SIERRA

The Ford Cortina was launched in the 1960s, and despite a number of modifications and new models its appeal declined progressively through the 1970s. At the same time Japanese car exports were beginning to dominate the European car market.

◀▶Fig. 1 The design sketches of the 1960s Cortina – now well out of date

▼Fig. 2 Twenty years on – the new Sierra

Between 1962 and 1982 they rose from 1000 cars/year to 956 000 cars/year. Ford decided that they needed a new car to get back some of the lost market. Eventually the Ford Sierra was launched twenty years to the day after the original Cortina was unveiled. It is described by Ford as ... an authoritative response to the Japanese. Like the Cortina it is a wholly integrated package that is not produced by whim or by chance, but by planning and thinking and by a total commitment to design ...' This is the story of the Sierra.

The development of the Sierra involved the design of 7500 separate parts. It took 52 months and cost 1200 million dollars (i.e. almost one million dollars per day for four and a half years). Such an enormous investment meant it was essential that the finished item should be right, so the attention to detail in the design and planning was exceptional.

The design started with a 'features list' which put in writing all the things that the car should contain or be able to do. This list is compiled by very careful analysis of other competing cars. It is no good producing a car that can do less than your opponents' version.

The overall concept of the new car was then created in a series of exploratory 'concept sketches'. This stage was reached in 1978. Once the concept sketches had begun to take a specific direction, the designers produced small scale models for testing in the wind tunnel and began full size profile 'drawing' using adhesive tape.

17.12.79-CS-2727-38

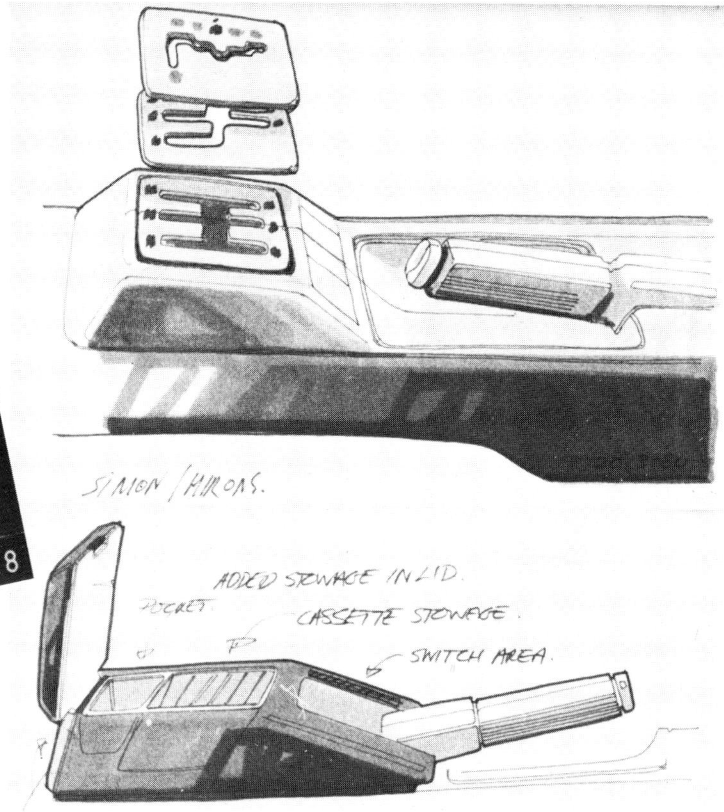

SIMON / MIRORS.

ADDED STOWAGE IN LID.

POCKET.

CASSETTE STOWAGE.

SWITCH AREA.

►Fig. 4 Design detail of the central storage area

▲▼Fig. 3 Styling the front end

▼Fig. 5 Design detail of the front seats

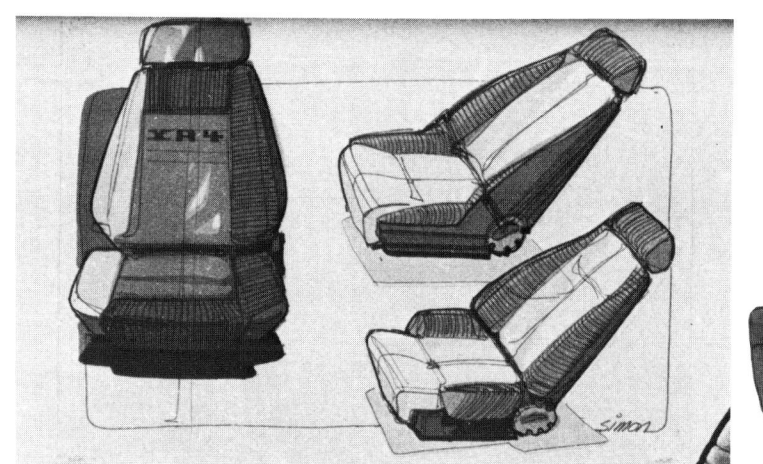

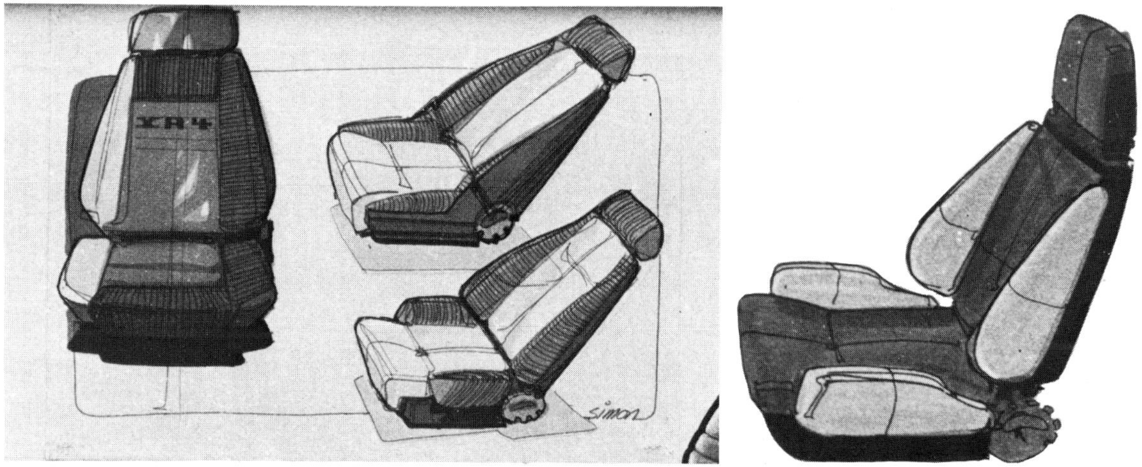

◄Fig. 6 Scale models are used to do the early tests of the aerodynamics of the design

▼Fig. 7

THE FORD SIERRA	
1978	
Oct	outline design strategy from production assumptions; originate a 'features list'; start 'concept' sketches
1979	
Feb	prepare cost assumptions; review safety laws; review initial 'concept' design ideas
April	launch market research
May	start interior design; analyse export potential
July	start full size clay model of exterior; start pricing study; complete interior design; specify engine/mechanical requirements
Nov	business studies of components to be 'bought in'
Dec	prepare sales/finance plan
1980	
Jan	testing and development of static 'concept' car (wind tunnel etc.)
March	body engineering studies – structure and layout
July	finalise chasis and structure; confirm production number
Aug	prepare final cost package
Oct	approval given by management for full mechanical prototype
Dec	final drawings to component manufacturers; all drawings approved for mechanical prototype; the name 'Sierra' is approved
1981	
May	first mechanical prototype built
June	analysis of parts to be changed
Dec	final pre-production prototype approved
1982	
June	first production vehicle produced
Sept	start pre-sell campaign European Press Announcement; Motor Show debut (Paris)
Oct	public sales in Europe

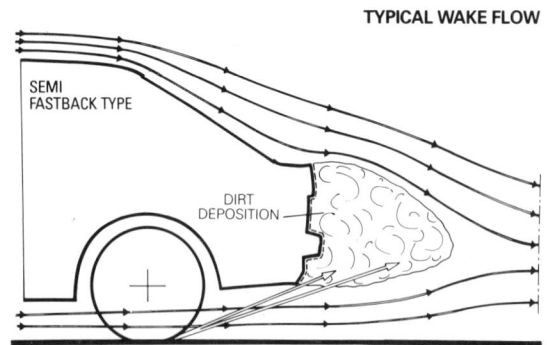

TYPICAL WAKE FLOW

SEMI FASTBACK TYPE

DIRT DEPOSITION

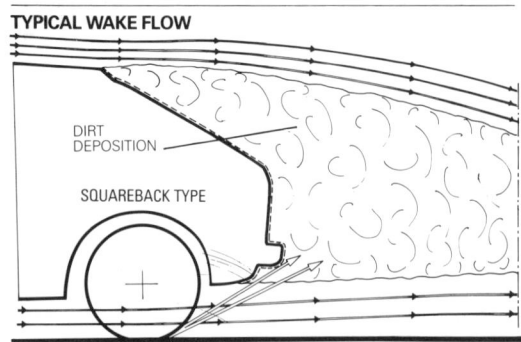

TYPICAL WAKE FLOW

DIRT DEPOSITION

SQUAREBACK TYPE

It was at about that stage that the Ford Safety Office began to study the needs of the new car in terms of safety, damage resistance, exhaust emission and noise. Every country has its own laws controlling these requirements. Designers have to be able to predict what the laws will be five years ahead and build in these requirements at the design stage.

'Package development' was the next important step. This was the development of the detail of the external shape of the car in relation to the internal space available for passengers, mechanical parts and luggage. The process began with full size wooden models on which various different solutions (for instrument panels, seats.) were fixed.

After eight months had passed, the overall form of the car was beginning to emerge and it was time to consider the detailed engineering aspects. Should the car have front or rear wheel drive? Did it need a new engine or would the present range be adequate? What sort of suspension system or heating or electronics would it need?

As these decisions were made by the product planners, work started on full size clay models. This stage is like sculpture and highly skilled craftsmen make the clay look like any material they choose – from glass windows to cloth seats or carpets.

By month 26 (i.e., after more than 2 years of development) a decision had to be made whether or not to go ahead with the car. It could still have been dropped at this stage. Several different clay prototypes had been developed and a final choice had to be made before the very expensive engineering design stage was

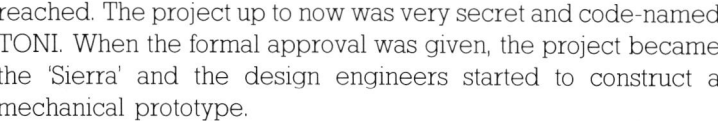

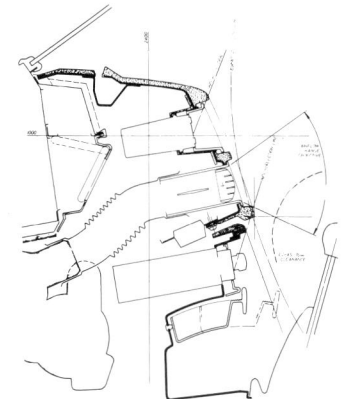

reached. The project up to now was very secret and code-named TONI. When the formal approval was given, the project became the 'Sierra' and the design engineers started to construct a mechanical prototype.

'Running metal prototypes', as they are known, are hand built and cost about ½ million dollars each. By this time all the marketing studies were under way and the costs calculated to the point where a sale price could be estimated. This unit price is calculated on the assumption that a certain number of cars will eventually be produced and sold every year. When the final detailing and testing of the running metal prototype was completed, the car was ready for production. The production line still had to be prepared. Special tools and components were brought in: press tools made for the giant presses that produce the body panels, robots installed and set to weld the panels together, and the moving production line organised and set so that the whole car could be assembled systematically. At this point the workforce had to be trained for the new production and assembly problems and on month 52 the first production vehicle rolled off the line.

▲Fig. 10 Detailed cross section through the instrument panel

►Fig. 11 Production and assembly

◄Fig. 8 Full size drawing with adhesive tape

▼Fig. 9 Full size detailed models, made entirely of clay

Even that is not the end of the story. A vigorous marketing campaign had been designed to tell the public about the new car. The campaign started in September 1982, a month before any of the cars could have been bought. The Paris Motor Show provided a suitable debut appearance.

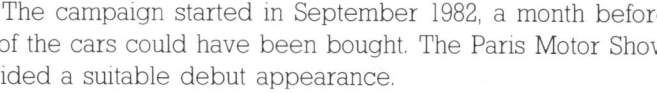
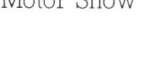

THE FLEXISTAND

We have seen how, in the story of the post box, the Post Office commissioned a major firm of design consultants to do all the designing and the production drawings. With Ford, the company is so large that it can afford its own design department with massive research and development facilities to perfect every model. But professional designers do not always work in such big organisations. In Britain it is quite common for small firms of designer/manufacturers to consist of just one or two people. Zygotek Ltd is one such firm which specialises in designing and making equipment for the handicapped. Malcolm Johnston, the founder of Zygotek, has been designing aids for disabled people for ten years, and for the last five years he has been largely involved in the design and development of the Flexistand.

WHAT IS IT?

A frame to support people who cannot stand or walk, in a normal

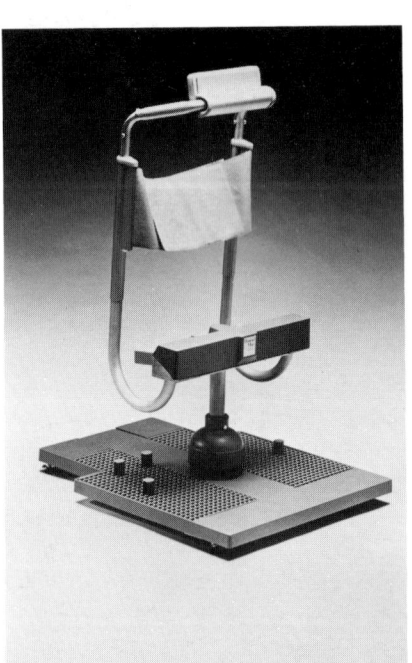

◀Fig. 1

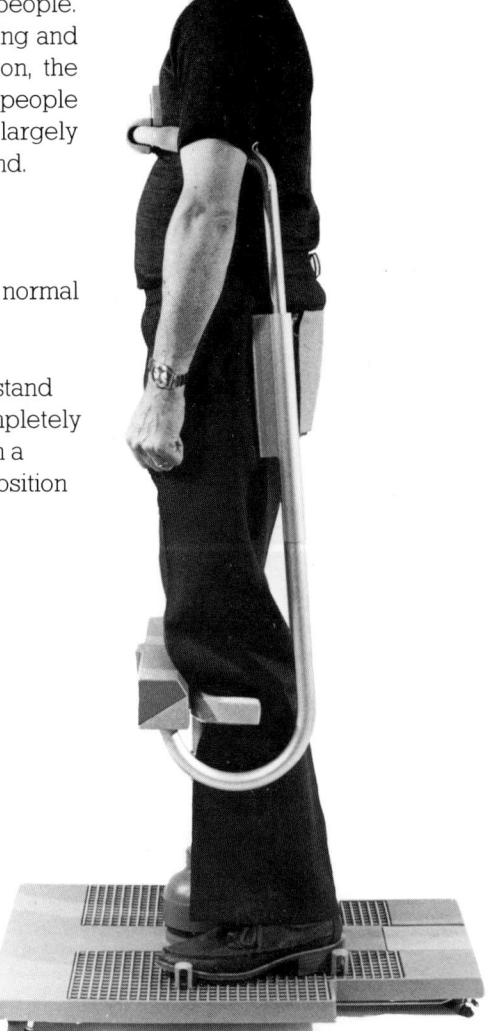

►Fig. 2 The Flexistand has to support completely disabled people in a normal standing position

WHY IS IT NEEDED?

There are many thousands of people who spend their lives in wheelchairs. If they can stand for an hour or so each day they can perform tasks which are difficult to do when seated. In this way they can also gain strength in their bones and muscles.

WHAT IS THE MAIN DESIGN REQUIREMENT?

When standing normally, the body is not completely still because the weight is constantly changing from one foot to the other and as the weight changes the body sways a little. The main design requirement was to support the body in such a way as to allow this normal swaying movement instead of holding it rigidly, which feels constricting and unnatural.

There were, of course, lots of other design considerations. For example, it has to adjust to fit most people between the ages of seven and adult. It must be as unobtrusive as possible, fit into as little space as possible and collapse to fit into a car. It must also conform to all the relevant safety standards.

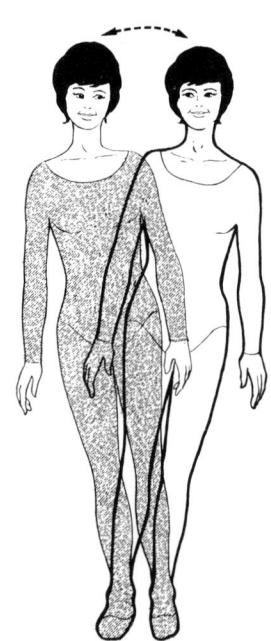

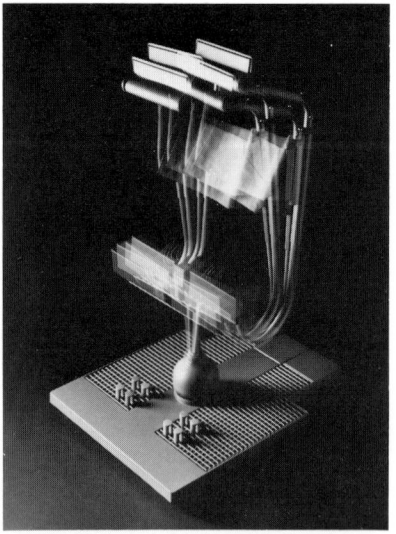

◀▲Figs. 3 and 4 The Flexistand has to allow normal body movement and still provide support

Flexistand Major
adjusts in height and in width

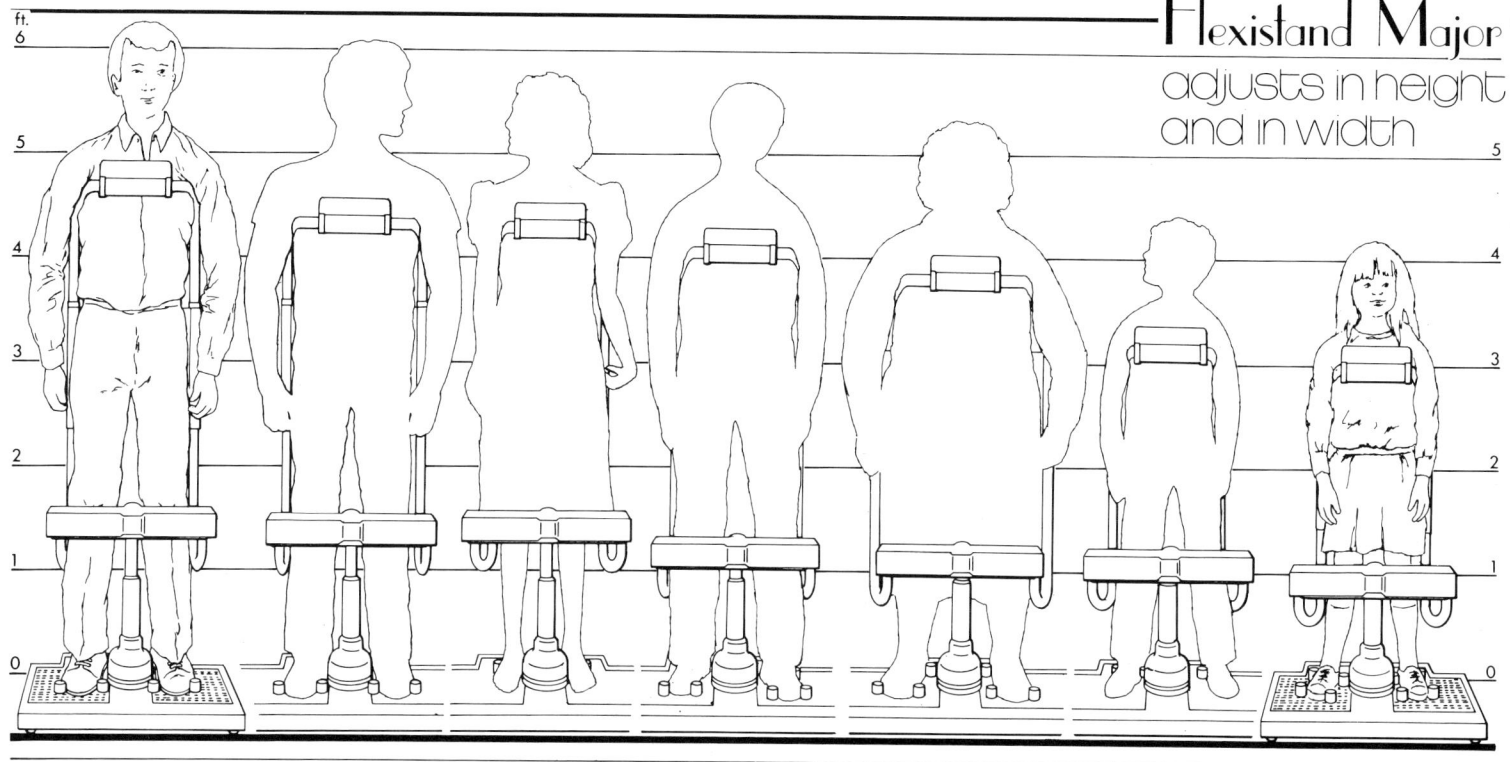

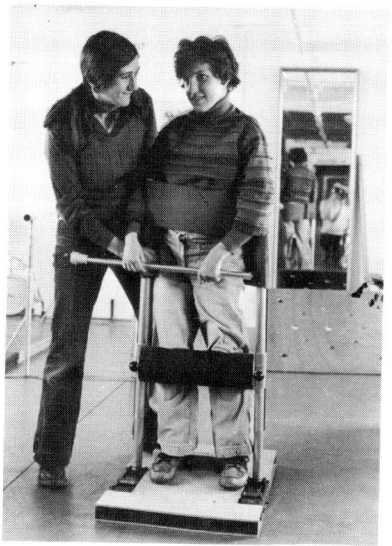

◀Fig. 5 The frame must hold people from 7 years of age up to large adults

▼Fig. 7 An early test rig with twin support poles and a low chest support

The first stage of the design required much detailed observation and measurement of bodies to discover the best ways of supporting the body. Imagine being totally paralysed from the neck down and you will see the problems involved in supporting such a body in a normal standing position.

HOW DOES THE FRAME HOLD THE BODY?

It was important to decide early in the design process exactly where the frame would support the body. The body can be seen as two sets of pivots: the upper one being at the hip, which links the trunk to the thighs. The lower pivot is the knees, which link the thighs to the lower legs. By controlling these pivots the body can be well supported.

Early experiments with body support methods showed that the chest support must be as high as possible, on a level higher than the armpits. With lower chest support the body tends to slump forward. Also the original idea of using two upright poles with

▼Fig. 6 The body must be supported in three places to stop it collapsing on its natural pivot points

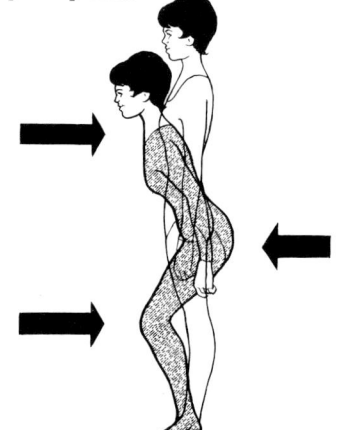

straps and supports between them proved to have several difficulties. The modified arrangement has only one pole going into the base but this connects to a double pole system for the retaining straps and supports. The height and width of the pole supports has to be fully adjustable for the range of human sizes.

FLEXIBILITY

Having devised a way for the support frame to pass around the body of the stander, there remained the problem of how to provide the adjustable flexibility at the base so the body could sway naturally. The original idea of a steel spring, apart from being difficult to adjust, was also too 'springy'. It was decided to use natural rubber instead of steel, as it can be mixed with various additives to provide the required movement whilst being just as resilient as the steel. However there was a special problem with this spring. As the Flexistand was to be used partly as a therapy instrument, it was important to be able to adjust the

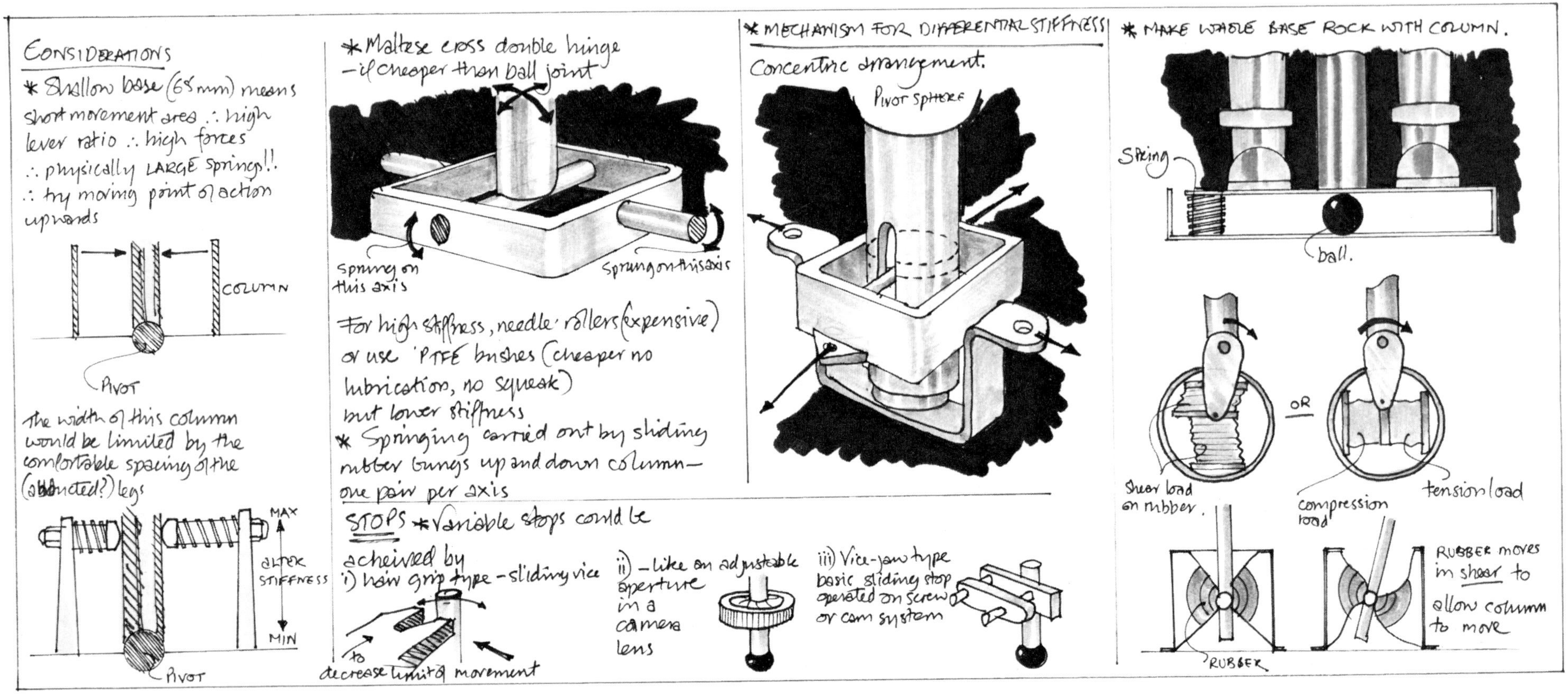

CONSIDERATIONS

* Shallow base (65mm) means short movement area ∴ high lever ratio ∴ high forces ∴ physically LARGE springs!! ∴ try moving point of action upwards

◀ COLUMN ▶

PIVOT

The width of this column would be limited by the comfortable spacing of the (abducted?) legs

MAX
ALTER STIFFNESS
MIN

PIVOT

* Maltese cross double hinge — if cheaper than ball joint

Spring on this axis

Sprung on this axis

For high stiffness, needle rollers (expensive) or use 'PTFE' bushes (cheaper no lubrication, no squeak) but lower stiffness

* Springing carried out by sliding rubber bungs up and down column — one pair per axis

STOPS * Variable stops could be

acheived by i) hair grip type - sliding vice

to decrease limit of movement

ii) - like on adjustable aperture in a camera lens

iii) Vice-jaw type basic sliding stop operated on screw or cam system

* MECHANISM FOR DIFFERENTIAL STIFFNESS

Concentric arrangement.

Pivot sphere

* MAKE WHOLE BASE ROCK WITH COLUMN.

Spring

ball.

Shear load on rubber.

OR

compression load

tension load

RUBBER

RUBBER moves in shear to allow column to move

springyness of the pole so that side to side movement is separate from front to back movement. As you can imagine, it was not easy to design a spring in which the stiffness could be separately adjusted for swaying from side to side and backwards and forwards. Four designs were made and evaluated, over several years, before the solution was found. As a result of detailed tests carried out on a prototype it was possible to iron out a number of small remaining problems and to explore a range of production methods. At this stage the design was finalised and the production drawings were produced.

For the users to get most advantage from the Flexistand, which by now had become a sophisticated product, it was clear that a simple instruction booklet would have to be supplied. This itself had to be designed and an illustrator was commissioned to show in simple drawings how the frame is adjusted and used.

▲Fig. 8 Developing ideas for the flexible column support

▶Fig. 9 A model used to explore the possibilities of a central spring

►Fig. 10 The first working drawing of the spherical spring

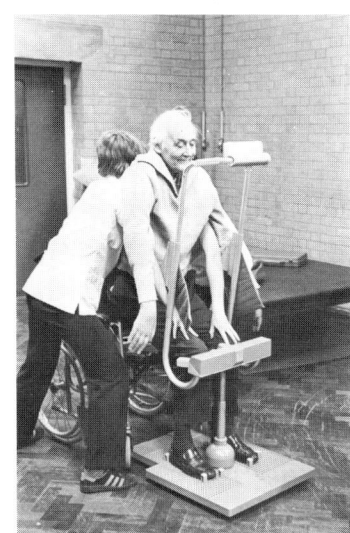

▼Fig. 11 Moulding the rubber spring in a steel mould

▲Fig. 12 A test rig to evaluate the flexing properties of the spring

At this stage ten pre-production prototypes were built from sample components produced by manufacturers. Assembly methods were developed and tested and extensive user tests carried out over several months. A small firm like Zygotek could not possibly produce all the components that would go into the Flexistand. Each one has over 100 components, most of which have been designed by Zygotek. However, once the components have been taken to working drawing stage, separate manufacturing firms actually produce them. All the assumbly and packaging is done by Zygotek in a small workshop.

PRODUCTION

Six months after the pre-production prototypes and four years after starting the design, the first production frames were made. There are now many hundreds of physically disabled people who are able to enjoy normal standing again or for the first time in their lives.

For Zygotek the immediate job is finished, but plans are already well advanced for two major developments for the Flexistand. A 'lifter' system is being designed to allow a disabled person to hoist him/herself into the frame, and the possibilities of a motorised mobile frame are being explored. For a designer, no job is ever completely finished.

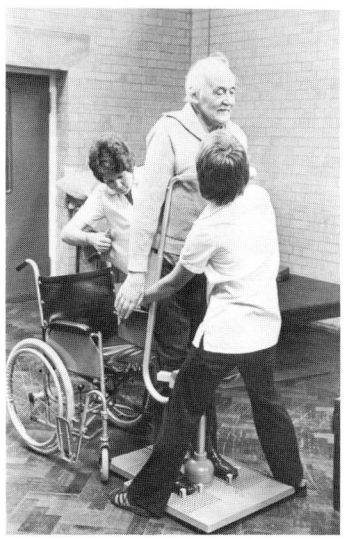

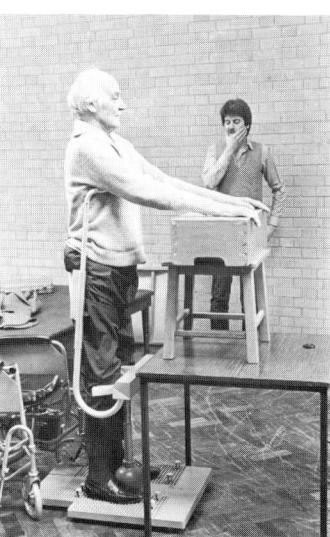

▲Fig. 13 Getting into the frame for some very important exercising

TWO

FINDING THE PROBLEM

THE SWIMMING CENTRE

The Stonesbury Swimming Centre is new. It was only opened in 1979 and it has been carefully designed to provide a range of swimming facilities. Nevertheless, there is plenty of opportunity in it for further designing and a group of fourth year students from a local school went looking for some design problems that they could solve.

▲Fig. 2 The main pool

▲▶Fig. 1 The new swimming centre

At the start of the visit they were shown around the complex (as a group) by the warden. He pointed out all the special facilities, including large pool, learner pool, changing rooms, showers, locker rooms, observation lounge and reception area. After this initial tour, the group divided up into smaller groups of two or three students to study particular areas in detail.

First, it was important to find out exactly how the different facilities in the complex are used by the public. This required careful *observation* of people using the complex and often direct

◄Fig. 3 The learners' pool

questioning of these people to find out how well the facilities worked and what PROBLEMS they had in using them. All this observation and questioning was carefully recorded with notes and sketches in a notebook. When problems were discovered, they had to be examined to see if they were suitable design problems for the groups to try to solve.

►Fig. 5 Lockers for bags and clothes

◄Fig. 4 The observation lounge

Questions

1 How else could all the information have been recorded other than by using notes and sketches in a notebook?

2 What would be the advantages and disadvantages of these other methods? What are the disadvantages of using notes and sketches and how can these be overcome?

3 What sorts of problems might exist in this situation that are not design problems in the sense of designing and making?

4 When people are being observed, it often affects their behaviour. How can you be sure that the people are behaving as they would be if you were not observing them?

OBSERVING THE SITUATION

Because of the size of the swimming centre and the number of different areas to be observed, the group of students needed to work in sub-groups of two or three people. Each group spent the rest of the morning studying one particular part of the centre in detail. They all had to make their notes under three headings:

1. Who did you see using the area?
2. What did you observe about the way they used it?
3. What problems did you identify from your observations?

For the rest of this project we shall follow the work of group C (Caroline and Michael) whose area was the learner pool.

WHO DID YOU SEE USING THE AREA?

During our visit we saw the baby swimming class, which took babies for 4 months to 1 year old. There was one instructor and lots of mums and dads with babies. Some parents had more than one baby

WHAT DID YOU OBSERVE?

(a) babies in the water with their parents.

(b) babies in playpens on the side of the pool, some playing happily, some crying.

(c) babies in carry-cots at the side of the pool, mostly on the benches round the wall.

(d) parents changing their babies' nappies - lots of towels, nappies, etc on the side benches.

(e) lots of movement in and out of the pool, especially by those mums with one baby in the water and one on the side

(f) the pool edge was a very unusual non-slip surface with drainage grids every few yards.

(g) babies swimming on their own at 6 months old !!

(h) the interior decoration is very plain bare brick, it's a bit uninteresting

(j) this learner pool is separated from the main pool by a glass partition screen, but there is free movement between the two pools

(k) the babies are not in the water for very long at a time, usually about 10 mins. Even though the water is quite warm (80°F) the babies get cold quite quickly so have to get warm at regular intervals

◄Fig. 6 Babies learning to swim in the learner pool

►Fig. 7 The babies cannot spend all their time swimming – they must be kept safe

◄Fig. 8 The babies need to be dried and changed

▲Fig. 9 The pool edge is non-slip, with drainage channels all round

Questions

1 If you were going to observe the activity in a swimming pool, what clothes would you wear and why?

2 What are the advantages of observing in small groups of two or three?

3 If you want to *observe* a situation and not influence it by your presence, you need to be as invisible as possible. How would you do this if you had to observe the following situations?

(a) A first-year science lesson in your school.

(b) An interview between an employer and an applicant for a job

(c) The normal working day of a librarian in a public library.

IDENTIFYING THE PROBLEMS

There were lots of problems. Caroline and Michael agreed these were the main ones in their area:

1. There was a lot of noise – crying, talking, squealing, shouting – and it all echoed around.
2. Babies did not like 'missing out' by being put in the play pens. They often cried or shouted to their mothers.
3. The babies cannot be left alone in the water – this was a problem if the mother had another child.
4. Toys from the play pens got thrown into the water.
5. There were not enough instructors for the number of babies in the class.
6. The towels and nappies often got dropped off the side benches and got wet.

By the end of the morning all the observations had been recorded. With all this information the students could now go back to school and talk about the problems with their Craft, Design and Technology teacher to see if they could come up with a real design problem that they could solve.

Caroline and Michael eventually decided on two problems that they could tackle.

DESIGN PROBLEMS

1. It is not possible at present for the baby to be involved in the general activity in the pool unless he or she is with an adult. It would be helpful if the child could sit in the water – in perfect safety – and watch the general activity. He or she would not feel so left out as when put in a play pen. *Design a baby seat that will hold the baby securely and which can be fitted to the edge of the pool in such a way that the baby can splash its legs in the water and watch what is going on from a position of complete safety.*
2. For the same group of babies it would be helpful to have a series of toys that are equally useful in and out of the water. *Design a push-along toy that will work on the pool side and will float acceptably when thrown into the water.*

PROBLEMS FROM THE OBSERVATIONS OF OTHER GROUPS

The morning spent in the swimming centre was just as useful for the groups who looked at other areas. These problems were decided upon by the groups who had to study the main pool, the observation lounge and the foyer of the centre.

1. When using the main pool it is not permitted to bring in bags of clothes and belongings. These must be stored in the lockers. The swimmers are only allowed to bring in a towel. Even so it is not uncommon for towels to get lost or stolen or taken by accident by the wrong person. *Design a hook or hook system that will ensure that your personal towel can only be used by you.*
2. Blocks of polystyrene (expanded) are commonly used as flotation or buoyancy aids for older children learning to swim. They are not ideal for several reasons. *Design a flotation aid that can be used in place of these polystyrene blocks and overcome their problems.*
3. In the pool observation lounge the No Smoking rule is strictly enforced, but there is a clear need for some waste containers for paper bags, sweet wrappers, crisp packets etc. *Design such a container bearing in mind the existing surroundings.*
4. A glance at the noticeboard in the foyer will show two things:
(a) The wide range of people and clubs that use the swimming centre noticeboard to advertise their activities: golf club, local

▲Fig. 10 How can the babies be held safely in the pool?

▶Fig. 11 Noticeboards are supposed to give information quickly and clearly

technical college, swimming teachers' association, and so on, as well as the various swimming activities such as the baby swimming class, OAP's swimming club, sub-aqua club etc.

(b) The information on display is jumbled and confusing. *Design an eye-catching noticeboard system that can be used by the clubs and classes* that use the swimming pool facilities, including an area for notices of general interest.

Later in the week, some of the groups returned to the swimming centre to get more information for the specific problem that they had chosen to tackle. The warden was very surprised about the number of problems that the design group had discovered. Michael and Caroline had a close look at the edges of the pool to see if any fixing points for a baby seat were available.

◄▲►Fig. 12 How can the seat be fixed to the pool side?

Questions

1 Why aren't the people in charge (like the warden at the swimming centre) necessarily the best people to ask about the problems that might exist?

2 Observe carefully a situation with which you are familiar, e.g. in your youth club, the sports club, the classroom or your bedroom. What problems can you find, and can you make them into DESIGN PROBLEMS that you could solve?

3 Can you think of the disadvantages of using expanded polystyrene blocks as buoyancy aids?

RESEARCH

Caroline and Michael decided to tackle the first of their two problems, the problem of providing a safe seat for the baby at the side of the pool. They analysed the problem and decided that there were five different things that they had to think about:

1. The seat must hold the baby securely and comfortably.
2. The seat must fix securely to the side/edge of the pool.
3. It must not be possible for the baby to unfix either itself or the seat.
4. The seat should be adjustable so that the baby can be raised and lowered slightly to allow for changing depth in the water or different sizes of baby.
5. The seat and fixings must be waterproof.

They knew that it was possible to buy baby seats for cars, and also that some manufacturers must specialise in producing equipment for swimming pools. So the start of their research was to write to these manufacturers (of seats and pool equipment) to find out what was available. Also they were able to ask about the important things they should build into their design. Figure 13 shows the sort of letter they wrote.

▶Fig. 13

Questions

1 Can you think of any other points the initial problem analysis could have contained? c

2 What other information would Michael and Caroline have needed before getting started on the design work? c

3 Apart from writing letters, how else could Caroline and Michael have got the information they wanted?

4 Do you think that writing letters was the most suitable means for getting the information they wanted? Explain why/why not.

5 If you were going to write to people or contact them in other ways, how would you find out who to contact?

6 When a company receives a letter from someone like you, how can you make them more willing to co-operate in your project? Remember that everything they do for *you* costs *them* money.

7 List the requirements for the flotation/buoyancy aid.

WINSTEAD COMPREHENSIVE SCHOOL
West High Street
Winstead

3rd October

Dear Sir,

We are students at Winstead Comprehensive School on an examination course in Design and Technology. We are writing to you for some help with our design project. We are trying to design and make a baby seat that will hold a baby on the edge of a swimming pool so that it can splash its legs in the water but at the same time it will be held safely in the seat. We think the seat will have to be slightly adjustable (up and down) so that the baby can be raised and lowered in the water.

It would be very helpful if we could see the details of the safety seats that you make, especially the system for holding the babies in safely. Also if there are any safety laws that we should know about for this project. We would be pleased if you could send us the information.

We enclose a large stamped addressed envelope for you to send us anything that you think might be helpful. Thank you very much for your help. We will let you see the project when we have finished it.

Yours sincerely,

Caroline Johnston
and
Michael Clark —

EXPLORING IDEAS

After they had received the replies and information from the manufacturers they had written to, and after they had got all the other information from the library that they thought might be useful, Caroline and Michael began to think about the design of the seat. It was clear that they could go about it in two quite different ways:

1. Get an existing safety seat and modify it so that it could be mounted on the side of the pool.
2. Design a new seat from scratch, with all the necessary features included.

Time was quite short, however. There were also many problems involved in making a seat from scratch. For both these reasons they decided to find an old seat and design around that. This is a small selection of their design sketches, which show the way their thinking developed.

▼▶Fig. 14

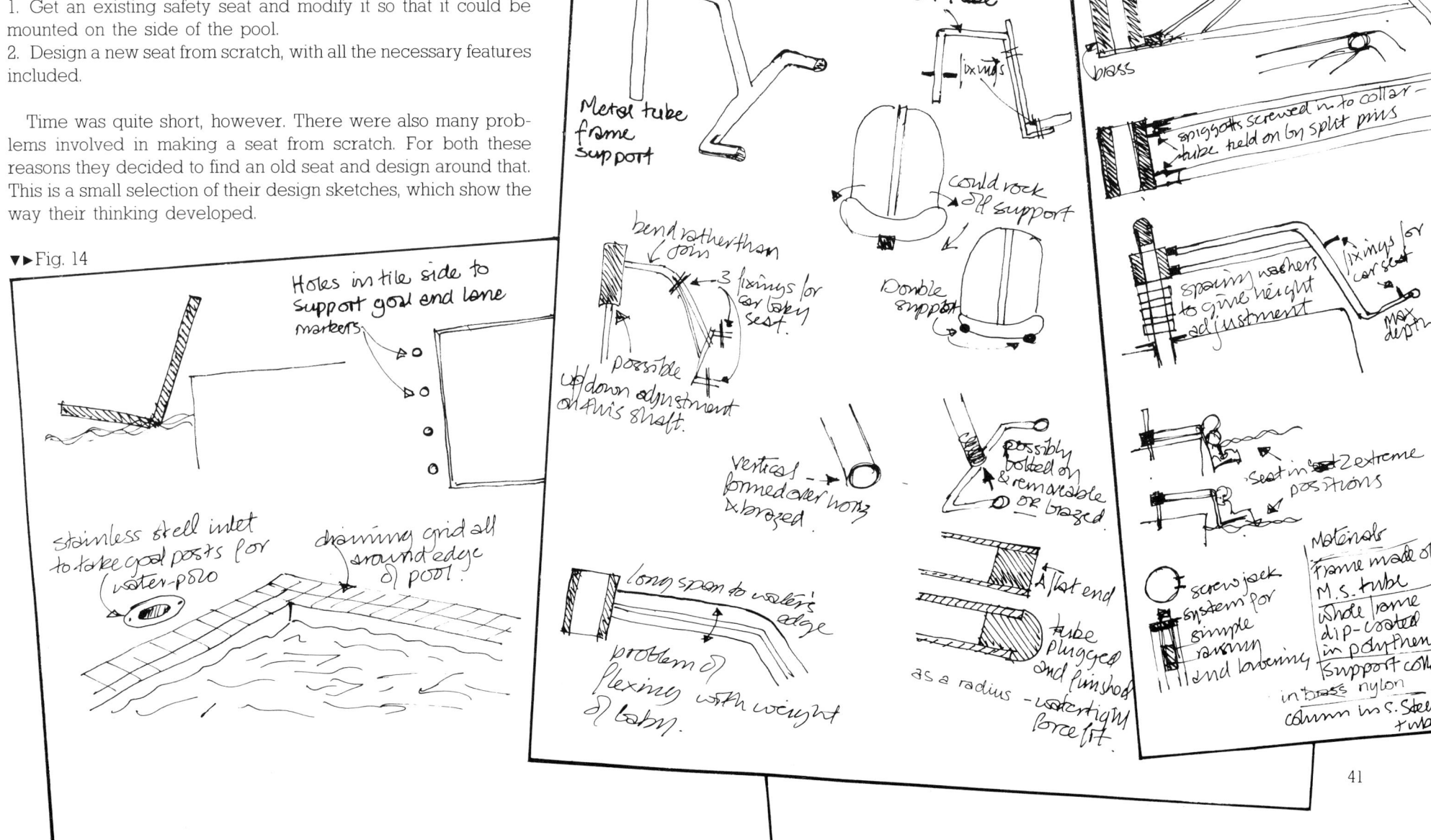

WORKING DRAWINGS

Having sorted out most of the problems for the pool seat, Caroline and Michael had to produce accurate drawings from which they could make the full size framework. Before doing the final drawings however, they went back to the swimming centre to check that they had got the important measurements right. The most important were the distance from the pool edge to the hole, the diameter and depth of the hole, and the level of the water below the pool side. They could then produce the working drawings.

▶Fig. 15 This information is vital and has to be accurate

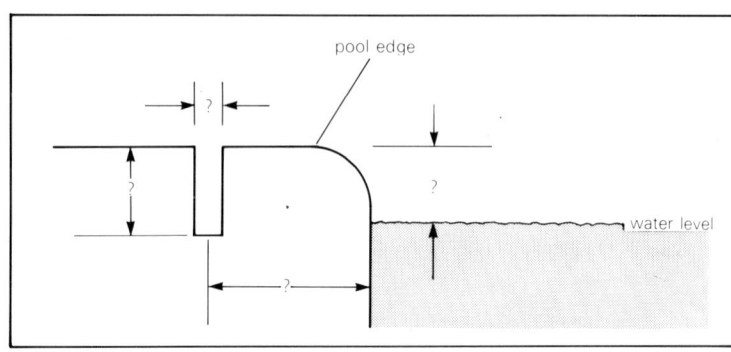

▼Fig. 16

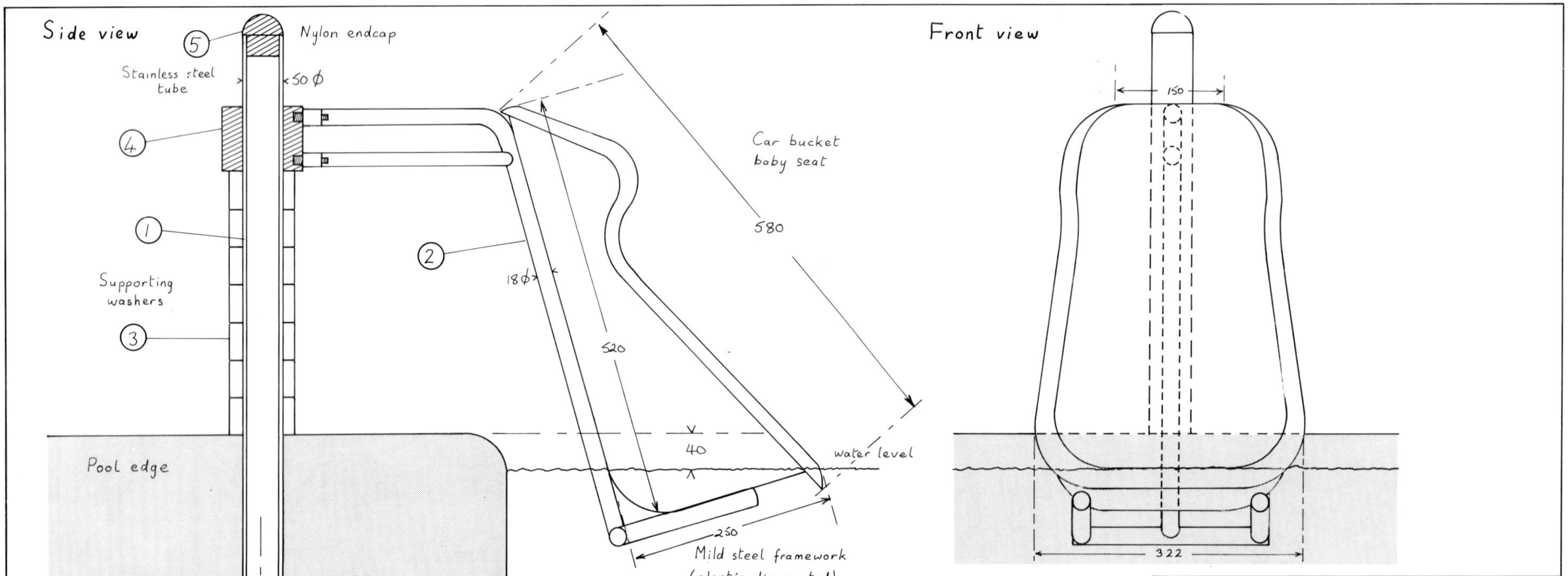

Side view

⑤ Nylon endcap

Stainless steel tube

◄50 ⌀

④

①

Supporting washers

③

②

180⌀

520

40

water level

250

Car bucket baby seat

580

Mild steel framework
(plastic dip coated)

Pool edge

300

Front view

150

322

5	Nylon	end cap	1
4	Nylon	collar	1
3	Nylon	washers	7
2	Mild steel	framework	1
1	Stainless steel	support column	1
Part No	Material	Description	No. off
Parts List			

Title of drawing. ADJUSTABLE BABY SEAT FOR SWIMMING CENTRE	
Scale of drawing 1:5	Dimensions in mm.
Name Caroline Johnson	Date 2-6-85

Questions

1 Examine the drawing. Are all the parts of the pool seat clear? Can you see how they all work? List all the points that are not clear to you (e.g. How does the tube framework fit to the nylon collar?)   **c**

2 Is it clear what materials are to be used? Why have these materials been chosen?   **c**

3 Working drawings use CONVENTIONS to simplify the presentation of information. (See chapter 4, pages 98–9.) Find some conventions on these drawings and explain why they are used. You will find another WD on page 33.   **c**

4 Caroline and Michael could have made a model to try out the structure of the seat and framework. If you were modelling this product, what materials would you use and what scale would you make it to? (See chapter 4, pages 96–7 for help.)

5 Why was nylon chosen as the material for the collar? Why do you think they changed their minds about using brass for this component?   **c**

6 Why do you think they decided *not* to plastic coat a mild steel tube for the column, but chose stainless steel instead?   **c**

7 How many components have they missed off the 'parts list' in the working drawing?

8 On this drawing, several components are too small to see properly, for example, the spigots holding the MS tube to the nylon collar. They need separate drawings. Produce accurate working drawings for the spigot and for the fixing units which hold the seat to the frame. You will have to sort out the design detail first.

PLANNING THE MAKING

Before they could begin to make the pool seat, Caroline and Michael had to make a list of all the things that they had to do in the making process. This PROCEDURE SHEET lists all the stages of making and in the right order. They must think through the whole making process before they start, and in that way they avoid problems arising at a later stage. They have both done a few design projects before, so they know roughly how long things will take to do.

PROCEDURE SHEET FOR POOL SEAT

Planned Action

Week 1. Get MS tube : cut to length and finish ends. Order stainless steel tube.

Week 2. Machine (lathe) the end plugs for tube and spigots for collar and fixing points for seat.

Week 3. Machine nylon collar and fit spigots.

Week 4. Bend MS tube. Braze joints and clean up.

Week 5. Have framework dip-coated in polythene and machine spacing washers.

Week 6. Cut off stainless steel tube to length. Machine and fit brass plug.

Week 7. Final assembly and checking of structure.

Questions

1 What sorts of problems does a procedure sheet help to eliminate?   **c**

2 Write out a procedure sheet for one of your past projects. Try to remember exactly what happened. Which parts of that project took you longer than you expected, and why?

3 Visit a local manufacturer and see how they plan their manufacturing procedure. What extra problems do they have?   **o**

4 Why did they decide to leave the work on the stainless steel column until week 6?   **c**

5 Some weeks will be harder work than others. Put them in order with the hardest week's work at the top and the easiest at the bottom.

MAKING

▲Fig. 17 Marking out must be accurate

▲Fig. 18 Cutting and filing the mild steel tube

▲Fig. 19 Using the tube bender needs teamwork

▲Fig. 20 Machining the end plugs is a precision job

▲Fig. 21 Brazing the framework

▼Fig. 22 They had to find someone to do the plastic coating for them

▼Fig. 23 The final assembly

Questions

To answer these questions, you will find it useful to read chapter 4, Making Skills.

1 How do you make the marking out lines show up clearly on mild steel (MS) tube?

2 Where will you get the stainless steel tube from?

3 What sort of fit should there be between the tube and the end plugs that seal it?

4 Describe in notes and sketches the stages of setting up a lathe tool for machining the plugs.

5 Describe the procedure for brazing the MS tube. What are the common causes of bad brazing joints?

6 What do you need to do to the MS tube before it can be dip coated in polythene? Where can this coating be done?

7 Why did they choose dip coating for this component?

8 (a) How is the finished frame to be fitted to the nylon collar?
   (b) Is this a permanent or a temporary joint?
   (c) What alternatives were there?

9 Do the plugs go into the tube before or after the joints are brazed? Explain your answer.

EVALUATION

When they had finished making the pool seat, Michael and Caroline tested it as much as they could in the workshop to make sure that it worked properly and was strong enough. However, the real test came when they took it back to the swimming centre and tried it out in the learner pool with some volunteer babies. They had a lot of questions that needed answering. This was done on a simple questionnaire which some of the parents and the baby class instructor filled in.

There were one or two small problems with the seat. It tended to swivel on the column and knock into the side of the pool. Also it was difficult to adjust the height of the seat with the baby sitting in it. Michael and Caroline began to think up modifications to the seat to overcome these difficulties. For the height adjustment they looked at systems for using a screw thread like some car jacks. This would make the seat more sophisticated but much simpler to adjust whilst the baby was in it.

▼Fig. 24 Checking the installation   ▼Fig. 25 The real test of the finished product

Questions

1 On page 40 you will see the five important design features that Caroline and Michael identified. Bearing these in mind, what questions would you ask to evaluate the performance of the pool seat? **c**

2 Who would you ask in addition to the parents and the instructor?

3 Would you ask the same questions of all the people? Look at pages 24–5 for some help on this. **c**

4 Think about one of your past projects and list all the questions that need to be asked to evaluate it fully. Say who you would ask.

5 If Michael and Caroline had thought about marketing this pool seat and getting a manufacturer to make it for them commercially, what questions would the manufacturer have asked about the seat?

6 Select a consumer product and design a simple questionnaire to evaluate it. **o**

7 The other groups at the swimming centre found several quite different problems and four of these are given on page 38. **c,x,o**

Problem 1 What systems exist in your local swimming pool to overcome this problem?

Problem 2 How do instructors teach children to use these buoyancy aids when learning to swim (a) the breastroke, (b) the backstroke?

Are they equally useful in both cases? Are there any special flotation aids to help handicapped children to learn to swim? Where would you expect to find details of those products?

Problem 3 Why is it important that the No Smoking rule is enforced in the swimming centre? Why is it more important here than in some other places? Draw a plan of the reception area in your school and mark on it the position of litter bins. Observe people using the area and decide if there are enough bins and if they are sensibly placed. How often are they emptied and whose job is that?

Problem 4 Do a detailed survey of the noticeboards used in your school. Are they well organised? Are messages easy to pass on to specific individuals or groups? Are they placed in the best position? How could they be improved?

THE PLAYGROUP

Several students were interested in carrying out a design project that would help a local playgroup. As the presence of a large number of observers would interfere with the smooth running of the session, two students, Jane and Tony, were chosen to visit the centre where the playgroup was based.

OBSERVING THE SITUATION

Before the morning session began, they talked to the leader of the playgroup who outlined the way the sessions worked. They then spent the morning watching carefully and making brief notes and sketches of their observations. Jane and Tony managed to spend some time talking to parents of children using the playgroup. They made careful notes on their conversations.

◄Fig. 1 Jane and Tony discussed playgroup activities with the leader

PLAYGROUP OBSERVATION

TUESDAY 20th JUNE 1983

9.30 Mums, Dads and children start arriving. It's wet, small waiting space, no seats, not enough room to hang up wet clothes. Helpers start to set up the hall. A lot to get out in a short while

10.00 - Parents have gone. 20 children left with 3 helpers plus 1 leader. Some children are crying and are being coaxed into activity. Others know what they want to do and do it. There seems to be a free choice of what to do.

11.00 - Half way through the session. Most children have tried 3 or 4 different activities. they seem to change when they want to. the few squabbles are dealt with by helpers. One child has been crying since his dad left at 10.00. Two other children have just sat and watched the others and not joined in.

11.30 - Noise level much higher now. 4 or 5 children being naughty.

11.45 - leader tells story to all children while helpers begin to put the equipment away. They find it difficult to check that some games equipment is complete.

12.00 - Parents arrive to collect children. Finding clothes is a problem despite assistance from helpers.

12.15 - Parents and children have gone. Helpers put away remaining equipment. Cupboards for equipment storage are too small.

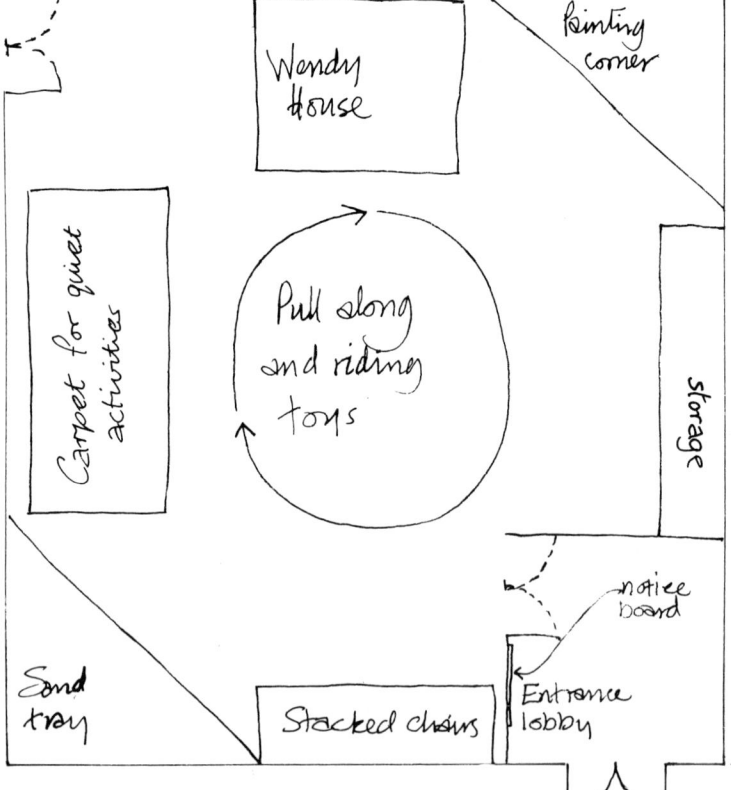

◄Fig. 2 Jane's plan of the playgroup drawn to scale 1:100, with the activities marked

Questions

1 The students used notes and sketches to record their observations. Other possibilities are photographs, videotapes and audiotapes. What are the advantages and disadvantages of these various methods? How might the disadvantages be overcome?

2 The presence of just two extra people might have had a disruptive effect on the playgroup. How can the observers find out if their presence upset the morning's session?

3 The storage of wet clothes caused problems at the beginning of the session. What were these problems? Suggest three ways in which they might be overcome?   c

4 The storage of equipment posed at least three problems. What were they? ·   c

5 One child cried for most of the session and at least two others were not involved in any activity. Suggest possible reasons for this. Is this a serious problem and, if so, what should be done about it?

6 What happens to the noise level towards the end of the session? What appears to happen at the same time? What solutions might there be to these 'end of session' problems?   c

7 A lot of time is spent getting equipment out and putting it away. Why not simply leave the equipment out? Can you think of any other people who might use the room?

8 Is there enough detail in the notebook? Remember Jane and Tony spent 3 hours at the playgroup.   c

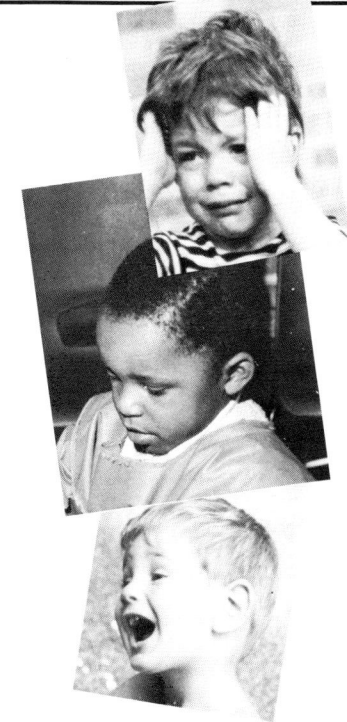

▲Fig. 4 What can you tell from these faces?

▼Fig. 3 The playgroup in action

1 How many different activities can you identify in fig. 3? List them.   c

2 Why might a playgroup need a wide range of activities?

3 How many children are not involved in an activity? How does this compare with the number that are involved?   c

4 Can you tell if there are enough toys and activities to go round?   c

5 What are the helpers doing?   c

Use the photographs in fig. 4 to answer the following questions.

6 What can you tell from the expressions on the faces of the children – boredom, frustration, anger, pleasure, interest, happiness? Try to identify the feelings of each child shown.   c

7 How might understanding these expressions help you to identify problems?

8 Can you tell how old the children are? Why might this be important?   c

IDENTIFYING THE PROBLEMS

Jane and Tony visited the playgroup twice more and from their observations arrived at the following list of problems.

1. Outdoor coats and shoes, often wet, have to be stored during a playgroup session.

2. The playgroup noticeboard for parents and helpers is badly damaged and unattractive.

3. In fine weather the playgroup wishes to play on the grass. Unfortunately this area backs onto a dangerous pond.

4. The storage facilities in the hall are inadequate.

5. The playgroup does not have enough toys to go round.

6. The playgroup has no large toys for use outside in fine weather.

7. The playgroup has no large indoor climbing activities.

Questions

1 For each of the above problems write a design brief that you could use as a starting point to solve the problem.   c

2 Use the observation notes on page 46 to find the observations that led to the identification of the problems listed above.   c

RESEARCH

Jane decided that she would try to design and make a storage unit for wet outdoor clothes and shoes. Her analysis of the brief suggested that there were five areas requiring further information:

1. the types of outdoor clothes and shoes worn by the children,
2. the size of such clothes for the 3–5 year age range,
3. the size of children's shoes and wellingtons for this age range,
4. the size of 'hanging' loops that manufacturers attach to children's clothes,
5. the height that children in the 3–5 year age range can reach.

Jane thought she could find the answers to (1) and (4) by observation at the playgroup. The other information was obtained by writing to a large children's outfitters and The Design Council.

In Britain The Design Council is an organisation set up by the Government to help industry improve the design of its products. Its address is 28 Haymarket, London, SW1Y 4SU. It helps industry in the following ways:

- by advising firms on the solution to design problems,
- by publishing information on design,
- by promoting and advertising outstanding British design achievements,
- by encouraging improvements in the training of designers,
- by stimulating interest in design among school students and their teachers.

The Design Council may be able to help themselves, or to suggest somewhere else you might write to for the information. The librarian in your local library could also be a useful starting point in your enquiries and may be able to suggest how to go about finding particular types of information (see chapter 4, pages 88–9, on researching). In this case, The Design Council suggested that Jane contact the Ergonomics Society, and they were able to provide the information Jane needed. Copies of the letters Jane wrote are shown in figs. 5 and 6. The reply from The Design Council is shown in fig. 7.

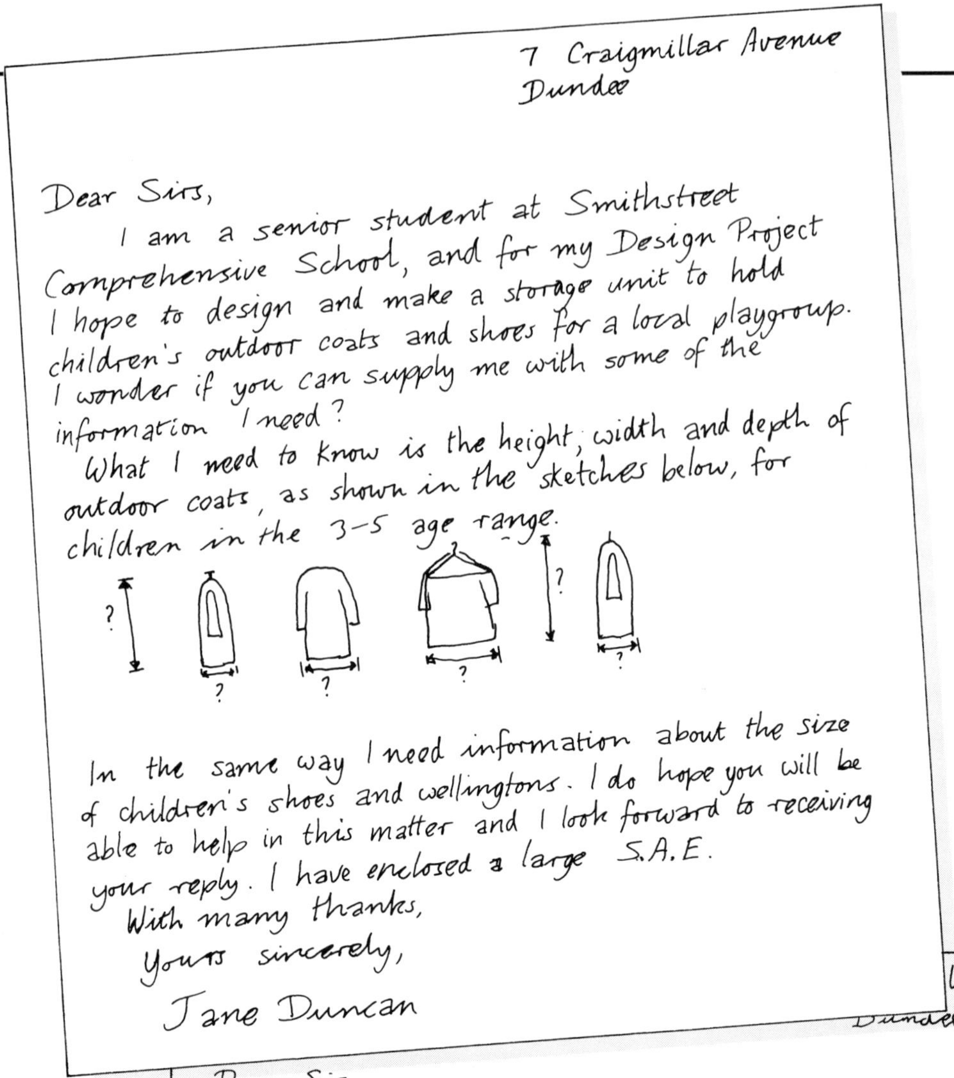

▶▲Fig. 5 Jane's letter to a children's clothes manufacturer

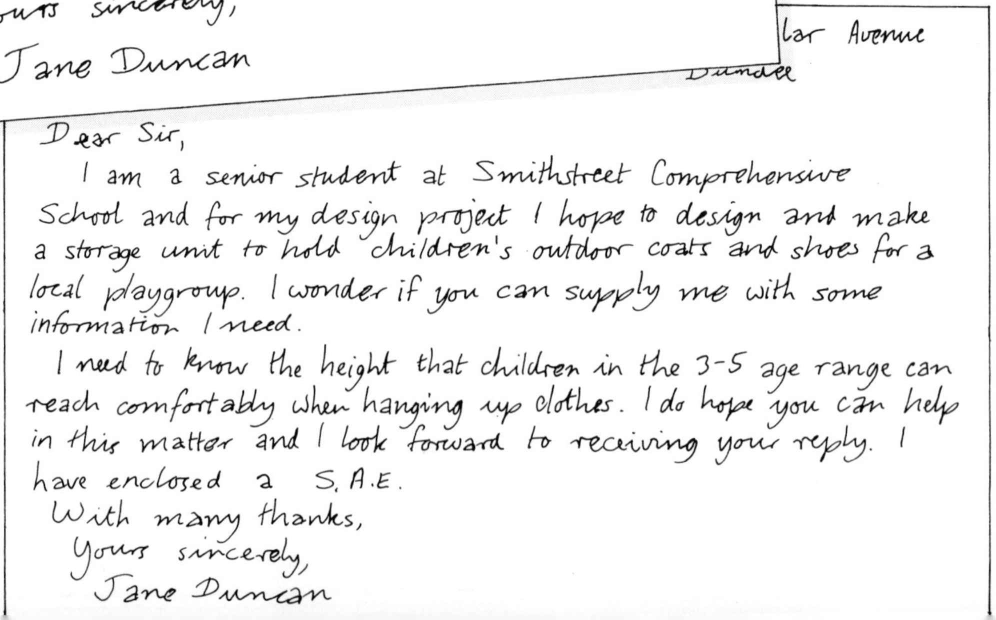

▶Fig. 6 Jane's letter to the Design Council

7 Craigmillar Avenue
Dundee

Dear Sirs,

I am a senior student at Smithstreet Comprehensive School, and for my Design Project I hope to design and make a storage unit to hold children's outdoor coats and shoes for a local playgroup. I wonder if you can supply me with some of the information I need?

What I need to know is the height, width and depth of outdoor coats, as shown in the sketches below, for children in the 3–5 age range.

In the same way I need information about the size of children's shoes and wellingtons. I do hope you will be able to help in this matter and I look forward to receiving your reply. I have enclosed a large S.A.E.

With many thanks,

Yours sincerely,

Jane Duncan

7 Craigmillar Avenue
Dundee

Dear Sir,

I am a senior student at Smithstreet Comprehensive School and for my design project I hope to design and make a storage unit to hold children's outdoor coats and shoes for a local playgroup. I wonder if you can supply me with some information I need.

I need to know the height that children in the 3–5 age range can reach comfortably when hanging up clothes. I do hope you can help in this matter and I look forward to receiving your reply. I have enclosed a S.A.E.

With many thanks,

Yours sincerely,

Jane Duncan

▼Fig. 7 The Design Council, as always, provides useful information

Information provided by the Ergonomics Society of the University of Technology, Loughborough indicated that children in the 3–5 year age range could reach a peg 120 cm above floor level. Jane carried out a survey of the outdoor coats and footwear used by the playgroup children in wet weather. Her results are shown in fig. 8. Using the information obtained from her research, Jane was able to identify the critical dimensions, shown in fig. 9.

▼Fig. 8 Jane's survey results

FOOTWEAR SURVEY	
Total number of children = 21	
Shoes	3
Wellies	15
Others	3

OUTDOOR COAT SURVEY	
Total number of children = 21	
Raincoats	8
Parkas	10
Kagools	2
Anoraks	—
Others	1

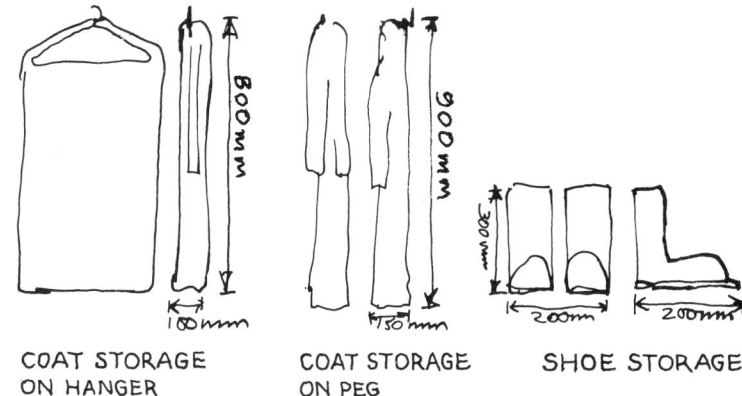

COAT STORAGE ON HANGER   COAT STORAGE ON PEG   SHOE STORAGE

▲Fig. 9 Critical dimensions obtained from Jane's research

Questions

1 Jane could have measured the clothes and shoes of the children who attended the playgroup. Suggest reasons why she did not do this. Explain why it is useful to have manufacturers' information. Why would it have been better to get information from both sources?   **c**

2 Suppose Jane had been unable to find out the height that playgroup children can reach. Devise a series of experiments and observations that would enable her to gather this information for herself. Remember that small children enjoy games and that a 'reaching' game might give her the information she needs.

3 In surveying the coats and footwear used by the children in bad weather, Jane recorded information on one wet-weather day. Why is this likely to give false information? What can be done to overcome this? What might be the consequences of using such false information?

4 Researched information showed that the maximum height for wellingtons was 25 cm, yet the space Jane allowed for footwear storage shows 30 cm. Similarly the maximum length for an outdoor coat was 80 cm, yet 90 cm was allowed. Explain clearly why the spaces allowed (the critical dimensions) are apparently larger than necessary.

5 Using the appropriate critical dimensions calculate the approximate length for a storage unit to hold 20 outdoor coats side by side (a) from hangers and (b) from pegs.   **c**

EXPLORING IDEAS

Jane has to use the information she has collected through her research. This section describes her thinking and highlights the decisions she made. Read it carefully and answer the questions to understand the reasons for the decisions.

Piling coats on each other is no good – they get crumpled, linings get wet, individual clothes are hard to find and I can't link coats with shoes.

I know – I need to use pegs or hangers!

If the coats overlap, linings will get wet.

Explain why this will happen. Jane decided to restrict hanging to side by side with no overlap.
Why does this rule out double hooks?
Why is this costly in terms of space?

Jane knew that clothes can be hung from pegs or hangers. Hangers can be loose or fixed as shown in fig. 10.

►Fig. 10 Possible coat hanger designs

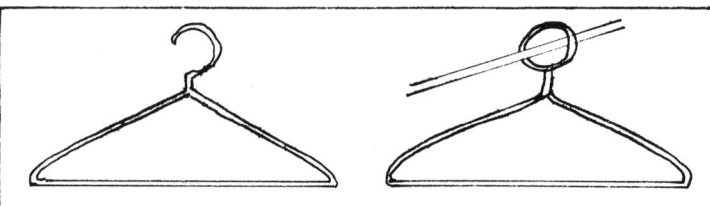

I'll use single pegs – Loose hangers will get lost and fixed hangers would be difficult for children to use. Coats will end up on the floor.

Jane has no evidence to support her opinion that children will find fixed hangers difficult to use. How can she find out?

What advantages are there in having a system that children can use easily?

I'll use a row of single pegs 120 cm above the floor.

The area for a pair of shoes is similar to the area needed by a coat hanging from a peg, as shown by Jane's sketch in fig. 11.

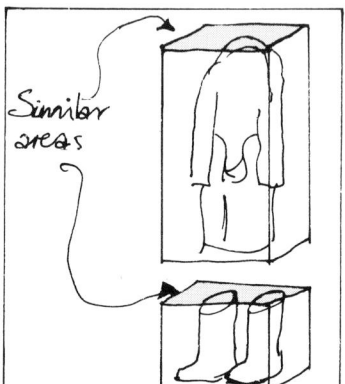

◄Fig. 11 Storage area comparisons between footwear and outdoor coats

If I put the shoes above or below the coats I can link them!

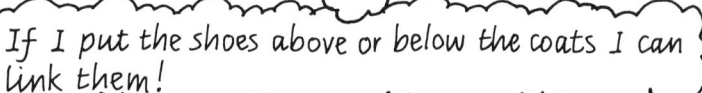

Do you think this 'one above the other' arrangement provides sufficient link?
How might this link be strengthened?

Jane reasoned that with a footwear compartment above a coat there is no possibility of water dripping into the shoes but there is the danger of the child pulling wet muddy shoes onto his face as shown in fig. 12. With the shoe compartment beneath the coat there is no safety problem, but the footwear will need protection from drips.

I wonder . . . is there room for a compartment beneath a coat?

She decided that there was.
What information did she have to use to make this decision? Where did she find this information?

In order to find out how much protection footwear would need from dripping clothes, Jane decided to find out how wet clothes dripped. (fig. 13.)

Design a series of experiments for yourself that finds out how a range of children's coats drip. Your experiments should find out:
(i) the area beneath each garment that receives drips,
(ii) whether different types of coat give different drip areas,
(iii) some of the factors governing the size and shape of the drip area.

A sheet of blue cobalt chloride paper placed beneath a dripping coat will reveal drip area. Talk to your science teacher about this.

From her experiments Jane decided that it was necessary to cover the whole of the shoes. She also discovered that within a playgroup session there was little chance of a 'soaked-through' coat drying out when hung on a peg. Jane has decided to use pegs. What problem has her discovery revealed? What can she do about it, or should she stick to her original decision?

Jane thought about getting shoes in and out of the compartment. She reasoned that if they were put in from the top the compartment would need a movable lid to act as a drip tray (see fig. 14A). She thought that if the shoes were put in from the front

▲Fig. 12 The hazards of overhead storage

▼Fig. 13 Just how do wet clothes drip?

the compartment could be fitted with a fixed drip tray (see fig. 14B). She decided that access from the front was the best solution.

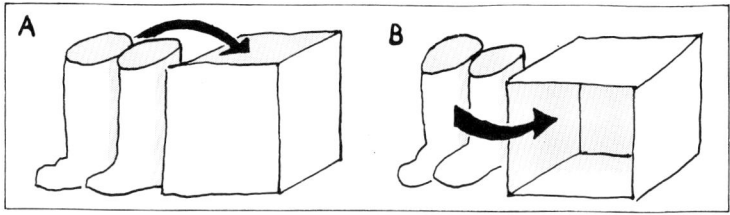

▲Fig. 14 Shoes in from the top or the front – which is best?

What disadvantages might there be in loose lids and hinged lids?

You could design the footwear compartments to be seats as well.

I wonder if he's right?

Jane rejected her friend's suggestion. There are several valid reasons why Jane is right to do this. What are they?

Jane was now in a position to write out a more detailed design brief based on her thinking and decision making so far. Remember, the starting brief was:
To design and make a simple inexpensive storage system for coats and shoes.
The more detailed brief now reads:
To design and make an inexpensive storage unit in which the coats hang side by side from single pegs without overlap; peg height to be 120 cm above floor level. Beneath each peg is a footwear compartment fixed with a drip tray top.
In what ways is this more detailed brief different from the starting brief?

THINKING ABOUT POSSIBLE ARRANGEMENTS

Jane now had to think about possible arrangements that would meet the requirements of her more detailed design brief. By asking questions about the way different arrangements will work and what their advantages and disadvantages might be Jane worked out the best general arrangement. Figures 15A, B and C show a series of extracts from her notebook. Read them carefully and answer the questions at the end of each section.

▶Fig. 15A

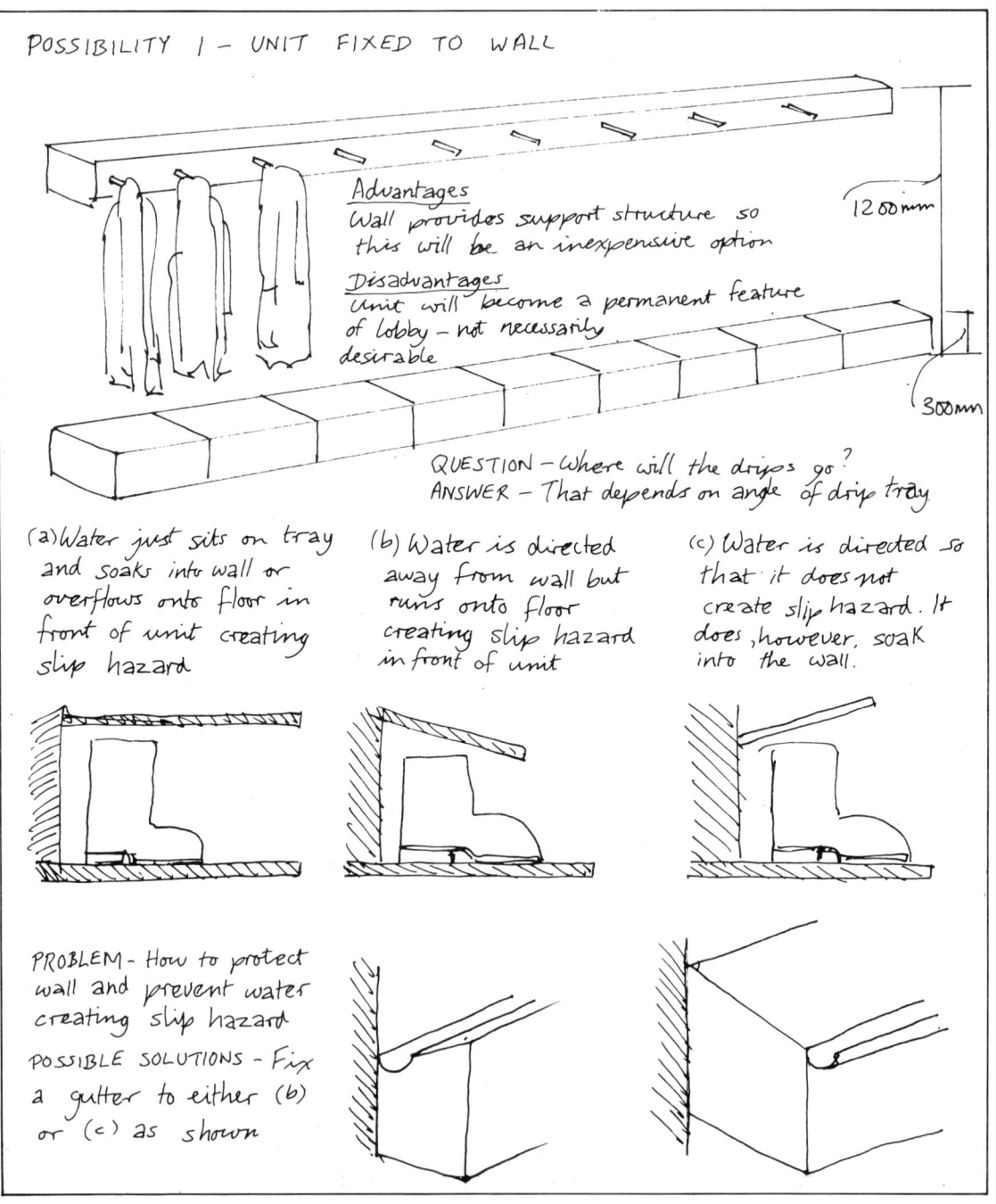

POSSIBILITY 1 – UNIT FIXED TO WALL

1200mm

300mm

Advantages
Wall provides support structure so this will be an inexpensive option

Disadvantages
Unit will become a permanent feature of lobby – not necessarily desirable

QUESTION – Where will the drips go?
ANSWER – That depends on angle of drip tray

(a) Water just sits on tray and soaks into wall or overflows onto floor in front of unit creating slip hazard

(b) Water is directed away from wall but runs onto floor creating slip hazard in front of unit

(c) Water is directed so that it does not create slip hazard. It does, however, soak into the wall.

PROBLEM – How to protect wall and prevent water creating slip hazard
POSSIBLE SOLUTIONS – Fix a gutter to either (b) or (c) as shown

Questions (fig. 15A)

1 Show clearly how you can calculate the length of wall required for a unit to take 20 coats.   c

2 Make a copy of the plan on page 46 and use it to decide if this length of wall is available in the lobby. Give reasons for your answer.   c

3 What is the maximum number of coats that can be hung in the lobby using this arrangement? Again use the plan and give reasons for your answer.   c

4 In this arrangement the unit cannot be moved from the lobby. What problems might this cause?   c

Questions (fig. 15B)

1 Calculate the approximate length and width of a 20 coat unit. **c**

2 Calculate the approximate room (volume) taken up by a complete 20-coat unit in this arrangement and the room taken up by 20 coat–shoe spaces. Explain clearly how these calculations show that the back-to-back unit is economical on space. **c**

3 Use your copy of the plan and a simple scale model of the unit to find the best position for the unit in the lobby. Give reasons for your choice of location. **c**

4 What advantages and disadvantages might there be in the unit being easily movable? **c**

▶Fig. 15B

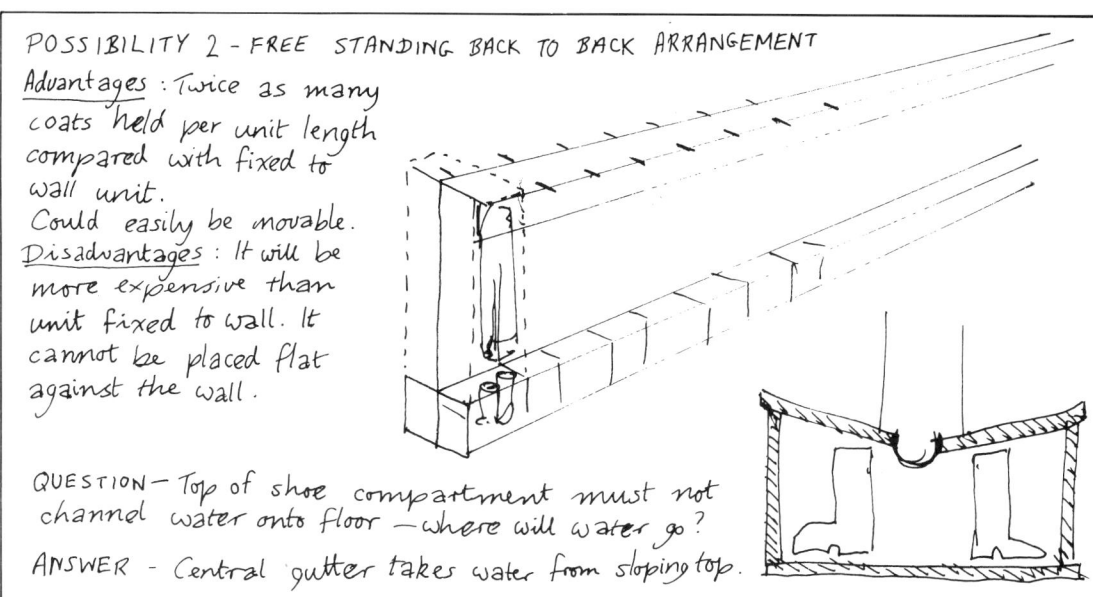

POSSIBILITY 2 – FREE STANDING BACK TO BACK ARRANGEMENT

Advantages: Twice as many coats held per unit length compared with fixed to wall unit.
Could easily be movable.

Disadvantages: It will be more expensive than unit fixed to wall. It cannot be placed flat against the wall.

QUESTION – Top of shoe compartment must not channel water onto floor – where will water go?

ANSWER – Central gutter takes water from sloping top.

Questions (fig. 15C)

▶Fig. 15C

1 Calculate the diameter of the circular unit if it is to hold 20 coats. Show your working clearly. Remember $2\pi r$ = circumference of a circle, where r is the radius. **c**

2 If a 20-coat circular unit is placed in a corner of the lobby, how many coat places would be 'blocked off'? **c**

3 How could a turntable arrangement solve this problem? What are the advantages and disadvantages of such an arrangement? **c**

4 Use your copy of the plan and a simple scale model of the circular unit to find the best position for the unit in the lobby. Give reasons for your choice of location. **c**

5 Calculate the approximate room taken up by an entire circular 20-coat unit. Compare this with the room taken up by 20 coat–shoe spaces. Explain clearly how these calculations show that a circular arrangement is wasteful of space. **c**

Jane decided that the best arrangement was a mobile back-to-back arrangement. Using the information given in pages 91–5, draw a perspective view of the lobby plus Jane's chosen unit. Use this to decide whether you agree with Jane's decision. **c**

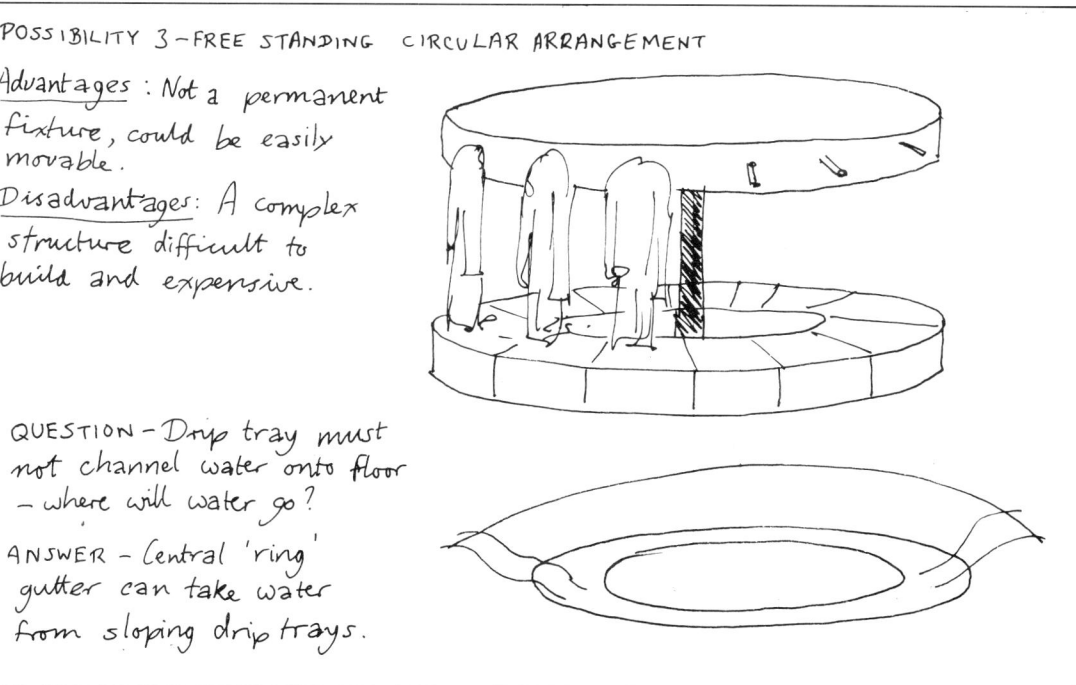

POSSIBILITY 3 – FREE STANDING CIRCULAR ARRANGEMENT

Advantages: Not a permanent fixture, could be easily movable.

Disadvantages: A complex structure difficult to build and expensive.

QUESTION – Drip tray must not channel water onto floor – where will water go?

ANSWER – Central 'ring' gutter can take water from sloping drip trays.

DEVELOPING IDEAS

Now that Jane had decided upon an arrangement for the unit, she had to work out the details of the construction. From these details she would be able to produce the working drawings, the plans, for the unit. The comments on her sketches (figs. 16–19) show how she decided upon the detailed plans. Read these carefully and answer the questions at the end of each section.

Questions about the stability of the unit (fig. 16)

1 Which is best – to increase the width of the base at the ends only or along the entire length of the unit? Give reasons for your answer.   **c**

2 Fixing castors to the base will make the unit movable. Bearing in mind your answer to question 1, use sketches to show where you would fix castors. Give reasons for your decision.   **c**

3 Use sketches to show how you would build 'triangles' into the unit to prevent the deformation shown. Explain clearly why your structure won't deform so easily.   **c**

4 Find out the meaning of the term 'centre of gravity' and explain how this affects the stability of an object.   **c**

Questions about the framework (fig. 17)

1 Which would you use for the frame – timber or steel? Give reasons for your decision.   **c**

2 If you were making the framework from timber, what joints would you use at A, B and C? Give reasons for your answer.   **c**

3 It is possible to use sheet material to make the 'triangles' shown. Suggest suitable sheet material.   **c**

4 What ways, other than brazing or welding, are there for joining a steel tube framework together?

5 In what ways could a steel frame be prevented from rusting?

6 In what ways could a timber frame be prevented from rotting?

7 Build a simple scale model of the framework using wire and soft solder. Use cardboard 'additions' to investigate the ideas shown in figs. 18 and 19.   **x**

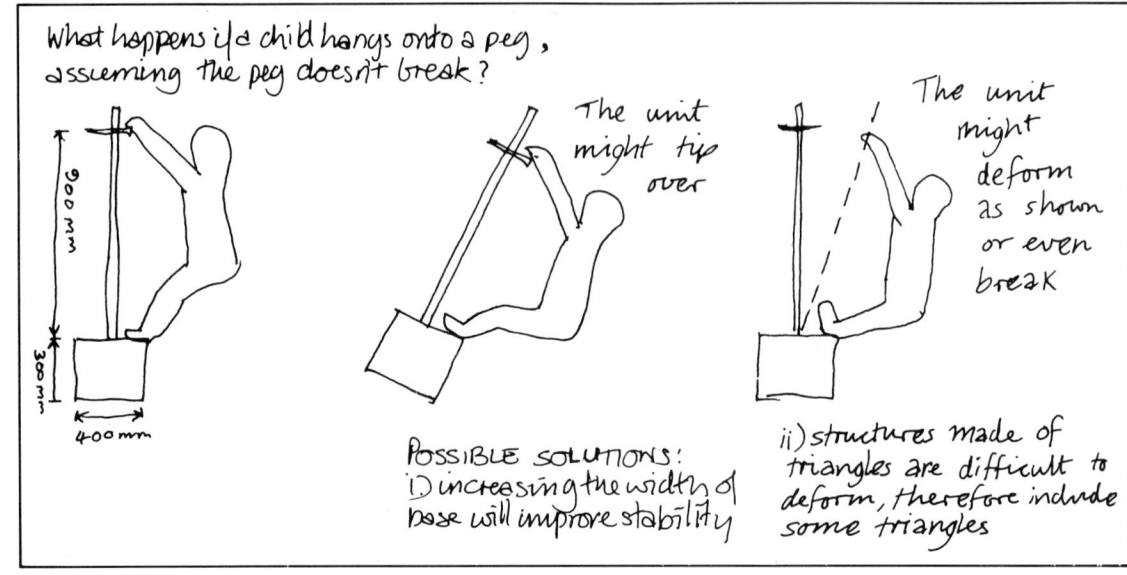

▲Fig. 16 How stable is the unit?

▼Fig. 17 What can be used for the framework?

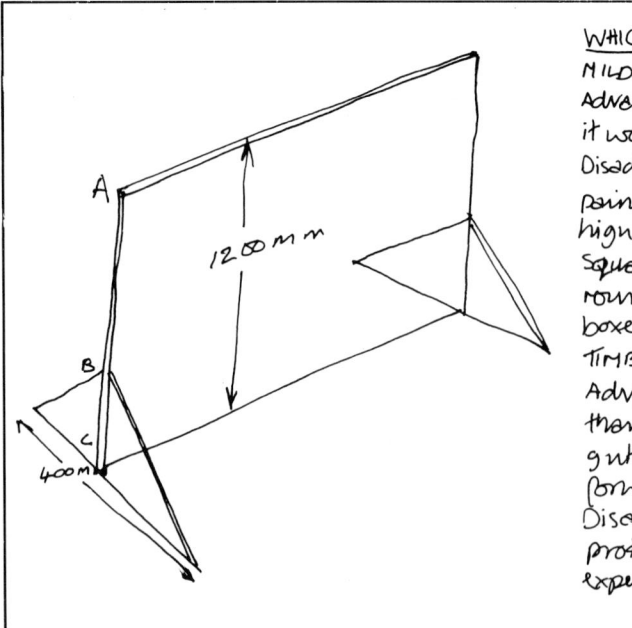

Questions about the shoe compartments (fig. 18)

1 Jane reasoned that whatever material she chose for the lid should have the following properties:

(a) water repellant and non-absorbent,

(b) resistant to corrosion or rotting,

(c) resistant to fracture, tough,

(d) resistant to distortion, it shouldn't warp or twist,

(e) resistant to abrasion, a durable surface finish,

(f) easy to work and fix to the unit,

(g) readily available in the required length,

(h) inexpensive.

Explain clearly the importance of each of these properties. **c**

2 Jane thought that one of the following materials would be suitable:

polyvinyl chloride sheet (PVC)

acrylic sheet (Perspex)

polycarbonate sheet

galvanised steel sheet

exterior quality plywood.

Bearing in mind the required properties, draw up a table showing the advantages and disadvantages of each material. Look at chapter 1, pages 12–13, and chapter 4 pages 102–105 for help. **c**

3 Jane believed that using the same or similar materials for the lid, bottom and sides of the shoe compartments is an advantage. Do you agree with her? Give reasons for your answer.

4 Jane decided that the best way to work out the minimum slope for the lid was by experiment. Give brief details of the experiments you would carry out to find out the slope.

Questions about the partition (fig. 19)

1 What properties should the partition material have? Give reasons for your answer.

2 Which of the materials suggested for the lid might be suitable for the partition? Give reasons for your answer. **c**

3 How might the partition be fitted to a frame made of square section steel tube and a frame made of timber? Why is it important for the partition to be removable?

4 Design a style of numbering that would be appropriate for a playgroup coat rack.

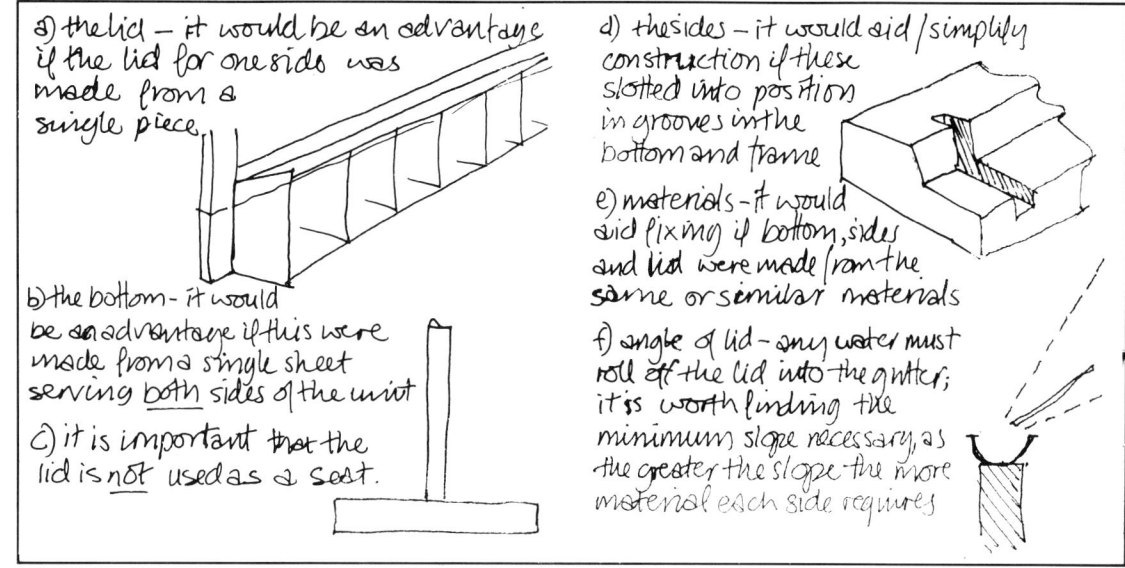

a) the lid – it would be an advantage if the lid for one side was made from a single piece.

b) the bottom – it would be an advantage if this were made from a single sheet serving both sides of the unit

c) it is important that the lid is not used as a seat.

d) the sides – it would aid/simplify construction if these slotted into position in grooves in the bottom and frame

e) materials – it would aid fixing if bottom, sides and lid were made from the same or similar materials

f) angle of lid – any water must roll off the lid into the gutter; it is worth finding the minimum slope necessary, as the greater the slope the more material each side requires

▲Fig. 18 Shoe compartment details

▼Fig. 19 The partition separating the coats

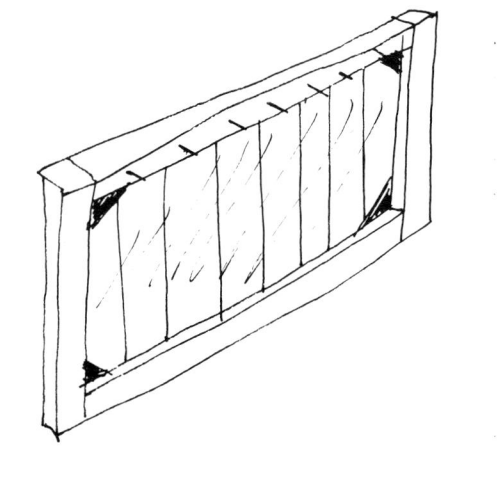

coats hanging opposite each other on either side of the unit might get tangled and/or make each other's linings wet. A partition running the length of the unit solves this problem.

If the partition were transparent this would provide an element of 'hide and seek' fun for the children.

The in-line arrangement of the pegs and shoe compartments can be strengthened by printing dividing lines on the partition. Numbers and/or pictures can be printed in each section.

5 Design a series of pictures that would be suitable for a playgroup coat rack.

▼Fig. 20 Coat pegs in local shops

Jane investigated the coat pegs available from local shops. Her findings are shown in fig. 20. Which peg do you think would be most suitable for her requirements?

▼Fig. 21 Jane's working drawing for the unit

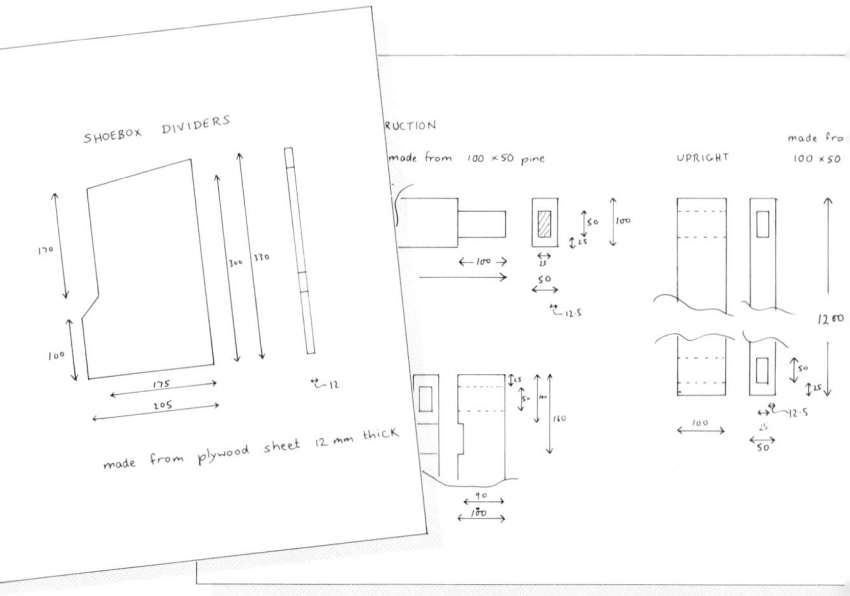

SKETCH	MATERIAL	METHOD OF ATTACHMENT	DURABILITY
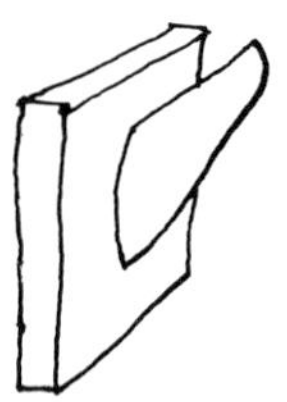	plastic	sticky pad	easily pulled off
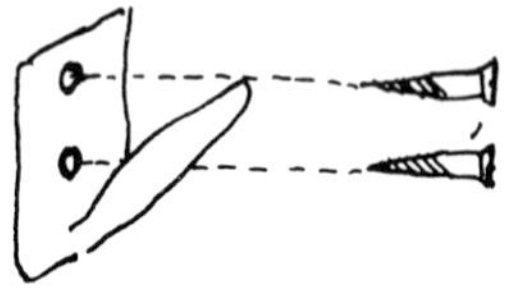	steel coated in plastic	woodscrews	firmly attached, might bend/break
	steel and plastic	steel holder screwed to surface, plastic peg slips over holder	firmly attached unlikely to break

WORKING DRAWINGS

With the details thoroughly worked out Jane was able to produce the working drawings. Some of these are shown in fig. 21. As the coat rack is a large item she scaled down the drawing and presented the details in insets as shown. Using the working drawings, Jane was able to produce the parts list shown in fig. 22.

Using the price list given in fig. 23, calculate the cost of materials and fixings required to make the unit. c

FIXINGS AND FIXTINGS

ITEM	DESCRIPTION	NO. OFF
steel c/s wood screws	No 8 50mm	11 (to fix base to frame)
brass dome head wood screws	No 8 50mm	8 (to fix end plates to frame)
"	No 6 30mm	14 (to fix end plate to cross piece)
"	No 4 25mm	10 (to fix gutter to frame)
steel c/s wood screws	No 8 30mm	8 (to fix cross piece to base)
brass machine screw and nut	M5 × 25mm	4 (to fix partition to supports)
Coat pegs (inc. screws)		20
Castors (inc. screws)		4
PVC adhesive tape		1 roll

▲Fig. 22 Jane's parts list for the unit

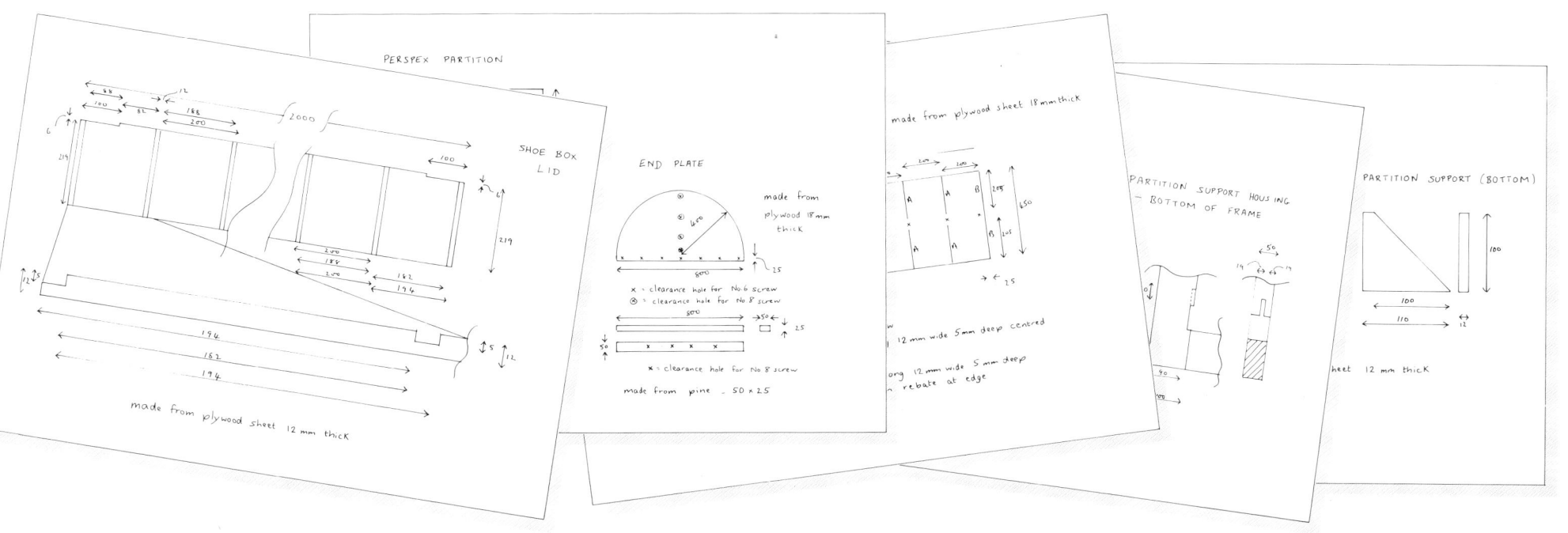

►Fig. 23 Price list for materials and fixings

CUTTING LIST

ITEM	MATERIAL	DIMENSIONS	NO.OFF
frame (upright)	pine	1200 × 100 × 50	2
frame (across)	pine	2000 × 100 × 50	2
gutter	pvc	1840 length	1
base	plywood	2000 × 450 × 18	1
lid	plywood	2000 × 225 × 12	2
dividers	plywood	330 × 205 × 12 (overall size)	22
partition	perspex	1795 × 995 × 5	1
partition support	plywood 12 mm thick	triangular plate 110 × 110 × 155	2
partition support	plywood 12 mm thick	triangular plate 105 × 105 × 150	2
end plate	plywood 18 mm thick	semicircular plate 400 radius	2
cross piece	pine	800 × 50 × 25	2
perspex numbers	perspex	500 × 250 × 5	1

pine 100 × 50	– £2.00 per lineal metre
pine 50 × 25	– £0.50 per lineal metre
guttering	– £1.50 per metre
plywood 18 mm thick	– £20.00 per 2m × 1m sheet
plywood 12 mm thick	– £12.50 per 2m × 1m sheet
perspex sheet 5mm thick	– £10.00 per 2m × 1m sheet
steel c/s wood screw No 8 50mm	– 0.03 each
No 8 30mm	– 0.03 each
brass dome head wood screw No 8 50mm	– 0.06 each
" No 6 30mm	– 0.04 each
" No 4 25mm	– 0.04 each
brass machine screw and nut M5 × 25mm	– 0.15 each
coat pegs	– 0.75 each
castors (and screws)	– £1.50 each
pvc adhesive tape	– 0.90 per roll
cascamite glue	– £2.50 small tin
Tensol	– £2.50 small tin
polyurethane varnish	– £6.00 large tin

PLANNING THE MAKING PROCESS

In order to build the unit efficiently, Jane produced a week-by-week plan of action for the complete process. Each stage in the plan is described with illustrations on this and the following two pages. When you draw up a plan of action it is important to bear the following in mind:

1. It should be as realistic as possible – each week should contain an amount of work that can be done in a week.

2. The order of operations should be carefully thought through. This will avoid wasting time and prevent errors.

3. It is important to keep each part of the process as simple as possible.

4. It is important to keep some time in reserve so that when parts of the plan take longer than expected you do not run out of time.

THE MAKING PROCESS

Read through the entire process carefully and then answer the questions on page 60.

WEEK 1   Mark out and cut frame pieces to size. Mark out and cut mortise and tenon joints and check for good fit.

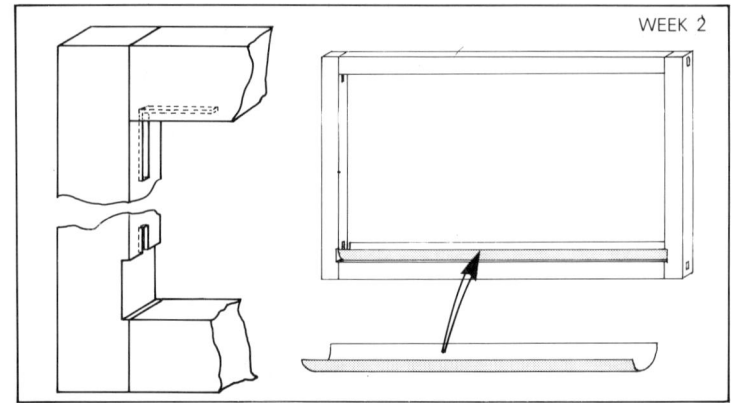

WEEK 2   Mark out and rout groove to take plastic partition supports. Mark out and cut housings to take gutter ends. Mark out and cut gutter to size. Check that it fits into assembly.

WEEK 3   Mark out and rout the slots in the frame for dividers and end compartment sides. Order pegs and castors for weeks 11 and 12.

WEEK 4   Mark out and cut partition supports. Check that they fit into assembly. Mark out and cut Perspex partition. Check that it fits.

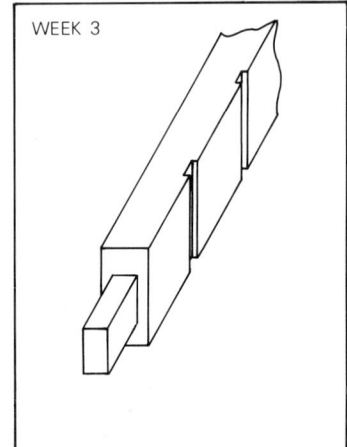

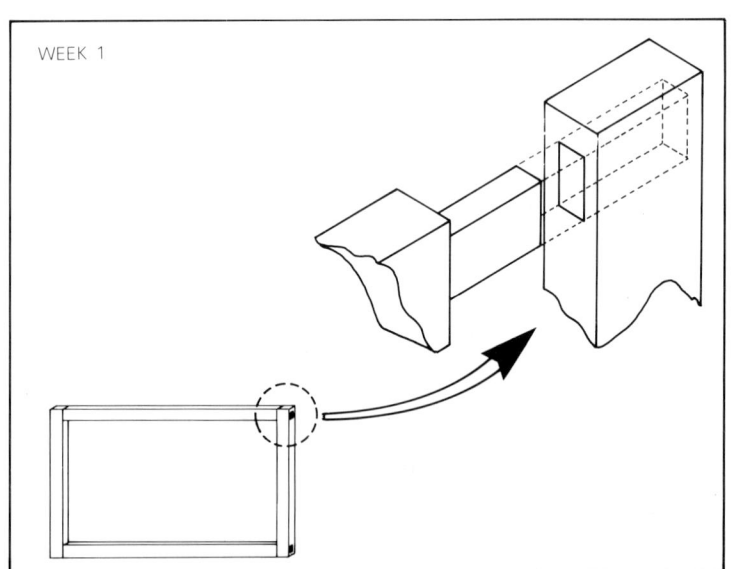

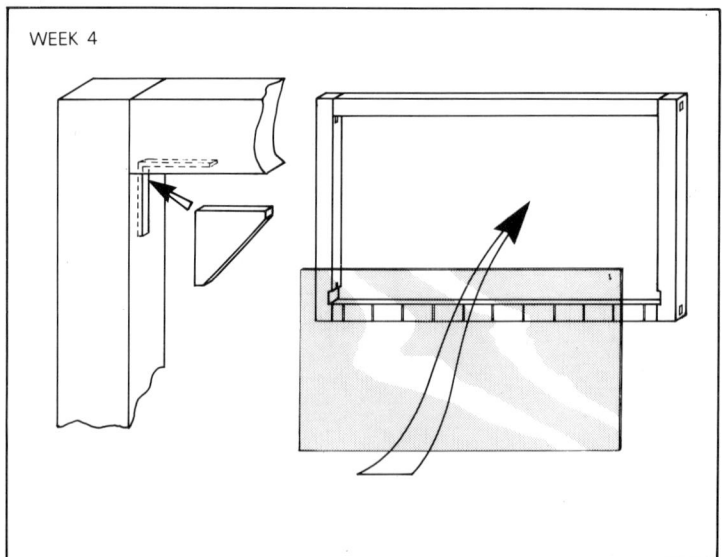

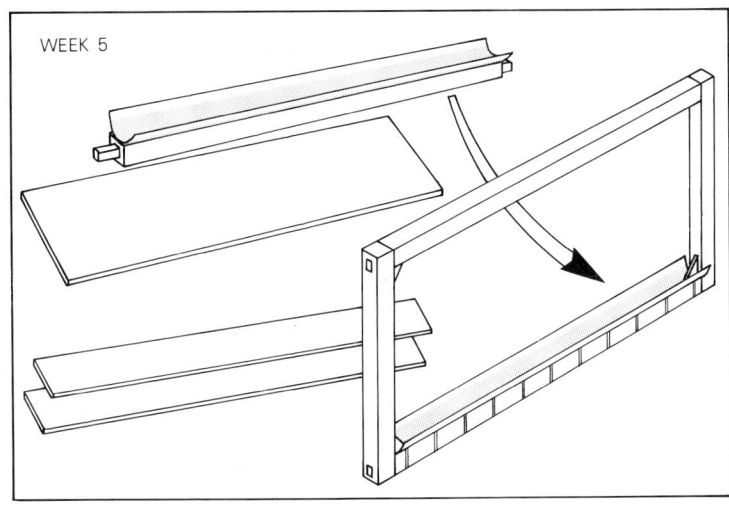

WEEK 5

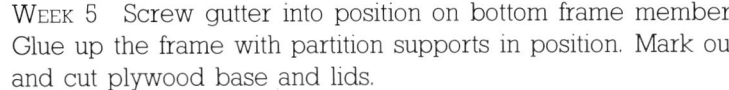

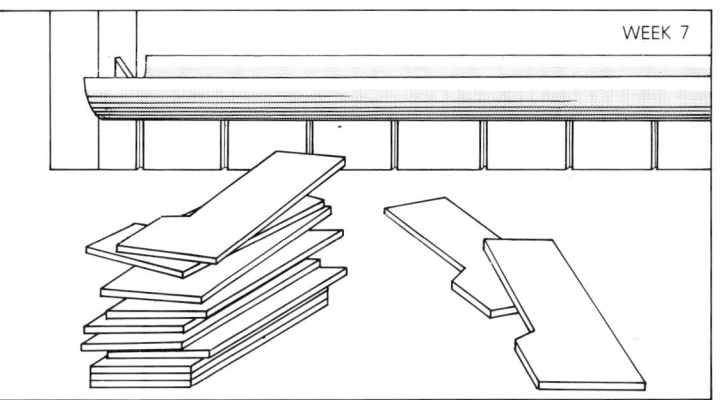

WEEK 7

WEEK 7 Give second coat of varnish to those parts varnished last week. Varnish base and lids. Mark out and cut 22 shoe compartment partitions.

WEEK 8 Give second coat of varnish to those parts varnished last week. Fix base to frame checking alignment of slots and fitting of partitions. Glue partitions and lids into position.

WEEK 9 Varnish partitions. Mark out and cut plywood end plate. Mark out and cut cross pieces. Drill clearance holes and countersink. Varnish these pieces.

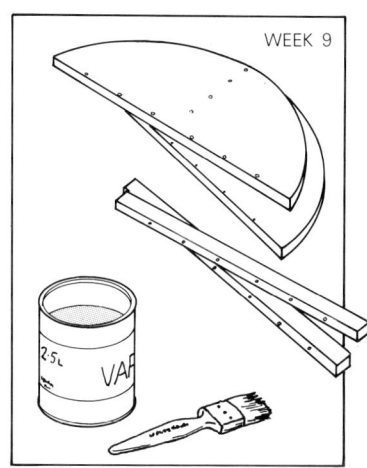

WEEK 9

WEEK 5 Screw gutter into position on bottom frame member. Glue up the frame with partition supports in position. Mark out and cut plywood base and lids.

WEEK 6 Varnish assembled frame avoiding areas yet to be glued. Mark out and rout slots in base and lids. Drill clearance holes in base and countersink. Drill pilot holes in frame.

WEEK 6

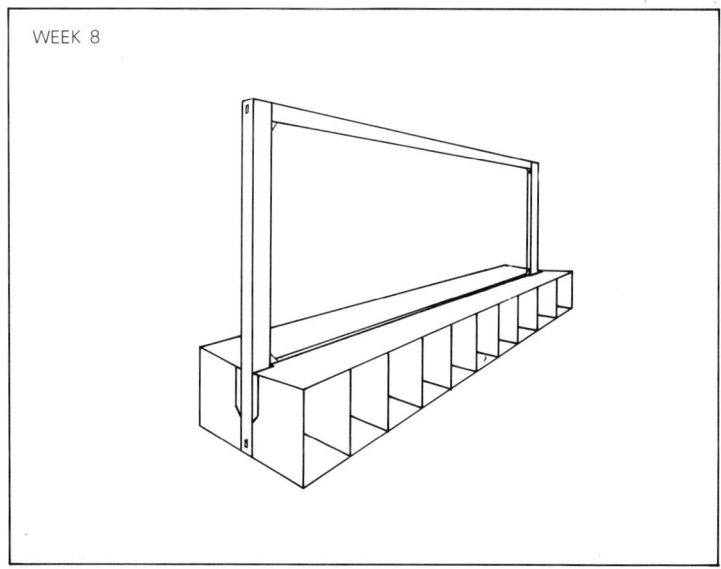

WEEK 8

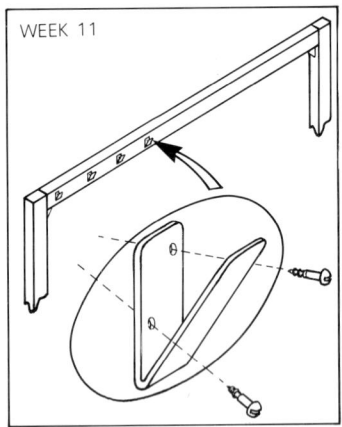

WEEK 11

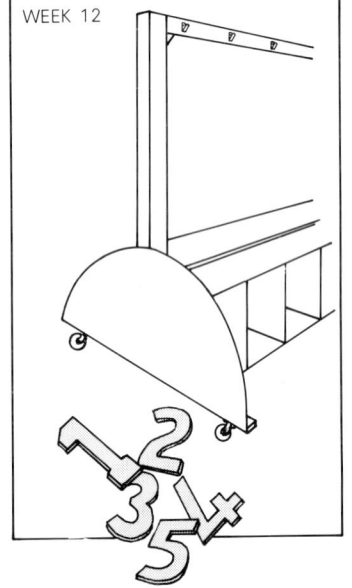

WEEK 12

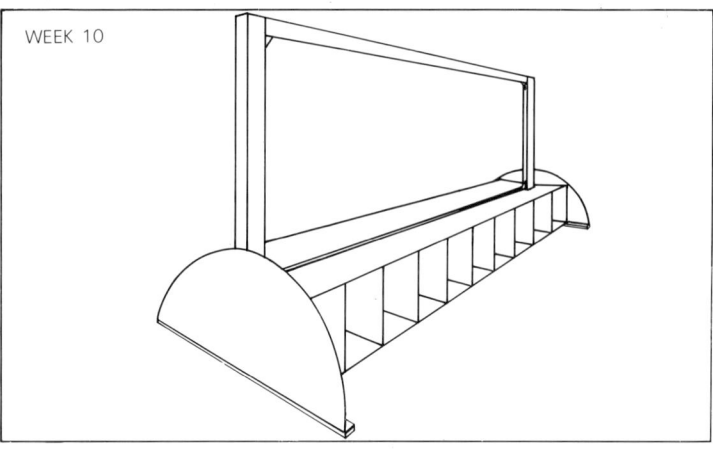

WEEK 10

WEEK 10 Give second coat of varnish to those parts varnished last week. Drill pilot holes in frame. Fix end plates and cross pieces onto frame.

WEEK 11 Mark out position of pegs. Fix pegs into position.

WEEK 12 Cut out Perspex numbers. Fix castors to cross pieces.

WEEK 13 Fix Perspex divider and remove protective wrapping. Tape on dividing lines. Fix numbers into position.

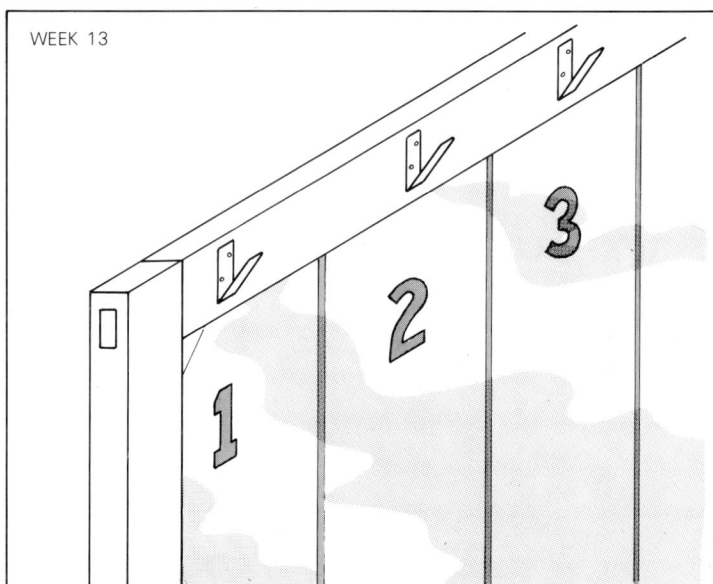

WEEK 13

Questions

1 What problems would have arisen if
(a) Jane had glued the frame together as soon as she had cut the mortise and tenon joints?   **c**
(b) She had waited until the unit was assembled before applying any polyurethane varnish?   **c**

2 Which of the following adhesives should Jane use: PVA woodwork adhesive, Araldite, Cascamite? (See chapter 4, pages 123–4)   **c**

3 What purpose does the polyurethane varnish serve? Why have two coats been applied?   **c**

4 The plastic guttering was not varnished – why not?   **c**

5 How could the strength of the mortise and tenon joints be increased?   **c**

6 The coat pegs were 'bought in'. What reasons are there for doing this rather than designing and making?

7 The plastic numbers were designed and made by Jane. She could have used 'bought in' stick-on numbers, the sort that have adhesive under peel-off backing. List the advantages and disadvantages of each, with reasons.

8 How did Jane prevent polyurethane varnish from touching and spoiling the Perspex partition?   **c**

9 What precautions should she take to ensure that the frame is kept square during the gluing-up process?

10 When the bulk of the frame is varnished, which parts should be kept free from varnish? Explain your answer.

11 Which size screws did Jane use to fix the base to the frame? What size pilot and clearance holes should she drill?   **c**

12 How can Jane ensure that the 22 plywood dividers she has to cut are of identical shape and size?

13 What difficulties might Jane experience in cutting plywood? How might this be overcome?

EVALUATION

When the unit was finished, Jane looked back at her more detailed design brief and checked that the product met all her requirements. She then took it to the playgroup for the children to try out. To find out how successful it was, she evaluated it in two ways:
1. Observing the way it was used.
2. Talking to parents, helpers and children.

►Fig. 25 Evaluating the unit

▼Fig. 24 The finished unit

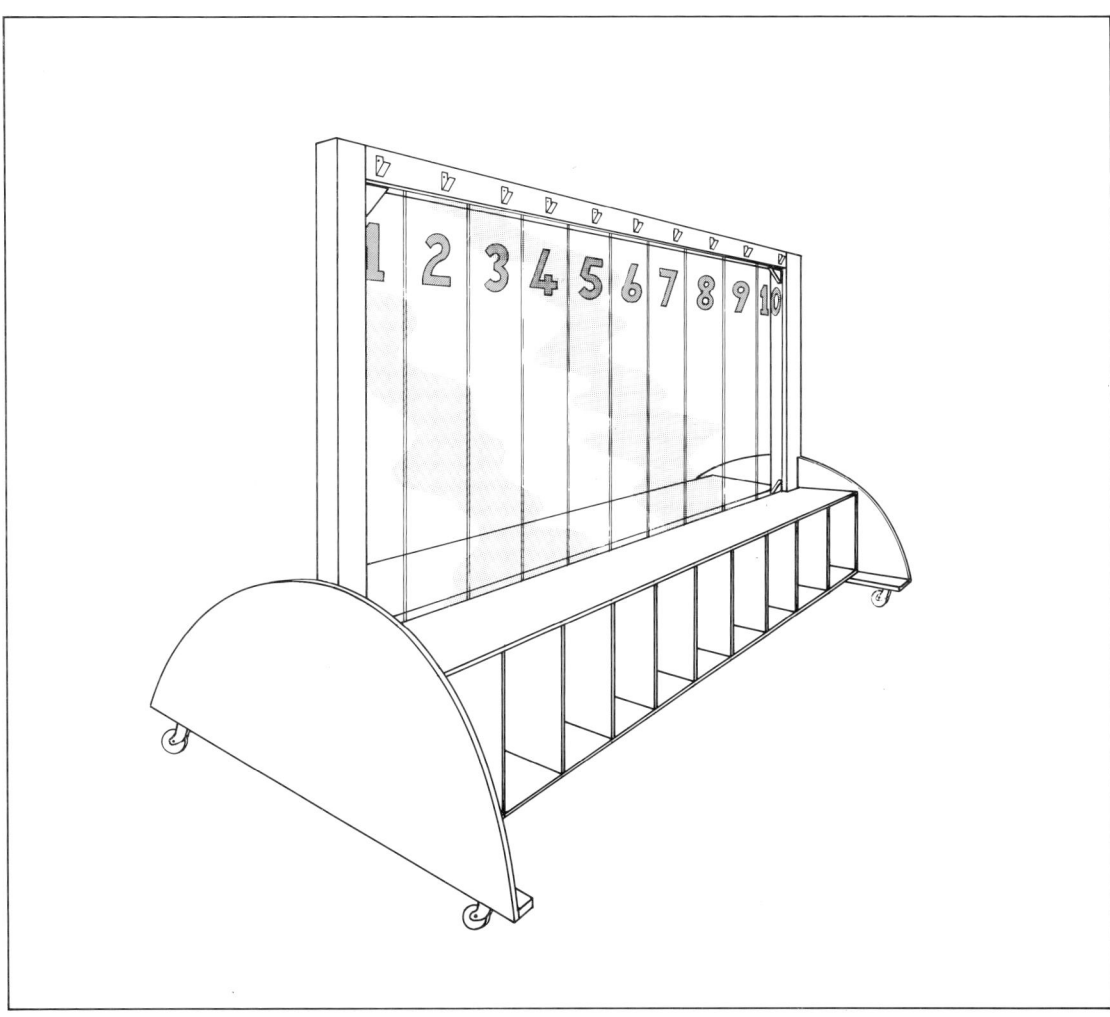

Questions

1 What questions should Jane ask parents and helpers? Should she ask the children the same questions? Give reasons for your answer.

2 Jane considered using a questionnaire which she could give out and then collect at a later date. She decided against this. What reasons might she have had?

3 What is the point of observing the unit in use? How might the information obtained by observing be different from that obtained by asking questions?

4 If you were a manufacturer in the business of making furniture you might be interested in designing a coat and shoe rack that can be mass produced. How suitable for mass production is the unit Jane has designed? **c**
What changes would you make if you wanted to manufacture 1000 units?

5 The appearance of an article is just as important as how well it does its job. What do you think of the appearance of Jane's unit? Make a list of ways in which the appearance might be improved. **c**

6 The cost of an article is important. Use the price list in fig. 23 and the parts list in fig. 22 to calculate the cost of the unit. Do you think the playgroup got value for money?

THE GARDEN

FINDING THE PROBLEM

We have seen how two very different design situations have been tackled thoroughly. This third project gives a much briefer outline of how yet another situation led one student into some detailed technological design.

A group of students looked closely at how their parents used and looked after their garden. Each house and garden was different, and each set of parents had different interests and styles of gardening. Some didn't like gardening much at all, so did their best to reduce the amount of time that they would have to spend doing it. Others were very keen gardeners who spent all their spare time growing plants and vegetables, some of which required a greenhouse to make them grow properly. Some of the gardens were small backyards that were largely covered in paving slabs, and some were larger gardens with big lawns and flower beds. The project was started by the students observing (and helping) their parents in the garden. The observations had to be precise and recorded in notebooks, with explanations about what was being done and why.

A number of problems were observed:
1. My dad was trying to grow a new bit of lawn and the birds kept eating the seed, especially the pigeons. It would be very useful to have some system for keeping them away.
2. My dad uses an electric hedge cutter. He has a long extension lead hanging on a hook in the shed, that he has to untangle every time he needs to cut the hedge. A cable winder that would keep it all tidy would be useful.
3. My mum's greenhouse gets very hot when the sun is on it but gets a lot colder at night. If she wants to keep a constant warm temperature for her plants she has to keep opening and closing the windows to adjust the temperature. It would save a lot of work if it could be done automatically.
4. If we put crumbs and food on our bird table, the small pretty birds get frightened away by the starlings. It would be good if we could have a bird table that only small birds could use.
5. We have got a big lawn and when we water it we have to keep moving the spray all the time to cover it all. A very big spray that did it all would be great.
6. My mum gets very cross when dad leaves the weedkiller and other chemicals lying around in the shed. He needs somewhere special to keep them locked up.
7. We have got a nesting box for blue tits on our fence. It's used every year but we can never see the babies hatching out until they are ready to fly away. I'd love to see them hatching.
8. My grandma loves gardening, but because she has to be in a wheelchair all the time she can't reach down to the flower beds. She needs some special extending garden tools that she can use for weeding and planting, and even for pruning.

Everyone in the group found a problem of some sort based on their own garden and how their parents had got it organised. In talking to the Design and Technology teacher at school they were soon able to tie down the general problems into very specific design problems that they could begin to tackle.

DEFINING THE PROBLEM

Peter's garden has a big lawn that needs watering, but the family has only a small water sprinkler. This always results in a lot of tedious movement of the hosepipe and sprinkler. Peter started by defining the problem carefully.

With a lawn of this size (see fig. 1) the sprinkler that they had (which was a spinning arm type that would cover about 10 m diameter) had to be moved three times to cover the whole area. This was made even more difficult if you had to turn the tap off each time so as to avoid getting soaking wet. What usually happened was that it would be put on to cover a particular area and then it would be forgotten about. This resulted in one area getting very wet indeed and all the rest of the lawn being completely dry. Peter decided that he wanted a system that did not require any moving at all. It would be turned on and (somehow) it would water the whole lawn.

Peter began his research in a big garden centre where he spent a long time looking at all the lawn sprinklers on sale. He found several different sorts that worked on quite different principles. They were all powered by the force of the water coming through the hose. The two most common types were the spinning arm type, and the moving spray bar type.

The spinning arm type works on the action and reaction principle. The water is fed into the spinning arm through the central spindle and it sprays out at the ends of the arm. However,

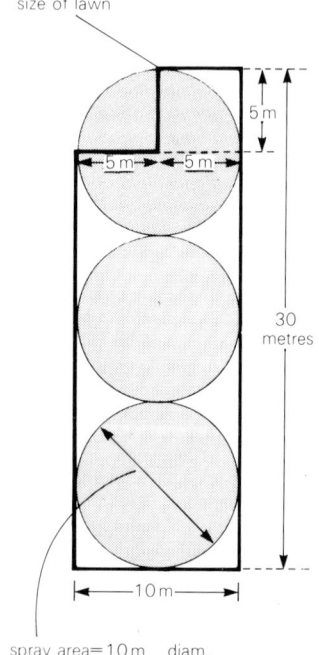

size of lawn

5 m

5 m 5 m

30 metres

10 m

spray area = 10 m diam.

▲Fig. 1 Even moving the spray three times still leaves some areas unwatered

▼Fig. 2 Spinning arm spray

▼Fig. 3 Moving spray bar sprinkler

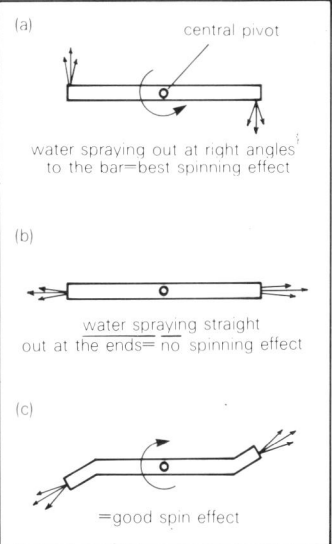

(a)

central pivot

water spraying out at right angles
to the bar=best spinning effect

(b)

water spraying straight
out at the ends= no spinning effect

(c)

=good spin effect

▲Fig. 4 Why does the arm spin?

if you look closely you will see that it does not spray straight out of the end, but at an angle. As the jet of water blasts out, it pushes the arm forwards. This pushing action works on both ends of the arm and causes it to spin around the central pivot. The greatest spinning force is created if the jets point at right angles to the arm. No spinning force would be created if the jet pointed straight out the end of the arm.

The moving spray bar type uses a quite different principle. The hose is connected into a box-like unit and the spray bar comes out the other side. The spray bar is a tube with many holes

◀Fig. 5

in it so that the water sprays out in lots of fine jets. However, these holes are all in line down the bar so if the bar stays still the jets would just spray straight upwards. To make the spray cover a wider area, the bar is made to roll from side to side (called oscillating). The jets of water therefore spray out left and right as the bar rolls over and back. This oscillating movement is generated inside the box unit and connected to the spray bar by a link mechanism.

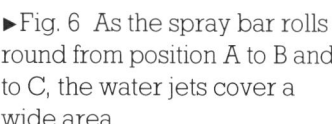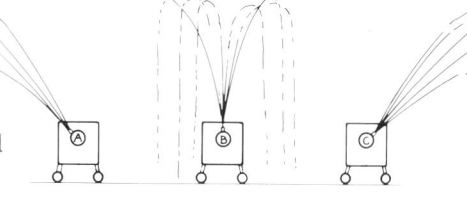

▶Fig. 6 As the spray bar rolls round from position A to B and to C, the water jets cover a wide area

Questions

1 Given the size of Peter's lawn and the area covered by the existing sprinkler, moving the sprinkler three times will allow most of the lawn to be sprayed. How many square metres will not get wet (assuming that there is no wind)? One way to work this out is to draw it out on squared paper.　　c

2 If the water pressure in the tap drops, and the spray only covers an area of 7 m diameter, how many times would it need to be moved and how much lawn would stay dry?　　c

3 You will see that the oscillating spray bar is formed into a curve. Why do you think that is? It is a very gentle curve with a radius of 0.5 m. What would be the effect on the spray area of increasing or decreasing the curvature of this bar?　　c

4 Why is it necessary to have an oscillating system at all? Why not just have many more holes in the bar, all set at different angles?　　c

5 How far over does the spray bar have to move in order to get the maximum possible sprayed area? Design a simple experiment using an ordinary hosepipe to find out what angle the water has to spray out at to carry the furthest distance.　　x

6 With the spinning arm type of sprinkler, why don't the jets point straight backwards at 90° to the arm? This would provide the best spinning action. On this type, how can you adjust the distance that the water sprays out from the arm?　　x

THE SEARCH FOR SOLUTIONS

None of the sprinklers that Peter examined could cover the area that he required, so he began to look at some new possibilities.

One was to put lots of holes all along the length of the hosepipe and lay it all over the lawn. Unfortunately not only would this result in a very uneven wetting, but also his dad thought it was a very silly idea as he needed the hosepipe for other things as well. Peter's most promising idea was to design a *moving* sprinkler that would cover a certain area in one position but gradually move along so that all the lawn got watered.

By going back to the plan of the lawn, Peter worked out that if a spray could cover the full width of 10 m then it would just need to crawl in a straight line down the middle of the lawn. None of the grass would be missed and it would save a great deal of effort. At this point Peter decided to separate the two major problems:

1. to provide a spray system to spread water over a 10 m wide lawn;
2. to provide a crawler system to move the spray along.

There were several types of spray system that Peter had already examined that solved the first problem. He decided that the easiest to make would be the rolling bar type. The bar rolls back and forth in a simple frame and the water sprays out of the holes and covers a wide area. He knew that the rolling bar was driven by the force of water in the hose, and he began to work on the idea that some of this force might be made to solve the second problem. He decided that he needed a much closer look at the working mechanism.

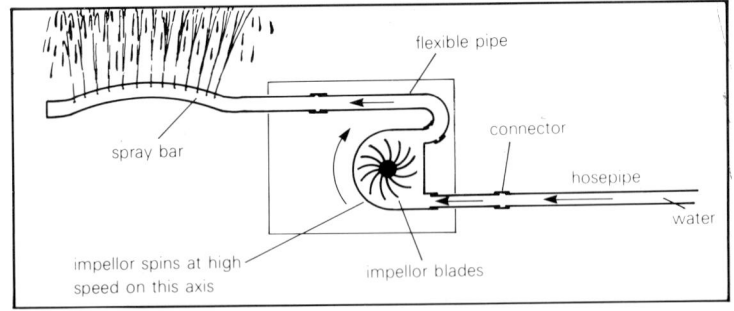

▲Fig. 7 The force of the water spins the impellor

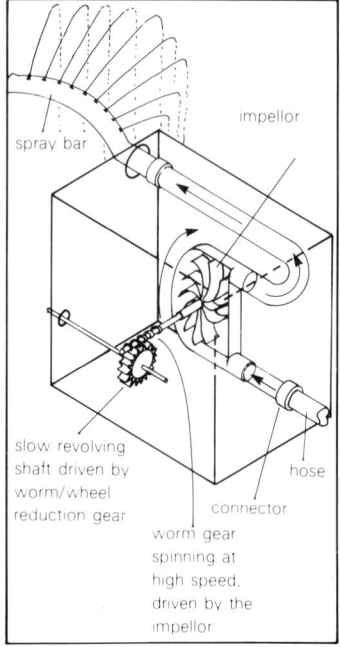

▲Fig. 8

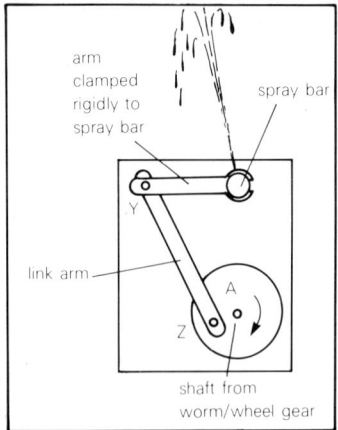

▼Fig. 9 The slow rotation of wheel A drives the spray bar to and fro

There were several different parts of the mechanism. The water jet from the hosepipe goes through an IMPELLOR (a sort of propellor in reverse). Some of the energy in the water jet is transferred to the impellor, which then begins to spin. This spinning action is very fast. Having gone through the impellor, the water goes through a flexible pipe and into the spray bar. The tiny holes in the spray bar let the water spray out in fine jets.

To spread the water spray over a wider area, the spray bar moves to and fro. The motion is driven by the impellor. The high-speed spinning action in the impellor is geared down with a worm/wheel gear to provide a slowly revolving shaft. The more teeth there are on the wheel, the slower it will revolve. This shaft then drives the link mechanism.

Figures 9 and 10 show how the link mechanism drives the spray bar to and fro. The wheel (A) is driven round by the shaft coming from the worm/wheel gear. Y and Z are free-moving pin joints. As wheel A spins, the sprinkler bar moves back and forth once every revolution of the wheel.

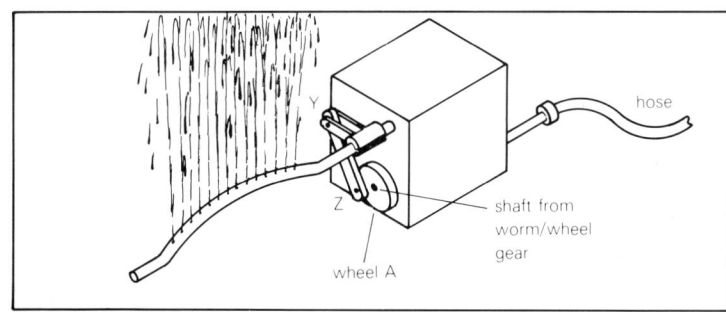

▲Fig. 10 Link mechanism fits into the front of the housing and clamps directly onto the spray bar

Peter's teacher provided him with a 'Meccano' building kit, and he was able to construct a similar system for himself, converting a high-speed wheel drive into a low speed. As well as experimenting with worm/wheel systems, he also had a go at other gearing arrangements which would give the same effect.

Once Peter fully understood the mechanism that drove the spray bar, he was ready to experiment to see if he could modify the system. What he needed was to make the mechanism drive some wheels to move the whole thing along. Peter went through a number of ideas that gradually led him to a solution. This involved taking apart the bits of the existing sprinkler and experimenting with different systems on his Meccano frame.

With the existing mechanism, the water pressure drives the impellor. By using a worm/wheel gear, the link mechanism moves the spray bar to and fro. (fig. 11)

The drive wheels to move the sprinkler along the ground must turn *very* slowly. Even the worm/wheel mechanism is turning too fast.

Using his Meccano kit, Peter tried other ideas:
1. Putting in a second worm gear. This is very slow indeed. (fig. 12)

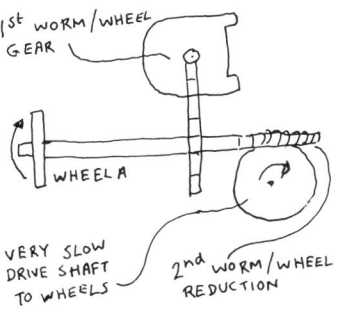

◄Fig. 12 A second worm/wheel gear makes the drive wheels much too slow

2. Changing the tooth ratio of the worm/wheel gear.
3. Putting in another gear on the same shaft. The speed of the drive wheel can be adjusted by changing the size of wheels X and Y. (fig. 13)

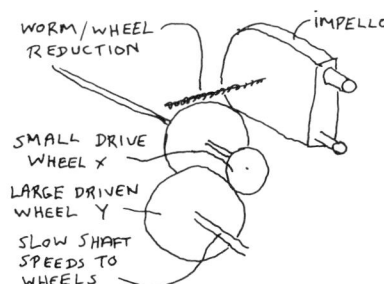

◄Fig. 13 Another reduction gear slows down the revolutions still further. This shaft could power some drive wheels

This last mechanism works in theory, but in practice the wheels are too far apart to be driven by the same small shaft. Also the hose gets in the way of the drive wheel. (fig. 14)

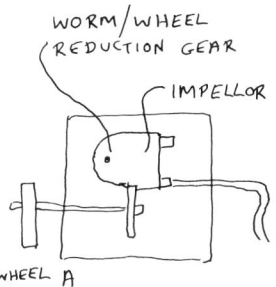

▲Fig. 11 Can drive wheels be powered by the same shaft that drives wheel A?

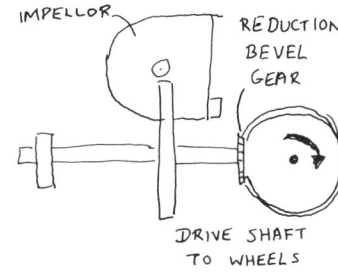

▲Fig. 16 Using a bevel gear, the drive shaft can come out sideways through the casing

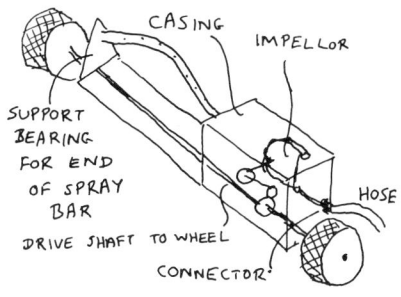

▲Fig. 14 This arrangement for the drive wheels is very awkward

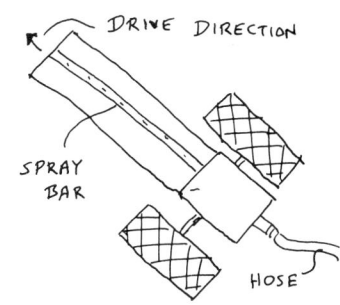

▲Fig. 15 This arrangement is *much* better

If the drive shaft could come out sideways from the body, both problems would be solved. (fig. 15)

Using a *bevel gear* instead of an ordinary gear, the drive shaft can come out sideways. (fig. 16)

Questions

1 The impellor in the mechanism is used to convert the linear motion of the water jet into rotary motion. Where else can you see this principle used? Look at some children's toys to see how they use it. **CX**

2 The impellor spins at 300 revs/min. With 50 teeth on the worm/wheel, the worm/wheel arrangement makes the shaft revolve at 6 revs/min. How big a wheel must you fit (i.e. how many teeth) to give a shaft rotation of:
(a) 5 revs/min
(b) 15 revs/min
(c) 20 revs/mins?
Try them out on a Meccano frame. **CX**

3 Figure 9 shows the link mechanism that drives the spray bar. Make a model of this mechanism from cardboard and drawing pins on a softboard base. Use it to answer these questions: **CX**
(a) What angle does the spray bar move through?
(b) If you increase the length of the clamping arm on the spray bar, does the angle change?
(c) What if you increase the length of bar YZ?
(d) What would happen if the wheel A had a bigger radius than the length of the clamping arm on the spray bar?

DETAILING THE DESIGN

Once the mechanical parts of the crawler and sprinkler had been worked out, it was necessary to see how they might be fitted into the overall form of the final product. Even though this project is mainly a mechanical one, it is important to remember that *all* products should look good as well as work well.

Lots of details still had to be worked out. These are some of them:

1. How is the front of the spray bar to be supported?

2. Does the unit need a front wheel as well as the two drive wheels?

3. How is the body that houses the mechanism to be made, and what materials could be used?

4. What gear ratios should be chosen to control the speed of the unit?

5. What material should the drive wheels be made of?

When all these details had been sorted out Peter produced his working drawing, which was in two parts. He did a 'general arrangement' drawing of the sprinkler body, scaled to half full

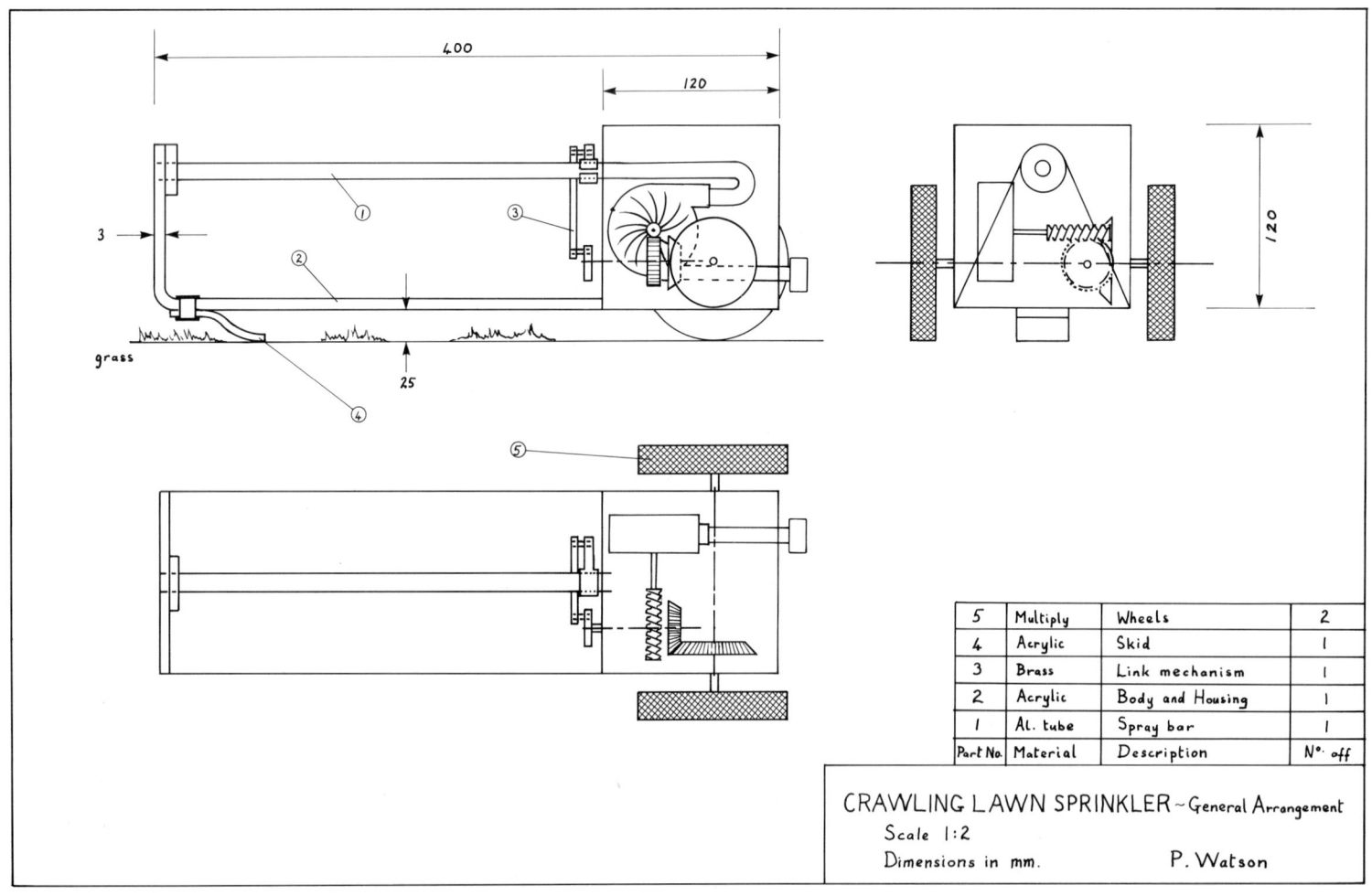

Part No.	Material	Description	N°. off
5	Multiply	Wheels	2
4	Acrylic	Skid	1
3	Brass	Link mechanism	1
2	Acrylic	Body and Housing	1
1	Al. tube	Spray bar	1

CRAWLING LAWN SPRINKLER ~ General Arrangement

Scale 1:2

Dimensions in mm.   P. Watson

◄Fig. 17 The general arrangement drawing is used to make sure all the parts fit together properly

size. However, this could not show enough detail in the mechanical parts, so he did a full size drawing just of the mechanical end showing how it all worked. He then had to plan the making.

Peter had already decided not to make the impellor and the gear wheels. He had got all these parts from the sprinkler he had taken apart. However, in making the body he had to be extremely careful to fit the mechanism accurately.

If the gear wheels don't meet properly, or if the bearing holes in the side of the housing are slightly out of line, then the mechanism simply will not work. This therefore needs *very* careful marking out and then great care in following the marked lines and centres. The procedure sheet had to take as much notice of the *order of assembly* and the time taken to do the assembly, as it did of the making.

When Peter had finished the unit, he took it home and tried it out on his lawn. Though his dad was very impressed to start with, gradually some problems became obvious.

◄Fig. 18

1. It is not possible to stop the crawler! As a result, if you need to use it to water a flower bed with the sprinkler sitting still – you can't do it. The drive wheels cannot be disengaged. Some system for putting the crawler wheels on and off would be a great advantage.
2. There was plenty of power for turning the wheels, but when the grass got wet the wheels tended to spin. They needed more grip.

3. In acrylic sheet the unit is fairly brittle and fragile. Peter decided that the housing would have been more durable in a more flexible plastic. Still he was pleased with his prototype.
4. As the weight of hosepipe that is being towed along builds up, the unit is inclined to do a 'wheely'. Peter had to improvise a weight to put on the front of the unit to stop it lifting.

Questions

1 Write out a procedure sheet for making the body of the sprinkler. Think carefully about the order in which you will have to do things. **c**
2 Design a simple system for engaging and disengaging the drive wheels. **c**
3 How could Peter have reduced the wheel spin? **c**
4 This unit was designed specifically for Peter's lawn, where it merely has to go in a straight line. How could the unit be made to go round a gentle curve? Design the modification. **c**
5 Design a brochure that Peter could use to advertise the crawling sprinkler unit. Make sure that all the special features (including any modifications that you may have included) are well illustrated. **c**
6 Why do you think Peter decided to use a straight oscillating spray bar instead of a curved one? Question 3 on page 63 may give you a clue to this one.
7 How can Peter find out what he might sell the unit for if he got a manufacturer to produce it for him, and how can he find out how many he might sell?
8 If he found out there was a large market for this product, he might decide to set up a small production line to make lots of them. How might the following points affect his plan of action?
(a) Bulk buying of mechanical components.
(b) Jigs to make assembly quicker and more accurate.
(c) Finding somewhere to do the work.
(d) Borrowing money to get started.

THREE

TACKLING ANY PROJECT

In this chapter we will look at a wide variety of projects tackled by students aged about sixteen years old. A summary of each project is given at the beginning of each double page. Down the left hand side is a flow chart of the total design process, with the part of the process that is being considered in detail highlighted. The complete flow chart is shown opposite.

As you already know, you begin the design process by carrying out RESEARCH into the problem. At first you do background research of a general nature, but almost immediately your research leads you to have ideas about possible solutions to the problem. Of course you have to explore each idea using rough sketches, simple models and investigations. This EXPLORING IDEAS stage will almost certainly lead you to carry out more research, but now the research will be aimed at answering specific questions.

It is easy to have so many ideas that you become overwhelmed and get stuck at the exploring ideas stage. So it is important to be selective and to choose the most promising ideas and develop them. When you are DEVELOPING IDEAS you will draw more detailed sketches, construct more intricate models and carry out more complex investigations. Sometimes you will find that ideas that looked promising have flaws which make them unworkable. At other times, however, you will be able to develop ideas to show that they will provide a good solution to the problem. Your final task in developing your ideas will be to draw up the detailed plans of the solution.

Once you have your detailed plans, you have to work out a plan of action for making your solution. When you are PLANNING THE MAKING for your project you must take into account many factors, including the time you have available, how long it takes you to do things, where you can get the materials and components, how long it will take to get them and so on. It is important that your plan is realistic and that you don't set yourself impossible targets. While it is important to organise your work so that you don't waste time, it is just as important to make sure that you don't have to rush things. For this reason it is wise to keep some time in reserve in case of mishaps.

MAKING THE SOLUTION is perhaps the most satisfying part of the design process because you see your ideas taking shape before your eyes. It is also a little frightening because you will be worried about making mistakes and just a bit scared in case your ideas don't work. But don't worry, most people feel like this, especially the first time they tackle a major design project.

Finally, you have to carry out an EVALUATION of your solution to the problem. You can find out more about the skills of research, communication, making and evaluation in chapter 4.

LOOKING FOR PROBLEMS

When it comes to choosing your project, it sometimes helps to think about where problems might be found. The most obvious place is your own home. Working on a problem in your own home is an example of a SITUATION BASED PROJECT. Careful observation of situations, as shown in chapter 2, soon reveals problems to be solved.

Some students find that they have enjoyed work on a particular part of the syllabus. If, for example, you have found work on structures or electronics particularly interesting, it would make sense to use this interest as a starting point for your project. An interest and investigation into structures might well be the starting point for the building of a large model suspension bridge for a playgroup toy.

If you have a hobby or interest that takes a lot of your spare time, you might base a project on this. For example, if you are a keen gardener with a greenhouse, the designing of an automatically controlled heating system would be a challenging HOBBY BASED PROJECT.

You will almost certainly use a lot of the information in the mechanisms and electronics parts in your syllabus as well. If you are particularly interested in science you may find that a scientific investigation is a good starting point. Such INVESTIGATION BASED PROJECTS usually involve considerable experimental work using apparatus you have designed and built yourself. One student designed and built a rig to investigate the power developed by a series of model aero engines – an investigation based project linked to a hobby.

A final group can be called INDUSTRY RELATED PROJECTS.

RESEARCH

EXPLORING
IDEAS

DEVELOPING
IDEAS

PLANNING
THE MAKING

MAKING

EVALUATION

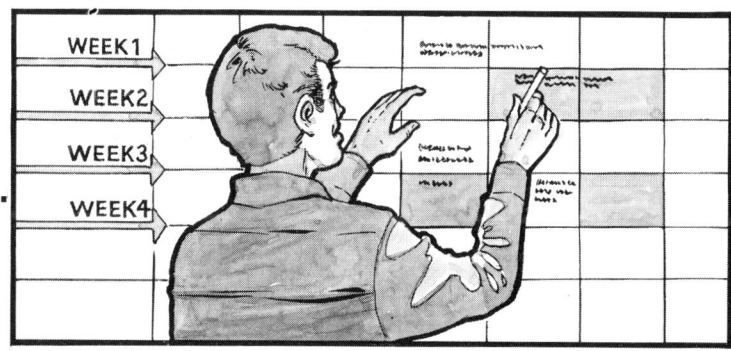

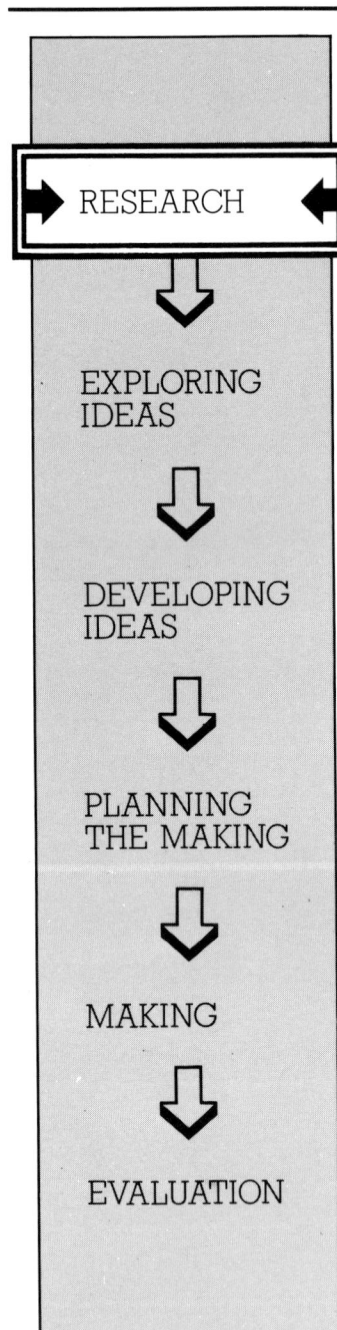

RESEARCH

EXPLORING
IDEAS

DEVELOPING
IDEAS

PLANNING
THE MAKING

MAKING

EVALUATION

PROJECT SUMMARY

Making lace is a skilled craft. One of the main tools of the craft is the bobbin that holds the thread that the lace is made from. Andrea got very interested in lacemaking and decided to research the area of lace bobbins to see if she could design and make her own. After initial research into how bobbins work and how they are traditionally made, Andrea had the idea that an attractive bobbin could be made from a transparent tube filled with different colours. She rejected the use of plastic tubing as it would be difficult to work and expensive. She chose glass tubing as there was a readily available supply in the science department. She rejected the use of coloured liquids as accidental breakage or leakage would be very messy. Andrea got the idea of using layers of coloured sand to fill the bobbin from the TV programme *Take Hart*. She solved the problem of sealing the sand in by making the top half of the bobbin from wood and using it as a stopper. On showing her designs to a group of local lacemakers, Andrea received orders for 50 bobbins!

GENERAL RESEARCH

To begin with, Andrea needed to find out what lace bobbins 'do' and how they do it. She found the answers by watching lacemakers at work and talking to them. She summarised her findings by the simple sketches shown in fig. 1. Next she visited Luton Museum which has a fine collection of bobbins used by English lacemakers during the 19th century. Some of the notes she made are shown in fig. 2. They explain how the appearance of the bobbin changed, although the way they 'worked' did not. Finally Andrea wrote to two bobbin makers who lived in the area. Copies of her letter and the reply she received are shown in fig. 3.

▼Fig. 1 Andrea's sketch to show the functions of a lace bobbin

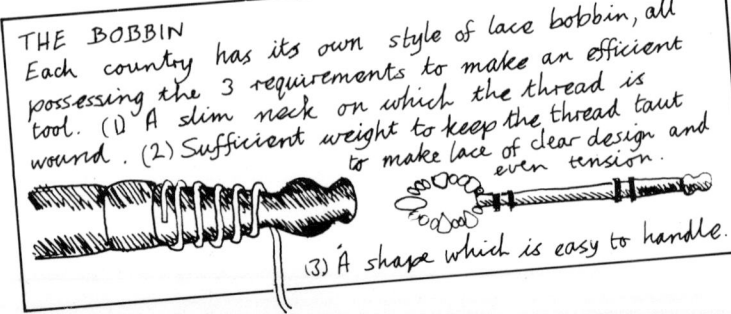

THE BOBBIN
Each country has its own style of lace bobbin, all possessing the 3 requirements to make an efficient tool. (1) A slim neck on which the thread is wound. (2) Sufficient weight to keep the thread taut to make lace of clear design and even tension.
(3) A shape which is easy to handle.

THE BOBBINS IN LUTON MUSEUM
The decorative wood and bone bobbins used by English lacemakers during the 19th century and still looked for by today's lacemakers and collectors.
The earliest surviving examples of local bobbins in the Luton Museum are Dumps or Bobtails.

These are heavy and plain. Often with a bulbous base resembling the Belgian type.

These gave way to a more slender bobbin, which had a spangle to replace the lost weight.

▲Fig. 2 Andrea's notes from the museum visit

▼Fig. 3 Andrea's research correspondence

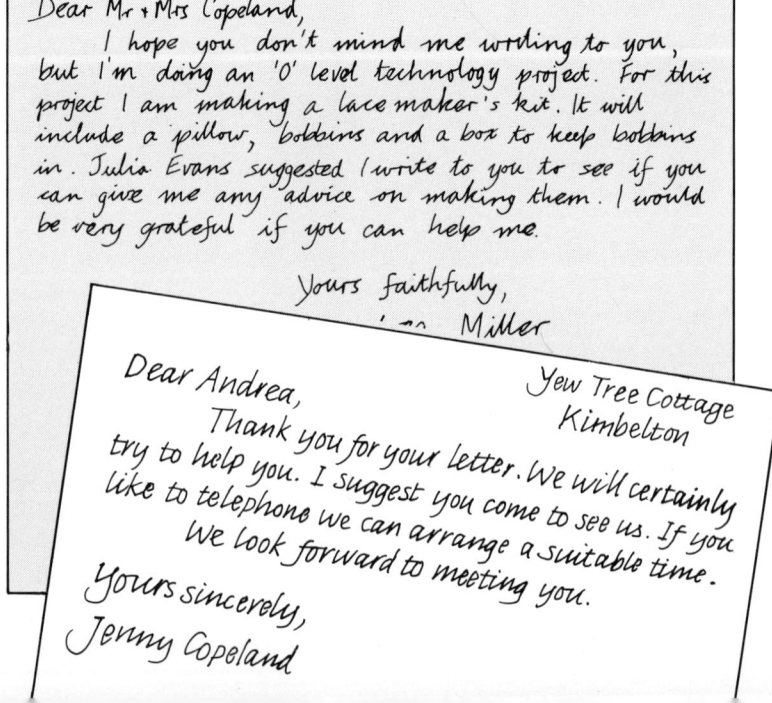

11 Barclay Road
Barlesham

Dear Mr & Mrs Copeland,
I hope you don't mind me writing to you, but I'm doing an 'O' level technology project. For this project I am making a lace maker's kit. It will include a pillow, bobbins and a box to keep bobbins in. Julia Evans suggested I write to you to see if you can give me any advice on making them. I would be very grateful if you can help me.

Yours faithfully,
[...]n Miller

Dear Andrea,
Yew Tree Cottage
Kimbelton
Thank you for your letter. We will certainly try to help you. I suggest you come to see us. If you like to telephone we can arrange a suitable time. We look forward to meeting you.

Yours sincerely,
Jenny Copeland

SPECIFIC RESEARCH

RESEARCHING GLASS WORKING TECHNIQUES

At a later stage in the project, when Andrea had decided to use glass tubing in her bobbins, she needed to learn about simple glass working techniques. She asked her chemistry teacher about this and he was able to show her the processes outlined in fig. 4. From then on it was a matter of using several CDT lessons to practise these techniques until she was proficient.

RESEARCHING THE COLOURING TECHNIQUES

From watching the TV programme *Take Hart*, Andrea knew that she could colour sand using food colouring. Her account of the process as she developed it is shown in fig. 5.

Colouring Sand

1. Add 3-4 drops of food colouring to half a test tube full of water.

2. Shake gently so that the solution is thoroughly mixed.

3. Add 6 spatula measures of sand to the liquid and leave overnight.

4. Filter off the coloured sand.

5. Place in a glass dish in an oven at 100°C overnight.

▲Fig. 5 Andrea's account of sand colouring

Red, yellow, blue, green, orange and purple food colourings were used. Andrea found that orange-coloured builders' sand could be coloured but that the results were dull. Silver sand, almost white in colour, borrowed from the science department gave brighter results. One of Andrea's bobbins is shown in fig. 6.

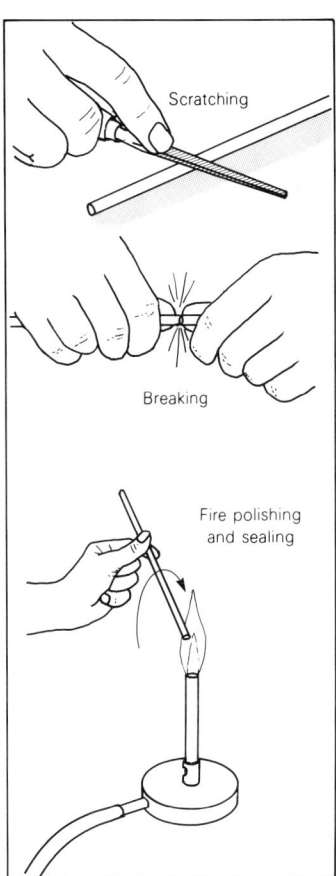

▼Fig. 4 The simple glass working techniques needed for this project

Scratching

Breaking

Fire polishing and sealing

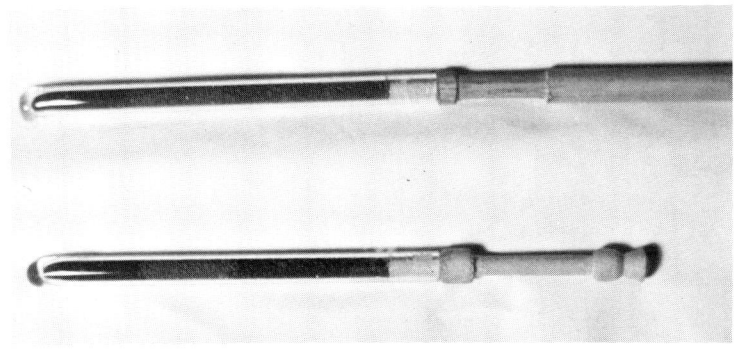

▲Fig. 6 A completed bobbin

Questions

1 In what ways might the museum visit notes be improved? c

2 In what ways might the account of research into sand colouring be improved? c

3 Andrea found that an empty glass bobbin was not satisfactory. Apart from not looking very attractive it did not work very well. Explain why. c

4 The density of any material used to fill the bobbin should be equal to or greater than the density of sand. Explain why. c

5 What other materials might be used to fill the bobbin? c
Which ones would you choose? Give reasons for your choice.

6 It is possible to put coloured paper into the glass tube. This would give a bobbin that was too light. How might this problem he solved? c

7 What research advantages are there in basing a CDT project on a popular local craft?

8 Andrea wrote 'thank you' letters to everyone who had helped her with her project. Why is this important?

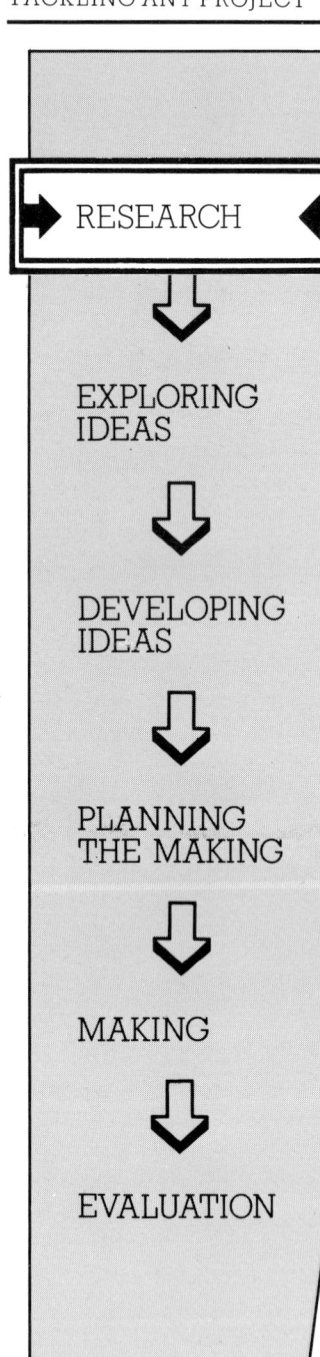

RESEARCH

⬇

EXPLORING
IDEAS

⬇

DEVELOPING
IDEAS

⬇

PLANNING
THE MAKING

⬇

MAKING

⬇

EVALUATION

PROJECT SUMMARY

Paul had found the work on structures very interesting and set himself the task of finding out how simple bridges worked. He began his project by using a construction kit to investigate the nature of the forces in simple bridge structures – the Warren girder, the Fink truss and the Howe truss. He was able to show which members were in tension, which in compression and how this changed depending on how the structure was loaded. In the second part of his project, he used his knowledge of structures to design and build a model rope bridge. This was supported on movable banks so that its behaviour over different spans could be investigated. The completed model is shown in fig. 6.

GENERAL RESEARCH

Paul started by going to the library and looking up bridges in the subject index. He also wrote to the Design Council to ask if they could suggest any sources of information. On this occasion they were able to help (fig. 1).

◀ Fig. 1 Paul's research correspondence

SPECIFIC RESEARCH

There are many construction kits for use in CDT courses (see fig. 2). They provide a useful way to explore ideas quickly. Paul was able to make a copy of a Warren girder bridge in about half

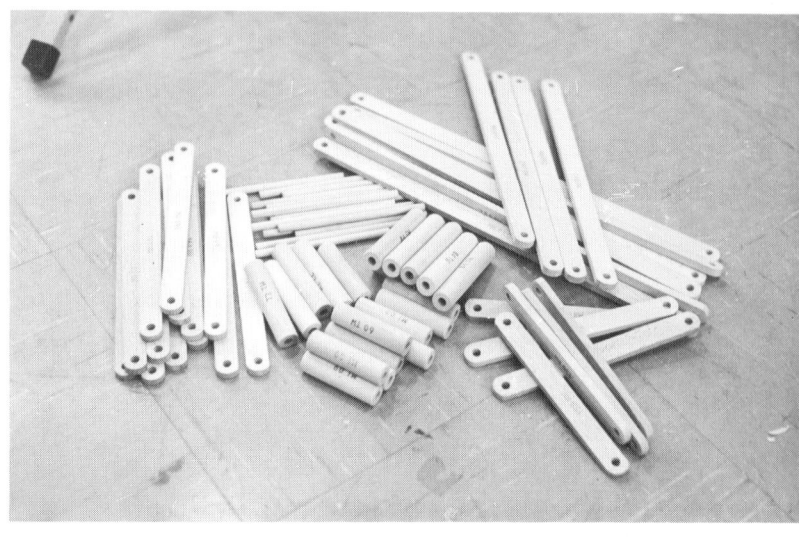

▲Fig. 2 A useful construction kit

an hour. Can you imagine how long it would take if he had used timber that required cutting to size? The photograph in fig. 3 shows his model set up for investigating the forces in the bridge,

TENSION AND COMPRESSION TESTS

In these tests my aim was to find out whether certain members of the Warren girder were in tension or compression. I replaced parts of members with string, loaded the girder and watched to see if the string became tighter or looser.

▲Fig. 3 Investigating the forces in a structure using a construction kit and some of his notes. Figure 4 shows a real Warren girder bridge and, as you can see, a designer can arrange the bridge to have an upper or lower deck. So Paul investigated the effect of loading his model at different positions on the lower deck. Some of his results are shown in fig. 5.

▲Fig. 4 A Warren girder road bridge

▼Fig. 5 Paul's results on different loading positions

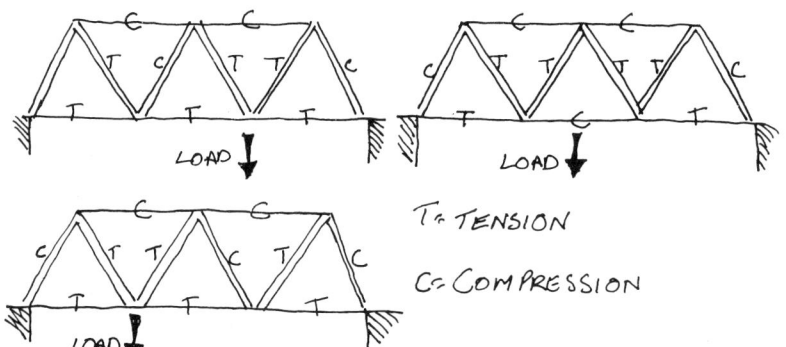

T = TENSION

C = COMPRESSION

▲Fig. 6 Paul's model rope bridge

Questions

1 Using Paul's results shown in fig. 5, identify those members that have changed from being in compression to being in tension and from being in tension to being in compression when the loading of the model changes. **c**

2 Cast iron is much stronger in compression than it is in tension. If a Warren girder was made from cast iron members, a designer might choose to make those members in compression thinner than those members in tension. What problems could this cause? **c**

3 By substituting string loops for a pair of members and then loading the structure, Paul was able to tell if those members (now the string loops) were in compression or tension. How was he able to do this? **c**

4 You can extend Paul's investigation by trying to find out if the forces in the structure change when the position of the deck in the Warren girder bridge model is altered. **c**

5 All Paul's investigations were qualitative. He only found out whether a member was in tension or compression, not how large or small the force was. How could he have extended his investigation to measure or calculate the forces in each member? **c**

6 Using the construction kit, Paul was able to build models of Fink and Howe trusses and investigate them. Find out what form these trusses take. **x**

RESEARCH

⬇

EXPLORING IDEAS

⬇

DEVELOPING IDEAS

⬇

PLANNING THE MAKING

⬇

MAKING

⬇

EVALUATION

PROJECT SUMMARY

Rachel had been set the problem of designing a 'pull-along' toy for young children. She decided to base it on an animal shape and chose a duck because of its familiar, non-frightening shape and interesting movements. She decided to build into the toy mechanisms that imitated the waddle and head-bobbing action of a walking duck. She explored a wide range of ideas on paper to include making the body, designing wheels to provide a waddle and a spring-loaded neck for the bobbing. From this wealth of ideas she had to choose those features she wanted in her final design. The completed toy is shown in fig. 4.

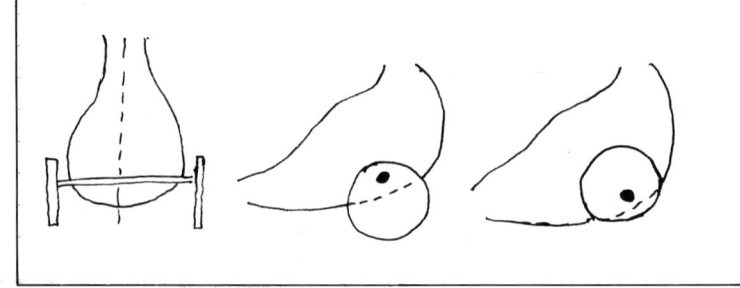

▲Fig. 2 Rachel's design to produce a waddle

▼Fig. 3 Rachel's ideas on how to make the wheels

HOLLOW BODY.
Can be formed on some kind of split pattern

Split pattern can only be made by time consuming hand-wasting process.

Once pattern is made body production is not very time consuming

SOLID BODY
Irregular shape can only be formed by time-consuming hand-wasting process

Solid body will be heavier than hollow shell. Is this an advantage or not?

As more than one body might be required use HOLLOW BODY

WAYS TO MAKE A HOLLOW BODY:

1. From glass reinforced plastic (G.R.P.):
Make wooden pattern of left hand side } → Make GRP female pattern } → Make GRP body shell of left hand side
Repeat process for right hand side

2. From thermoplastic sheet (vacuum or drape formed)
Make wooden pattern of left hand side } → Vacuum or drape form } → Thermoplastic body shell of left hand side
Repeat for right hand side

3. From thermoplastic sheet (blow moulded)
Make wooden pattern of left hand side } → Make GRP female pattern } → Reinforce to give blow mould } → Blow mould to give left hand side of body shell.
Repeat for right hand side

a) Cut from sheet material with adjustable spigot cutter.
Possibilities include:
acrylic sheet - would need to be laminated
plywood
chipboard

b) Cut from material in rod form
Possibilities include:
steel
brass
aluminium
nylon
polythene

c) Made by fluid forming (casting)
Possibilities include:
thermosetting resin
aluminium
brass

▲Fig. 1 Rachel's ideas on how to make the body

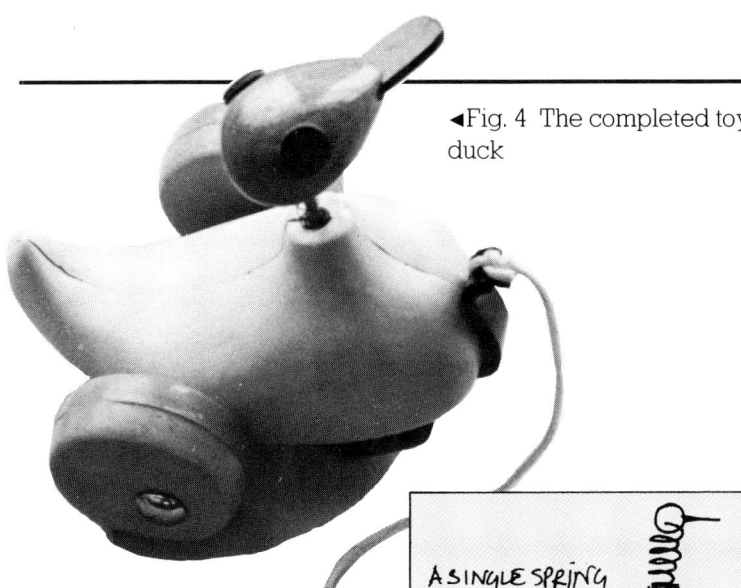

◀Fig. 4 The completed toy duck

2. existing skills,
3. availability of materials (including cost),
4. availability of equipment.

She did not choose the simplest or the quickest way to make the wheels. Which ways do you think are the quickest and simplest? Which method would you use in your school?

Some of Rachel's ideas for ways to join the head to the body are shown in fig. 5. Her chosen solution combined a spring-loaded rod with a stand that prevented the duck from falling over when pushed, as shown in fig. 6. Do you think this will give the required bobbing effect?

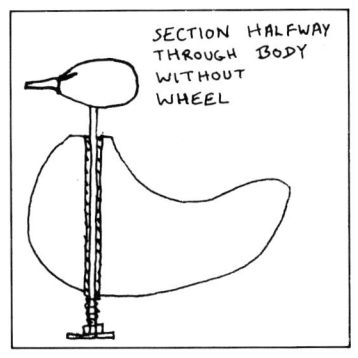

SECTION HALFWAY THROUGH BODY WITHOUT WHEEL

A SINGLE SPRING

Up and down motions from wheels will give a wobble to the spring. This wobble will be "all over the place"

A SPRING WRAPPED AROUND A ROD

Up and down motion of wheels will give wobble to spring but rod will restrict this to up and down movement

◀Fig. 5 Rachel's ideas on joining the head to the body

▲Fig. 6 Rachel's neck design – will this give the required bobbing effect?

Rachel's ideas on how to make the body are shown in fig. 1. She chose to make a hollow body from glass reinforced plastic (GRP). Here are some of the factors which may have influenced her decision:

1. strength and toughness needed in the final form,
2. availability of materials (including cost),
3. availability of equipment,
4. what the equipment available will do.

Are there any ways to make the body that she has not thought about? Which method would you use in your school?

Rachel thought that the waddling motion of the duck was really an up and down movement. Do you agree with her? She decided that the simplest way to produce this was to have two circular wheels with the axles mounted off centre as shown in fig. 2. How else could she have done this?

Rachel considered several different ways to make the wheels and these are shown in fig. 3. She decided to use hollow wheels made from glass reinforced plastic. The following factors probably influenced her decision:

1. compatibility with body,

Questions

1 The joins where the body halves and wheel halves meet are very obvious. What can be done to hide these defects? c

2 The waddling motion of a duck involves some side-to-side movement of the tail. Design a movable tail that could be attached to a hollow body and a mechanism that would cause side-to-side movement in the tail as the toy was pulled along. c

3 The head-bobbing motion of a duck involves a forwards and backwards movement as shown in fig. 7.

▲Fig. 7

Design a head–body jointing system and mechanism that causes this movement as the toy is pulled along. c

4 What problems might you have in fitting the mechanisms you have designed in questions 2 and 3 into a GRP body shell? c

5 One criticism of the toy is that the head should be made of plastic to be in keeping with the body and wheels. (Rachel made it of wood.) Show by means of notes and sketches several different ways of making a plastic head. State clearly which one you would use, with reasons. c

75

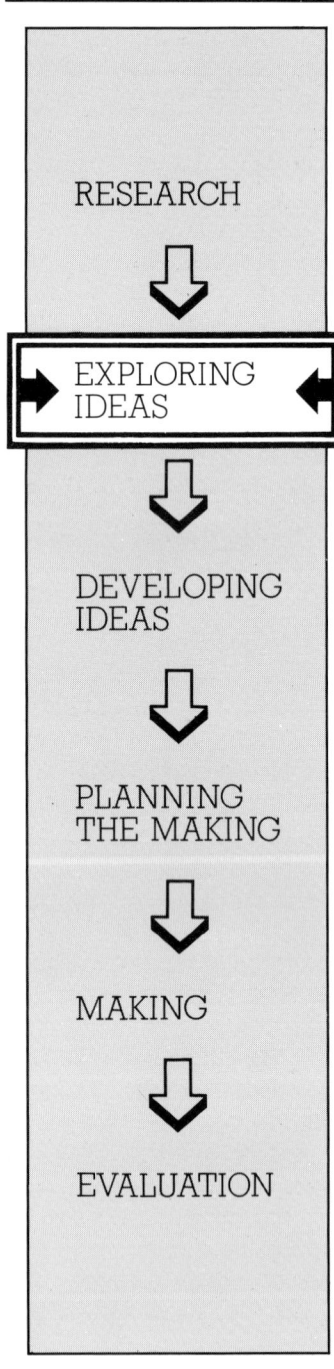

RESEARCH

⬇

EXPLORING IDEAS

⬇

DEVELOPING IDEAS

⬇

PLANNING THE MAKING

⬇

MAKING

⬇

EVALUATION

PROJECT SUMMARY

Antonia was interested in designing an automatic door for the garage at home. She knew that she would have to produce a working model before her father would let her loose on the garage itself. These pages show how she explored lots of different ideas for solving her problem. She realised that there were two parts to the project – the mechanism by which the door opened and closed and the control system which governed *when* the door opened and closed. First she investigated a range of possible mechanisms by building a series of Meccano models. She then investigated possible control systems by building a range of circuits. At this stage she had all the ingredients for an automatic sliding door and was in a position to assemble a working model. She could then build her final design.

Antonia's first Meccano model is shown in fig. 1. She reasoned that for the door to slide it would have to be in some sort of track and on some sort of bearing. She used Meccano to make both the track and the bearing wheels at the base of the door. Will she need a similar set at the top of the door?

▼Fig. 1 Antonia's model track system

▼Fig. 2 Antonia's winding system

The simplest way to move the door was to pull it along. So Antonia designed the simple winding arrangement shown in fig. 2. It pulled the door quite smoothly. However there were problems in getting the door to close. What happens when the direction of the winding motor is reversed? Two motors could be used to solve this problem. How?

▲Fig. 3 Antonia's first rack and and pinion design

Antonia rejected the use of two motors and decided that a rigid movement system was required. She investigated using a rack and pinion. Her first attempt is shown in fig. 3. The rack is attached to the rail. The pinions are mounted on the door. In this arrangement the motor has to be attached to the door. There are many disadvantages to this arrangement – what are they? Antonia reasoned that by putting the rack on the bottom of the door she would be able to move the door by pinions driven by a fixed motor. Her sketch for this idea is shown in fig. 4.

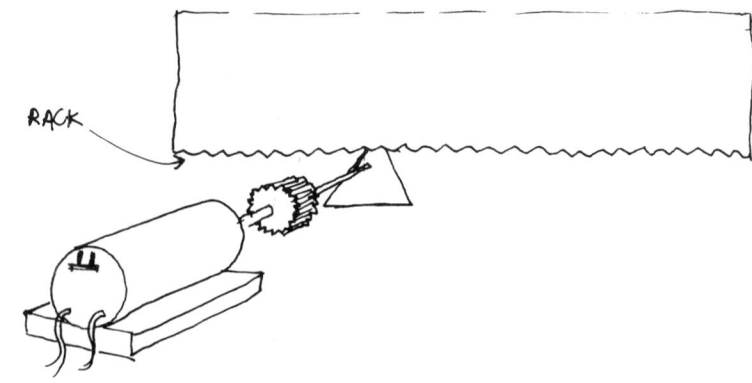

RACK

▲Fig. 4 Antonia's second rack and pinion design

Finally she considered the problem of stopping the door while the motor was running. Why is this necessary? She decided that this could be achieved by means of a belt drive from the motor to the pinion shaft. There would be sufficient friction for the belt to drive the pinion when only the door had to be moved. Any increased resistance to motion would cause the belt to slip. Her design sketch for this is shown in fig. 5.

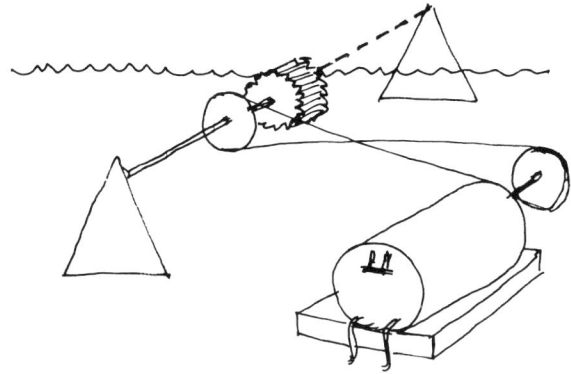

▲Fig. 5 Antonia's design to prevent the door closing on people

Antonia wanted the sliding door activated by a light (why?) but also capable of push button control. So that any circuits she built up were permanent, she soldered components to pins in matrix board.

First, Antonia investigated a circuit including a light-dependent resistor (ldr). She made the simple circuit shown in fig. 6. When she shone a bright line on the ldr the lamp came on. When she removed the light source the lamp went out. Can you explain why this happens? She realised that she could replace the lamp with a motor and so control the motor by light. She also realised that she could build a push switch into the circuit and short circuit the ldr and so give manual control. Draw the circuit diagram for this arrangement.

Antonia knew that in a real situation the motor operating the door would need a much larger current and voltage than that operating the ldr. So to make the model as realistic as possible she decided to use the ldr circuit to operate a relay which would then switch on the motor. The ldr circuit and the motor circuit would then have independent power supplies. A diagram of the circuit she built to do this is shown in fig. 7.

►Fig. 8 Details of a rack and pinion arrangement

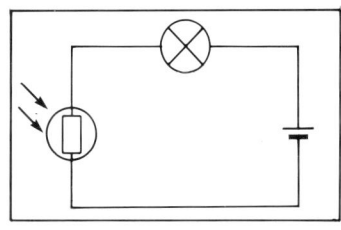

▲Fig. 6 Antonia's first simple circuit

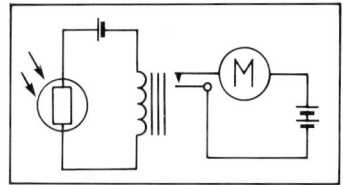

▲Fig. 7 Antonia's second more complex circuit

Antonia connected her rack and pinion operated door (shown in fig. 5) to the light operated control circuit (shown in fig. 7). She found that the light could be used to open the sliding door. There was however no way of turning off the motor other than removing the light source. Why is this not a practical proposition for a head-light operated garage door? She decided that a micro switch operated by the door when it reached the limit of the sliding movement could be fitted into the system. All that remained now was to find a way of getting the door to close, either automatically after a pre-set time delay or by a manually operated switch. Can you do it?

Questions

1 Figure 8 shows a close-up of a rack and pinion arrangement.　　**c**

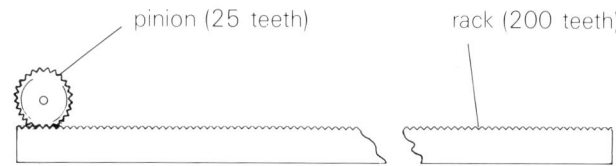

(a) In what direction must the pinion rotate to move B towards the pinion?
(b) How many revolutions must the pinion make before point B is directly under the pinion?
(c) If the pinion rotates at 60 rpm, how long will it take to achieve this?
(d) If you wanted the rack to do this movement in half the time, what ways are there to achieve this? What are their advantages and disadvantages?
2 (a) Draw a clear circuit diagram of the control circuit that Antonia has developed so far.　　**c**
(b) Design a switch system that allows the direction of the motor to be reversed.
(c) As soon as the light source is removed the motor will stop working. Design a switch system that will allow the door to be closed.
(d) When the sliding door has reached the closed position, how will the control system know this and turn the motor off? Design a system that solves this problem.

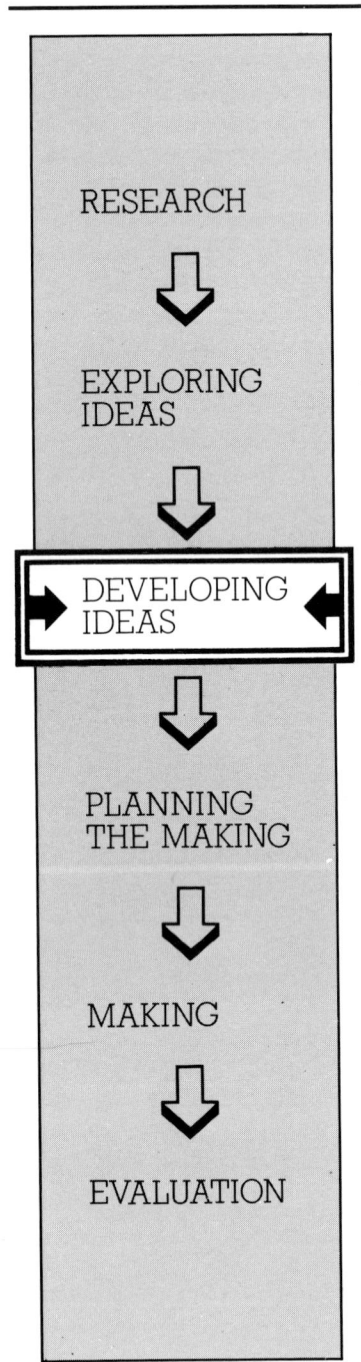

RESEARCH

⇩

EXPLORING
IDEAS

⇩

DEVELOPING
IDEAS

⇩

PLANNING
THE MAKING

⇩

MAKING

⇩

EVALUATION

PROJECT SUMMARY

Ronabir wanted to produce a series of unusual containers for sweets and fruits. He had explored several ideas before he came across the idea of making a container by using layers of sheet material – a bit like a liquorice allsort! As he wanted the containers to be visually interesting, he developed this idea to produce 'stepped' containers by building up layers of sheet material like the contours on a map. He developed a way of cutting rings from sheet timber using a face plate on a bowl-turning lathe. He developed a similar face plate technique on a metal-turning lathe for the production of rings from plastic sheet and sheet metal. A finished container is shown in fig. 5.

▲Fig. 1 Ronabir's card model

▼Fig. 2 Ronabir's drawing of
the rings needed to make
a stepped container

▼Fig. 3 Ronabir's cross-section developments of two stepped containers

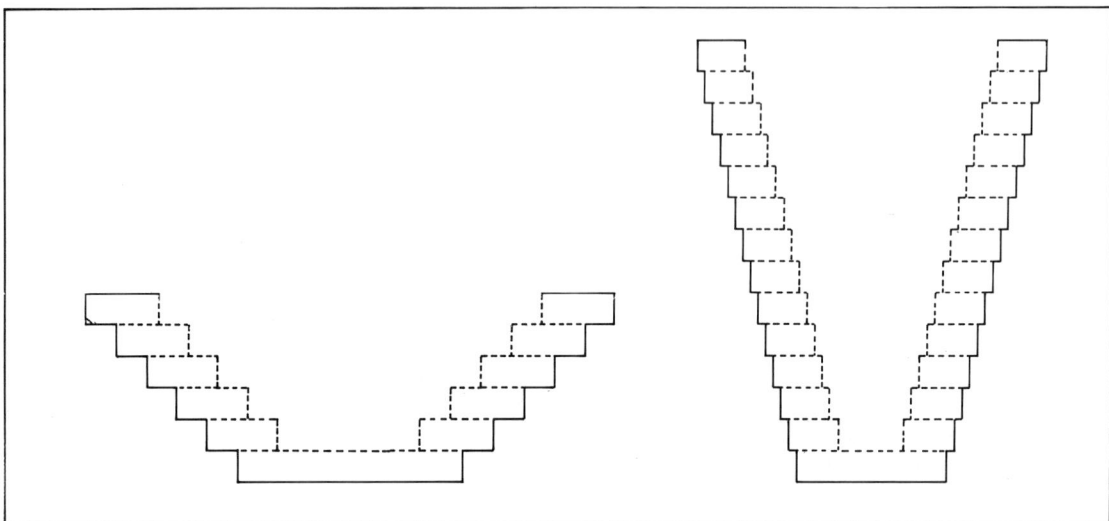

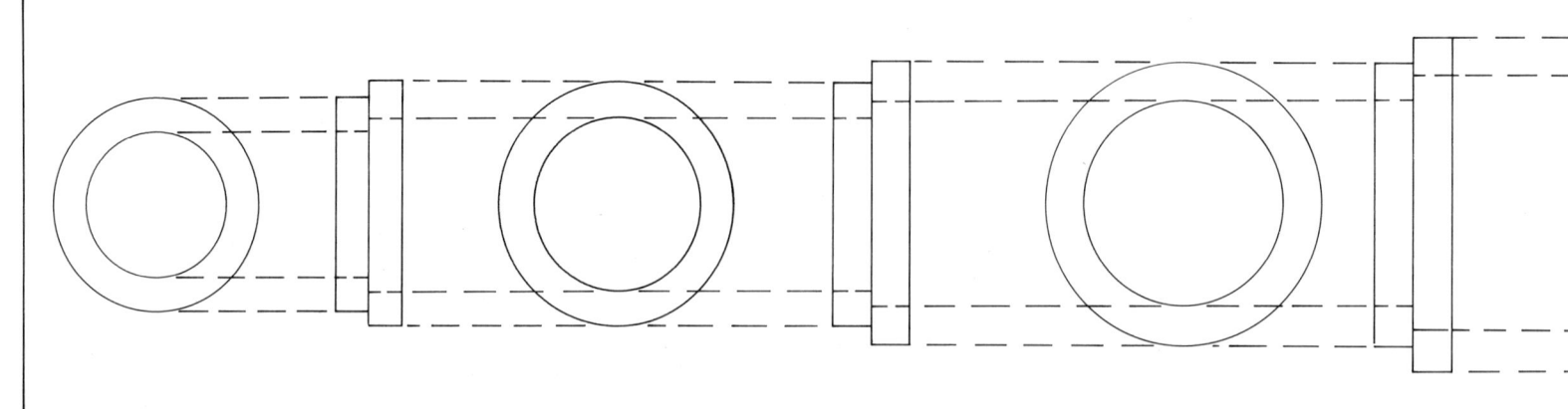

As a first step in exploring the idea, Ronabir produced the card model shown in fig. 1. He soon realised that he would have to make rings of sheet material of exactly the right size if he was to be successful. To do this he produced the drawings in fig. 2 (full size) so that he knew the size of each ring. Notice how the amount of overlap between adjacent rings can be clearly seen. He then realised that he did not need to draw the overhead view each time – a cross-section view would give him all the information he required. Figure 3 shows his cross-section developments of two forms; the first is tall and thin with slightly sloping sides (10° to the vertical), while the second is less tall, wider and has sides sloping 45° to the vertical. By drawing such cross sections he was able to develop a wide range of forms. Can you explain how the slope of the side affects the 'step' size?

In order to show the overall effect of using different materials, Ronabir produced some shaded side elevations. Some of these are shown in fig. 4. These drawings helped him to decide which combinations of materials would look attractive.

▼Fig. 5 A finished container, made of chipboard and painted

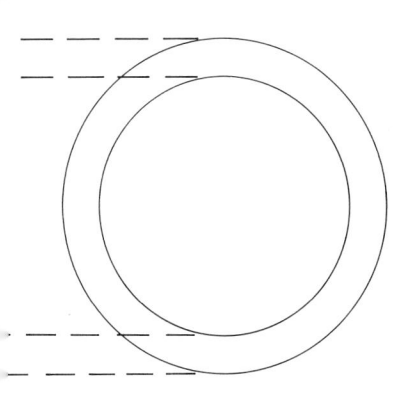

►Fig. 4 Ronabir's sketches showing possible effects of using different materials

PLYWOOD

DARK AND LIGHT WOOD

ACRYLIC SHEET

METAL SHEET AND ACRYLIC SHEET

Questions

1 Explain clearly why it is impossible to assemble a stepped container as shown in fig. 3 from concentric rings cut from a single piece of plywood. **c**

2 Using 10 mm thick plywood, calculate the size of sheets you would need to make the containers shown in fig. 3. **c**

3 Using isometric paper, draw a 3D sketch of the containers drawn in cross section in fig. 3. **c**

4 State which adhesives you would use if you were to assemble stepped containers from the following materials:
(a) hardboard, (b) plywood, (c) Perspex, (d) nylon, (e) Perspex and nylon, (f) plywood and brass, (g) brass, Perspex and plywood. Give reasons for your choices. **c**

5 With the aid of sketches, describe how you would position rings on top of one another so that they could not slip out of position. **c**

6 Ronabir wondered if he could hold plywood rings together without glue, simply by using screws. Use sketches to work out the details of such an arrangement and comment on its advantages and disadvantages. **c**

7 Draw up a table showing the size and number of rings you would have to produce to assemble the forms shown in fig. 3, using 10 mm thick sheet material. **c**

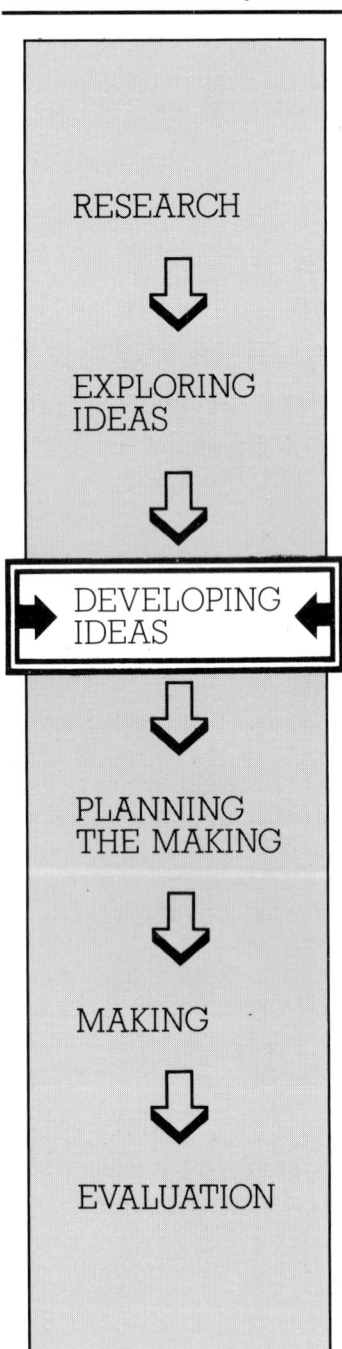

RESEARCH

⇩

EXPLORING
IDEAS

⇩

DEVELOPING
IDEAS

⇩

PLANNING
THE MAKING

⇩

MAKING

⇩

EVALUATION

PROJECT SUMMARY

Mary was in the same class as Rachel and also had the problem of designing a pull-along toy for young children. She began her project by looking at the range of pull-along toys in her local toy shops. She spent several Saturday mornings observing the re-actions of young children and their parents who came in to look at and buy pull-along toys. She found that children were attracted to toys that moved 'up-and-down' as they were pulled along and those with a friendly appearance. Parents were concerned that toys should be hard wearing and present no safety hazards.

To meet the needs of both adults and children, Mary designed a pull-along caterpillar whose body segments moved up and down as it was pulled. It was made from glass reinforced plastic (GRP) which is hard, tough and non-toxic. She designed a friendly face and made sure there were no small detachable parts. The finished caterpillar is shown in fig. 1.

▲Fig. 1 Mary's caterpillar toy

Mary's original design sketch for the moving body segments and the body shape she wanted are shown in fig. 2a. It proved impos-sible to make segments with this shape, as once cast they could not be released from the mould. (Can you work out why?) She developed a segment form which could be released and this is

shown in fig. 2b. She realised that this solution would lead to a body form like that shown in fig. 2c and that this was very dif-ferent from the body shape she wanted. She also realised that there would be less movement possible for each segment in this body form.

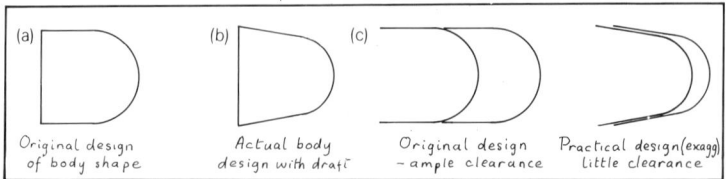

▲Fig. 2 (a) Mary's original body segment design (b) Mary's altered body segment design (c) The body shape produced by the altered segment design

Mary's solution to this problem is shown in fig. 3. When three segments with spacers are joined together as shown in fig. 4a, the first section appears longer because it is fully exposed whereas the others are only partly exposed. Mary chose to exaggerate

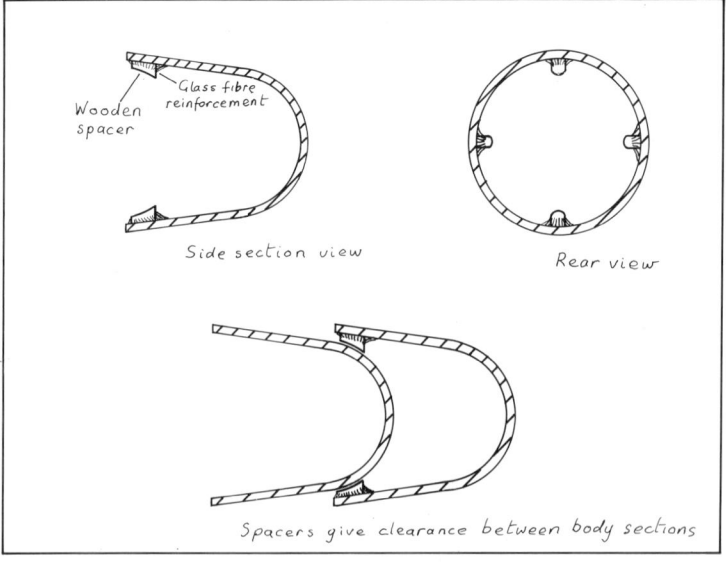

▲Fig. 3 Mary's solution to the body shape problem

this effect by making the rear segment shorter so that the segments appear to decrease uniformly as shown in fig. 4b.

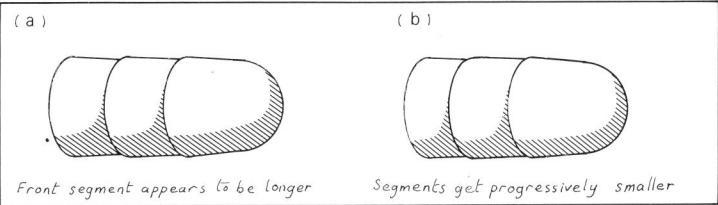

▲Fig. 4 (a) Body shape with equal size segments (b) Body shape designed to make segments appear smaller nearer the tail

The 'up-and-down' motion of the body segments is achieved by having each segment supported by eccentric wheels. In her early sketches Mary showed the wheel fixed somehow to the body. The details of the attachment had to be worked out. The details of the axle and wheel arrangement she designed are shown in fig. 5. In one of her early sketches Mary had shown the wheels held on to the axle by means of an axle nut. On reflection she decided to glue the wheels to the axle. Can you explain why?

▶Fig. 5 Mary's design for the axle and wheel arrangements

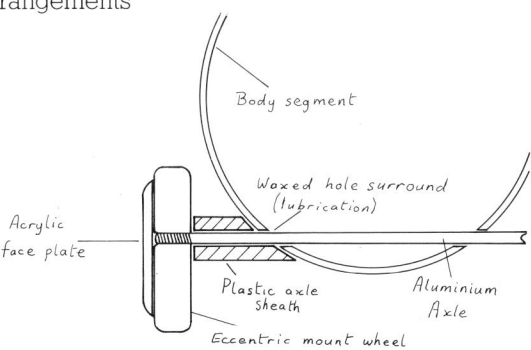

In the early stages of developing her ideas Mary thought she could use a single rubber band or a single piece of string to joint the segments together. Can you explain why she decided against both of these options and used the arrangement shown in fig. 6? Why is it necessary to have a piece of aluminium tube in the rear section?

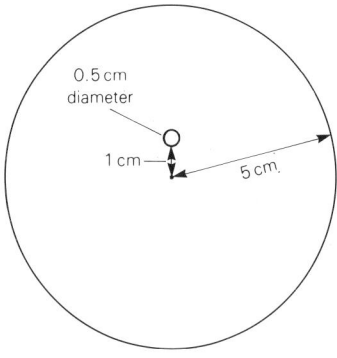

▲Fig. 7 An eccentric wheel

▼Fig. 6 Mary's chosen solution for linking the segments

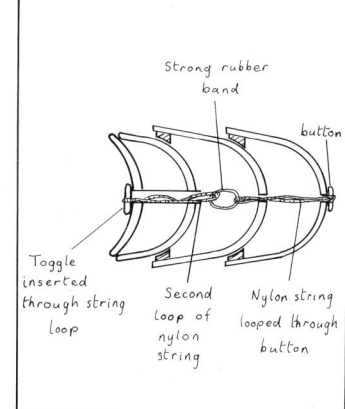

Questions

1 Starting with a tracing of fig. 3, work out the limits of movement, both up and down, that a body segment can make. Card cut-out models will help you. **C**

2 Mary designed the caterpillar body so that the segments appeared shorter towards the rear. Present a series of sketches to show the segment form necessary:
(a) for the segments to appear the same size,
(b) for the segments to become longer towards the rear. **C**

3 A friend criticised Mary's design because there were not lots of segments 'like in a real caterpillar'. Present a sketch that shows a ten-segment caterpillar and comment on the consequences of increasing the number of segments. **C**

4 The 'up-and-down' movement was produced by eccentric wheels. For the wheel shown in fig. 7 work out the amount of 'up and down' movement possible. How may the wheel design be changed (a) to increase and (b) to decrease the amount of 'up and down' movement? **C**

5 Show by means of sketches why both the amount of 'up-and-down' movement and the wheel size have to be considered when deciding on axle position in the body segment. **C**

6 Show by means of sketches that it is important to keep in mind the limits of up-and-down movement as governed by the segment form with the amount of up and down movement provided by the eccentric wheels. **C**

7 The details of the wheel and axle arrangement are shown in fig. 5. What advantages and disadvantages are there in using an aluminium axle instead of a steel one? What is the purpose of the plastic sheath? In her original design Mary had the plastic sheath covering the whole axle. Can you explain why she changed her mind? **C**

8 A friend suggested that oval shaped wheels would look more like legs. Use sketches to investigate this suggestion. **C**

9 What precautions should be taken to ensure that knots in the nylon linking string do not come undone? How easy do you think Mary's linking system will be to repair when the rubber band breaks? **C**

10 A friend suggested that with more segments it would be possible to design a simple linkage system that allowed a child to take the caterpillar to pieces and put it together with the segments in any order. Present sketches to show ways of doing this. **C**

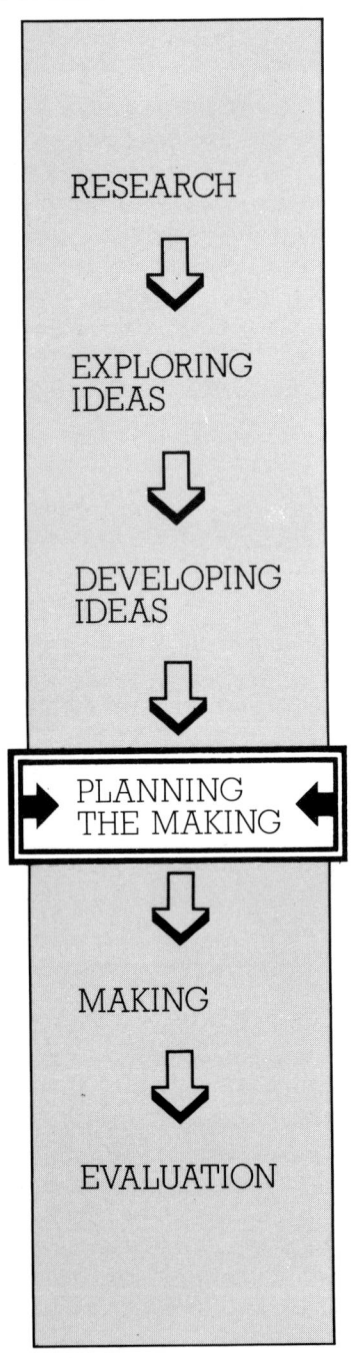

RESEARCH

⬇

EXPLORING
IDEAS

⬇

DEVELOPING
IDEAS

⬇

➡ PLANNING
THE MAKING ⬅

⬇

MAKING

⬇

EVALUATION

PROJECT SUMMARY

Michael's parents wanted a garden bench seat with an adjustable back rest. They specified a price limit of £10.00. Michael's research and idea exploring produced lots of different ideas. He developed the best ideas and produced a working drawing. The finished product is shown in fig. 1. To keep within his price limit Michael chose cheap materials – 50 mm × 25 mm softwood for frame construction and 75 mm × 25 mm softwood for the seat/bench top. As the piece was to be used outdoors, he stained the frame with wood preservative and treated the seat with polyurethane varnish.

▲Fig. 1 The completed bench seat

Any complex assembly like this bench seat cannot be fixed together all at once. It has to tackled in stages. Each stage is called a SUB ASSEMBLY. So in planning the making of his bench seat Michael drew up a procedure sheet in which he listed each sub assembly. This is shown in fig. 2. From this and the working drawings Michael was able to draw up a cutting list and a fixings and finishes list. These are shown in fig. 3. Use the information provided to complete the 'totals' column and find out if Michael's design is within his budget. The exploded diagram in fig. 4 will help you identify all the parts.

Michael was able to buy all his materials, fixings and finishes from the school, so he could buy exactly what he needed at rock bottom prices. However, if he had bought from the local DIY store it might have been much more expensive. Use the following information to work out the probable 'real' cost, taking into account the following hidden factors. 50 mm × 25 mm softwood is sold in lengths of 1 m 90 cm only, £0.70 per length. Brass hinges are sold in packs of four at £1.50 per pack. No. 8 50 mm brass countersunk screws are sold in packs of 20 at £1.60 per pack. Most schools provide sandpaper and glue free of charge. A packet of medium and fine sandpaper each cost £1.00 and a small tin of Cascamite glue would cost £2.50.

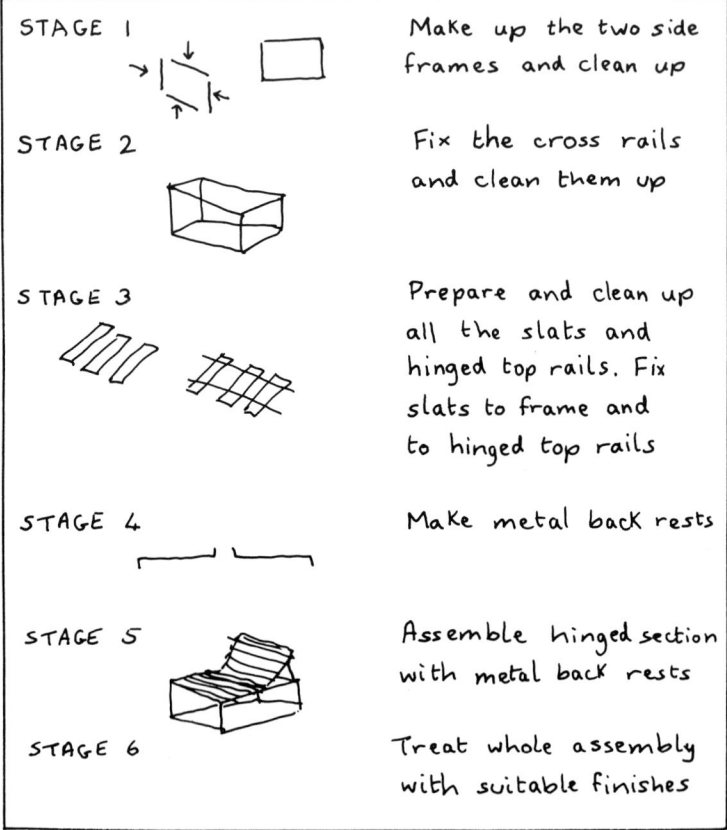

STAGE 1	Make up the two side frames and clean up
STAGE 2	Fix the cross rails and clean them up
STAGE 3	Prepare and clean up all the slats and hinged top rails. Fix slats to frame and to hinged top rails
STAGE 4	Make metal back rests
STAGE 5	Assemble hinged section with metal back rests
STAGE 6	Treat whole assembly with suitable finishes

▲Fig. 2 Michael's sub-assembly list

CUTTING LIST

Material	Part	Size	No. off	Cost	Total
softwood	siderail	1000 × 50 × 25 mm	4	0.35/m	
softwood	endrail	500 × 50 × 25 mm	4	0.35/m	
softwood	hinged toprail	500 × 50 × 25 mm	2	0.35/m	
softwood	crossrail	500 × 50 × 25 mm	2	0.35/m	
softwood	seat slats	500 × 75 × 25 mm	12	0.45/m	
mild steel	backrest	500 mm × 10mm dia.	2	0.10/m	

FIXINGS LIST

Fixing	Size	No. off	Cost	Total
dowel	1000mm × 6mm dia.	1	0.20/m	
brass hinge	50 mm	2	0.20 ea	
c/s brass screw	No.8 50 mm	48	0.02 ea	
c/s brass screw	No.6 20 mm	8	0.01 ea	
plastic slot	10mm dia.	4	0.05 ea	

FINISHES LIST

Finish	Amount	No. off	Cost	Total
Polyurethane varnish	large tin	1	2.30	
wood stain	small tin	1	1.00	

◄Fig. 3 Michael's cutting, fixings and finishes list

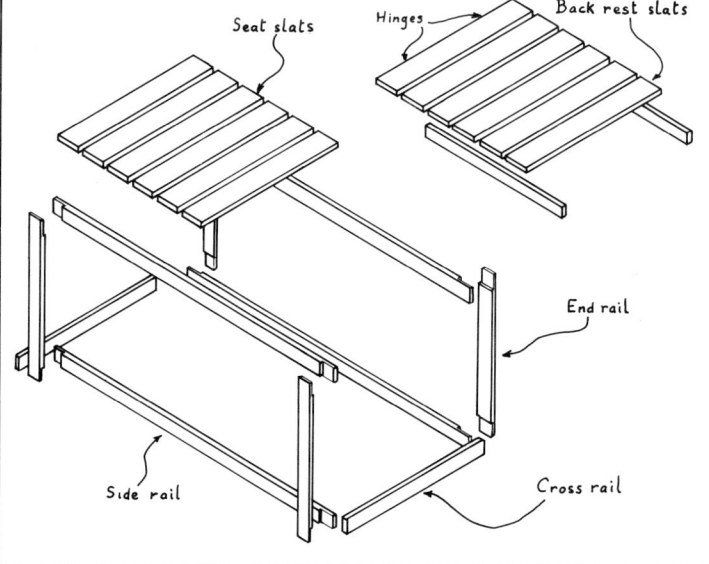

◄Fig. 4 An exploded diagram of Michael's bench seat

Questions

1 The details of each sub assembly stage have not been spelled out. For each stage list *all* the things to be done.　**c**

2 Using your answer to question 1, estimate the time taken to complete each sub assembly. Organise your 'time taken' into lessons-worth of time assuming a lesson is about 1 hour long. If Michael has two CDT lessons per week, how many weeks will he spend making the seat? How many weeks should he allow for the making process?　**c**

3 State clearly which tools and equipment you will need for each stage. Are these readily available in your school workshop? If not, how will you overcome this problem?　**c**

4 At the end of each sub assembly it is important to 'clean up' the sub assembly before moving on to the next stage. Why is this? Michael assembled and clamped the frames together without glue at one stage and cleaned up the insides of the frames before final gluing together. Explain why.

5 What sort of glue should Michael use? Give reasons for your answer.

6 What problem might Michael meet once he has applied a suitable finish to the seat? What facilities does your school have to cope with these problems?

7 Prepare a procedure sheet for the making of the following, showing clearly how you would divide the procedure into sub-assemblies: (a) Andrea's lace bobbins (page 70), (b) Ronabir's stepped containers (page 78), (c) Mary's toy caterpillar (page 80), (d) Rachel's toy duck (page 74), (e) David's card robots (page 84).　**c**

RESEARCH

⇩

EXPLORING
IDEAS

⇩

DEVELOPING
IDEAS

⇩

PLANNING
THE MAKING

⇩

→ MAKING ←

⇩

EVALUATION

PROJECT SUMMARY

David was interested in technical graphics and its use in packaging and advertising. He designed and made a series of cardboard cut-out model robots to be used as part of an advertising campaign for a new breakfast cereal – Roboflakes. He developed several cardboard model robots, one of which is described here. The model had to be designed so that all its parts fitted on the back of the packet. The instructions had to be clear and the model itself sufficiently interesting but not so complex that it was impossible for children aged 10–14 years to assemble.

▲Fig. 1 Science fiction magazines provided ideas for David's robot

▼Fig. 2 David's procedure sheet

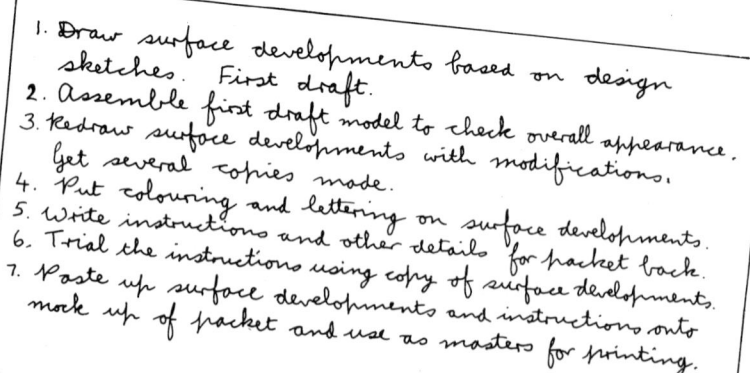

1. Draw surface developments based on design sketches. First draft.
2. Assemble first draft model to check overall appearance.
3. Redraw surface developments with modifications. Get several copies made.
4. Put colouring and lettering on surface developments.
5. Write instructions and other details for packet back.
6. Trial the instructions using copy of surface developments.
7. Paste up surface developments and instructions onto mock up of packet and use as masters for printing.

David read through lots of science fiction material as a source of design ideas. Some of these are shown in fig. 1. He produced a plan of action. This is shown as a procedure sheet in fig. 2. Read through this carefully and decide for yourself how long each stage will take. Talk to your teacher about how this plan can become part of a 'slip chart'.

The making part of this project breaks down into three stages:
1. making the cardboard robots,
2. making up the instruction sheet,
3. printing and making up the Roboflakes packet.
None of this making involves hard materials or machine tools but it still requires just as much thought, care and accuracy as projects that do. The procedure sheet will tell you *when* to do something: it will not tell you *how*. It is important that you seek advice whenever you are not sure how to do something.

David needed to get help in two areas. Firstly, before colouring the surface development he talked to the art teacher about how to use an airbrush and proper masking out methods. In order to obtain a professional finish he wanted to use rub down lettering rather than a stencil. Again he consulted the art teacher. Both these processes are shown in fig. 3. All through the making process it was important to work carefully and slowly. A single slip when cutting or scoring could cause disaster. The use of too much glue would result in sticky surfaces that gathered dust and fluff. The completed robot is shown in fig. 4.

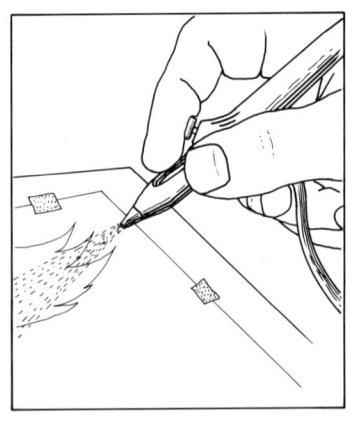

▲Fig. 3A Airbrushing

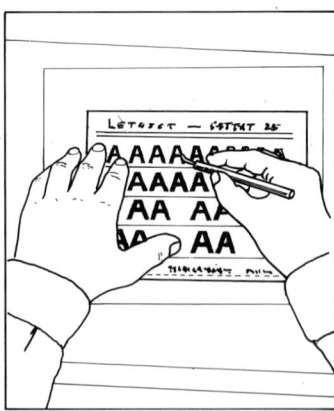

▲Fig. 3B Rub-down lettering

◄Fig. 4 David's completed robot

▼Fig. 5 David's layout for the back of the cereal packet

Questions

1 A more permanent model could be made using thin sheet metal. What problems are likely to be met and how might they be overcome?

2 How might a sheet metal model robot be mechanised? Here are some points to consider: wheels or moving legs? clockwork or electric motor? if electric, where will batteries be stored? What other motions – arms, head – might be included? What mechanisms will be needed for these?

3 Take a cheap clockwork toy to pieces and discover exactly how it works. You will be surprised at the ingenuity! **x**

4 How could you make the body, head and neck of the model robot from solid materials such as aluminium or nylon? There is more than one way. Describe each method in detail.

5 The arm design is shown in fig. 6. Explain how it can be assembled to give coloured detail on both sides. **c**

▼Fig. 6

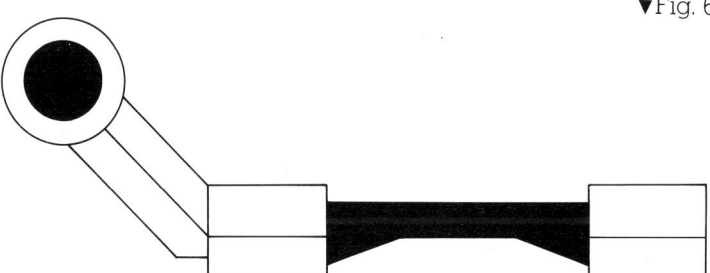

Tubular arms were not used for several reasons. Work out what these reasons might be.

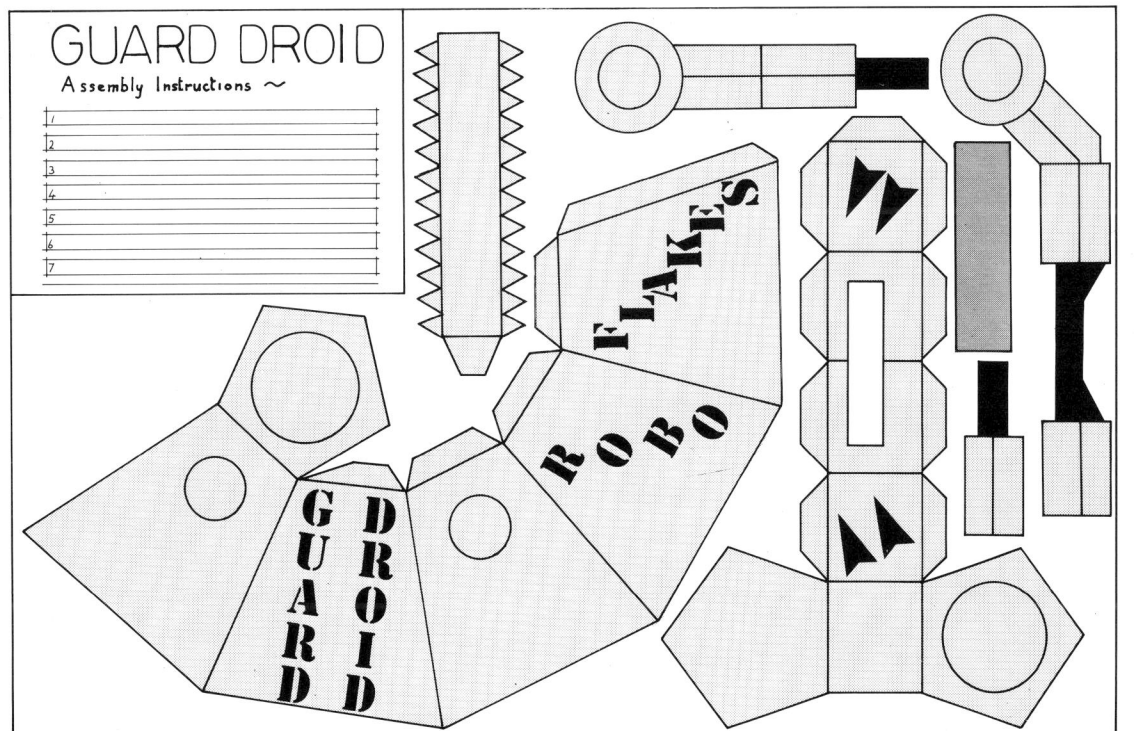

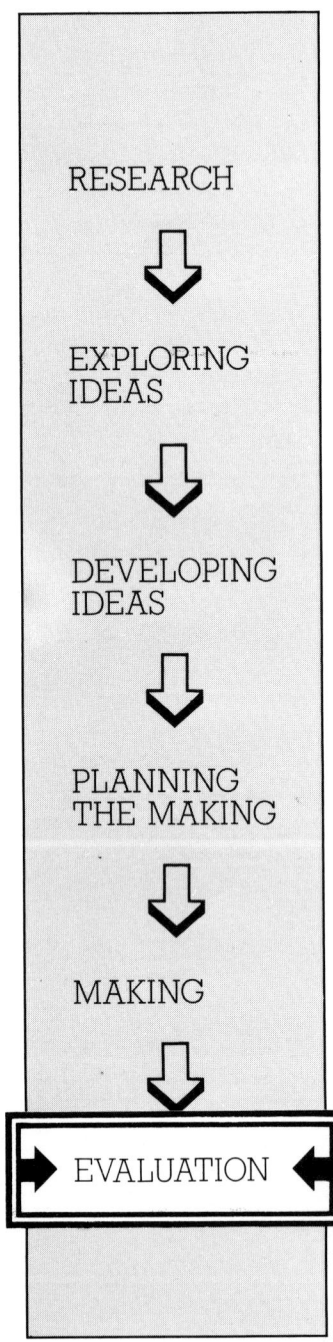

RESEARCH

⬇

EXPLORING
IDEAS

⬇

DEVELOPING
IDEAS

⬇

PLANNING
THE MAKING

⬇

MAKING

⬇

➡ EVALUATION ⬅

PROJECT SUMMARY

Martin became interested in robotic arms after visiting an exhibition. He decided to explore the possibilities of such an arm. He designed and built one using a hydraulics construction kit powered by a windscreen wiper pump. It took a long time to investigate the kit and understand how the control valves could be used to operate the drive cylinders. He used Meccano parts for all the framework, but designed and made the gripping hand from sheet steel and rubber. It took four weeks to develop a successful Meccano framework that could be fitted with hydraulic cylinders. It took another three weeks to produce a hand that worked well. Mounting the arm on a base board and tidying up the arrangement so that the plastic pipes carrying the hydraulic fluid did not interfere with the movement of the arm took another

▼Fig. 1 Martin's robotic arm

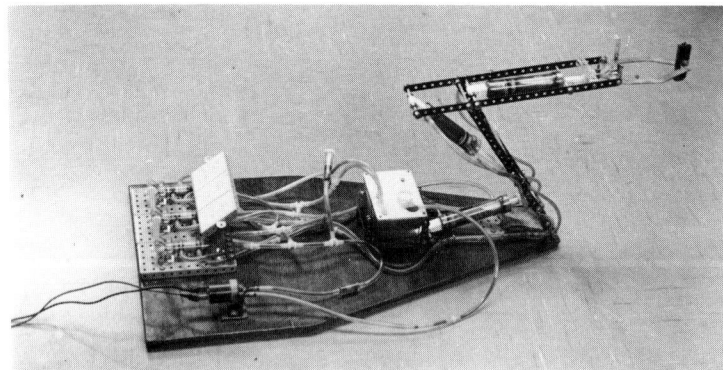

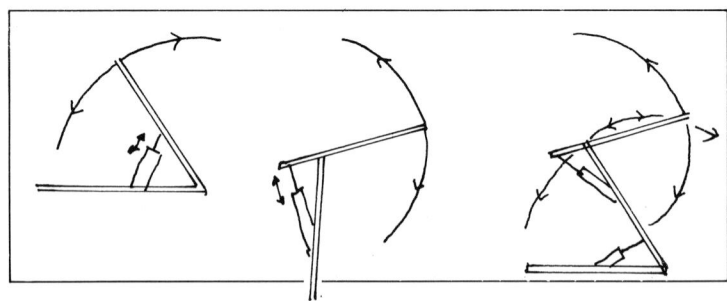

▲Fig. 2 Martin's design sketches on arm movement

three weeks. The rest of the time was spent evaluating the performance of the arm.

▼Fig. 3 Martin's design for the 'hand'

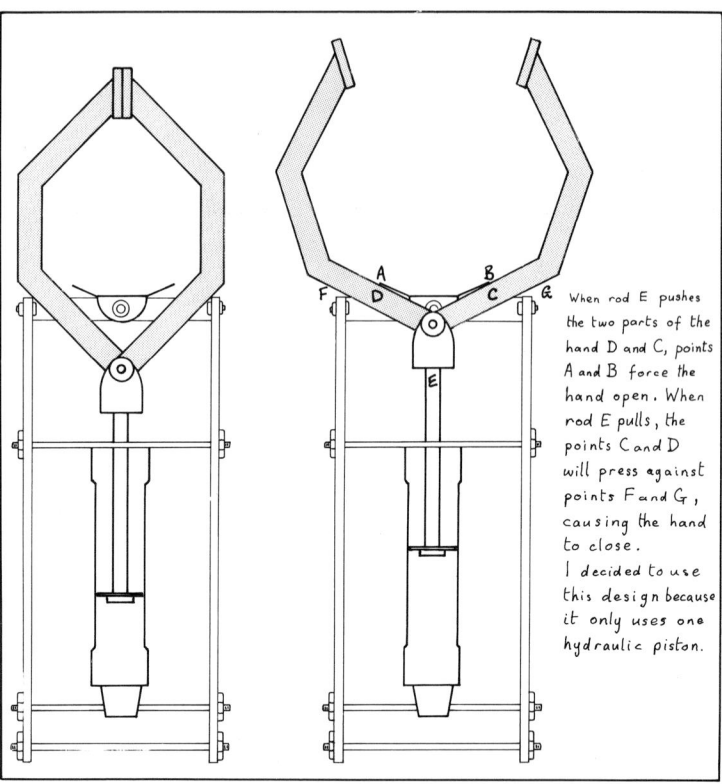

When rod E pushes the two parts of the hand D and C, points A and B force the hand open. When rod E pulls, the points C and D will press against points F and G, causing the hand to close.
I decided to use this design because it only uses one hydraulic piston.

The evaluation of the robotic arm was broken down into four sections:
1. ease of control, 2. effect of practice on performance, 3. arm power, 4. measurement of the workspace.

EASE OF CONTROL

Martin's comments on the ease of control read:

The arm was easy to operate. Without a lot of practice I could lift a 50g mass from the floor to 40cm above floor height and replace it in the same position without difficulty. Many other people thought it was easy to control.

EFFECT OF PRACTICE ON PERFORMANCE

For a given operation, e.g. lifting a small mass from one shelf and replacing it on a lower shelf, Martin found that his performance improved with practice as his results table indicates:

1st attempt	40 secs	4th attempt	27 secs
2nd attempt	37 secs	5th attempt	26 secs
3rd attempt	30 secs	6th attempt	27 secs

ARM POWER

This was measured by timing how long it took to lift various masses through a given distance. An incomplete version of Martin's results table is shown below:

MASS m (g)	FORCE $\dfrac{m \times 9.8}{1000}$ (N)	DISTANCE d (m)	WORK DONE force × distance (N × m)	TIME t (s)	POWER (Nm/s)
300		0.45		30	
250		0.45		20	
200		0.45		14	
150		0.45		9.5	
100		0.45		7	
50		0.45		6	

Martin carried out further experiments in which the time taken to lift loads through 45 cm was measured for masses from 50 g to 300 g at 10 g intervals. He plotted the mass lifted against time taken and drew a smooth curve through the points as shown in fig. 4.

MEASURING THE WORKSPACE

By fixing a felt-tip pen at right angles to the arm, Martin was able to trace out the area that the hand could reach. This is called the workspace. His scale diagram is shown in fig. 5.

►Fig. 5 Martin's measurement of workspace

▼Fig. 4 Martin's graph comparing weight lifted with time taken

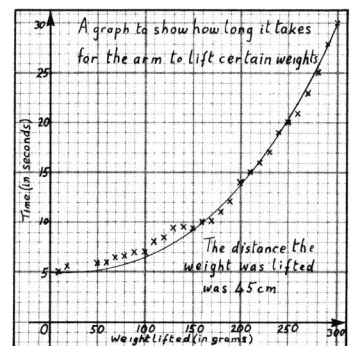

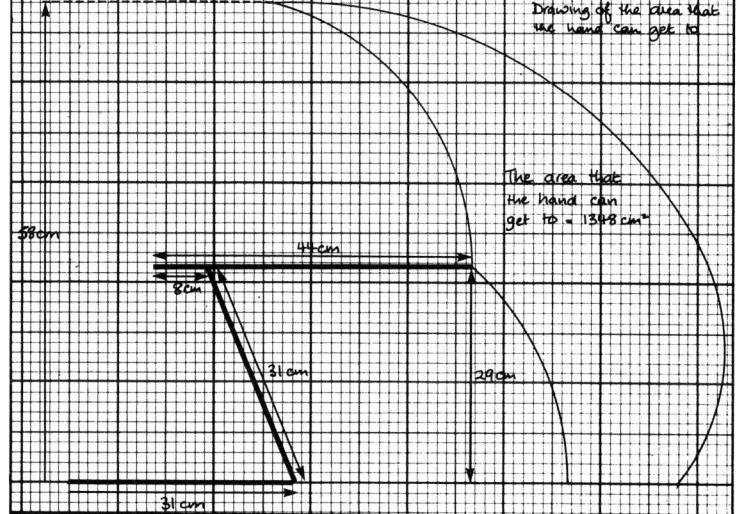

Questions

1 In what ways could the evaluation of ease of control and the effect of practice on performance be widened? What advantages might there be in (a) trying more complicated manoeuvres? (b) observing other students operating the arm?

2 In evaluating the power of the arm, only a single set of measurements is presented. Why would it be better to repeat the measurements many times and take an average result?

3 Copy and complete the arm power results table. Use the data to suggest an optimum working load for the arm. **c**

4 You can extend the evaluation of the workspace by considering the effect of limb dimension on the shape and area of the workspace. How would the shape and area of the workspace change if **c**
(a) limb A was made 22 cm long?
(b) limb A was made 66 cm long?
(c) limb B was made 15 cm long?
(d) limb B was made 46 cm long?

5 The evaluation as presented here is incomplete. What do you think about the following: **c**
(a) the appearance of the arm,
(b) how easy it would be to make,
(c) the situations and circumstances in which it could be used?

FOUR

LOOKING FOR THE RIGHT SKILLS

RESEARCH SKILLS

As you know, at the beginning of the design process comes the research stage in which you seek out the information you are likely to need to complete the design brief. However, as we shall see, research has to be carried out at all later stages as well. In fact, you are unlikely to complete all your research right at the beginning of a design project. This section is designed to help you learn the skills of researching so that whenever you need them, you can put them into practice.

Research for design projects can be divided into two sorts. GENERAL RESEARCH is used to get the 'feel' of the subject and to help you generate ideas. For example, if you have the problem of designing toys for young children you will need to know about the following:

1. child development and how this relates to possible play activities,
2. the sorts of toys that are already available,
3. whether such toys are appropriate for the age group you are designing for.

There is also SPECIFIC FACTUAL RESEARCH which is used to answer clearly defined questions. For example:

1. Which paints are permitted on children's toys?
2. Which materials will stand rough handling?
3. Which mechanisms convert rotary to reciprocal motion?

It is not difficult for you to decide what knowledge you need for any particular project. That is really a common-sense decision. Where to look for that information is much more tricky. There are three places to find information. These are summarised in fig. 1. We will look at each one in turn.

At present there is more information stored in books and magazines than anywhere else, and the majority of these are housed in libraries. Every library has a classification system for its non-fiction books and the most commonly used in this country is the Dewey Decimal System. Each main subject area is given a three-figure number. This allows 1000 areas (000–999) to be listed. Sub-sections within a subject area are defined by decimal numbers after the main three-figure number. For example: 668.4 – Plastics Technology.

▲Fig. 1 Information stores

Library assistants are there to help you find the information you need, so don't be afraid to ask.

Once you have been directed to where the books on your subject of interest are, the task of finding the right book from all the shelves can look even more daunting. Some of them will be too difficult, others too easy. You certainly won't have time to read them all. At this stage it is important to read the introductions and scan the contents pages of a few of the books. Both the introduction and the contents page will come at the beginning of the book. The introduction will tell you at what level the book is aimed: primary school, secondary school 'O' level or 'A' level, Higher Education BTEC courses or degree courses.

Once you have identified two or three books at your level, you can scan the contents pages to find chapters that are relevant to your research needs.

Suppose you needed to find out which wood to use for a garden seat, as Michael did in chapter 3 (page 82). He found a book in his local library called *How to Make Your Own Garden Equipment.* Figure 2 shows part of the contents page of this book. Can you tell which chapters the information Michael wanted might be in?

▼Fig. 2 Contents pages provide a quick guide to the information in a book

CONTENTS

If the information you require is very specific then you should use the index of the book. Indexes are at the end of books and list in alphabetical order the page numbers where various pieces of information are to be found. When you are ordering from large catalogues, it is essential to use the index to avoid tedious flicking through the pages.

If the first books that you select don't have the information you require, then it is a very simple matter to go back to the shelves and choose a higher or lower level book.

Once you have identified the part of the book that has the information you need, then you have to study that part in depth. This is not casual reading or scanning: it is a highly concentrated activity and you should make notes on what you are reading. To begin with you will probably find yourself copying out parts of the book, but you should try to avoid this. The best approach is to put the information in the book into your own words and to make your own diagrams. It is unlikely that you will be able to do more than 30 minutes in-depth reading and note taking without a break.

Individual magazines seldom have indexes, so scanning their contents pages is an important skill to develop. However, many magazines produce an index once a year which covers all the contents of the preceding year's issues, and these are often very useful. Scanning is important for extracting information from newspapers, as they generally have no contents pages or indexes. The skills of using an overall classification system, scanning and in-depth reading/note taking have their counterpart in high-technology information retrieval systems. Figure 3 shows a student learning to obtain information by using the Prestel system.

Information that is stored in people's heads is often the most difficult to obtain. To begin with you have to find out which people have the information you need and then you have to use the right approach to obtain the information. The *Yellow Pages* produced by British Telecom is a very convenient source of information about local industry. For example, suppose you were designing and making aluminium jewellery and wanted to colour the aluminium. Chemistry books would tell you about the principles of anodising, but you could look up 'Anodisers' in the *Yellow Pages* and find the addresses of local firms that specialise in anodising. If approached properly, they will give you the practical details of the process and probably practical assistance as well.

Well-presented letters, explaining who you are, what infor-

▲Fig. 3 Using high technology to obtain information

mation you require, why you require it and enclosing a stamped, addressed envelope for a reply will almost certainly get a positive response. The local colleges of further education, the local polytechnic and the local university are full of people who are willing to share their expertise with you if approached in the proper manner. So it is always worth taking time and trouble over letters requesting help. Do them in rough, discuss the rough draft with your teacher who will be able to suggest improvements, show the final versions to your teacher before you send them off and keep a copy of each one in your design folder so that you can refer back to them when you need to. Professional designers use expert help whenever they need to.

For some design briefs that you will tackle, you will have to discover things for yourself because the information that you need is not in any book or anybody else's head. This is often the case when you are designing fittings to go in your home. The preliminary measurements must be carried out by you and the way different parts of your home are used can only be found out by detailed observation on your part. Such measurements and observations are an important part of the research stage in many design projects and it is necessary that they are noted down carefully. The information obtained will play a key part in developing solutions to the design brief.

One final area of research is developing your own practical skills in the particular processes that will be required to make your chosen solution. Finding out the right way to carry out a making skill, be it wood turning, lost wax casting or soldering, and practising that skill until you are thoroughly proficient, is an important part of the research programme for any design brief where the designer is also the maker.

Questions

1 What sorts of information, both general and specific, would you need if you were designing the following:
(a) furniture for a play school,
(b) gardening tools for handicapped people,
(c) a bottle opener for people with arthritic hands,
(d) a control system for automatic greenhouse heating. **x**

GRAPHIC COMMUNICATION SKILLS
DEVELOPING IDEAS ON PAPER

When designing, you will need to communicate with all sorts of different people, and each situation will probably need a different sort of communication. We saw in chapter 2 how the *research* of a project involved written and spoken types of communication in order to get all the information needed. This section is concerned with the range of *graphic* communication skills that you will need. There are lots of them, but the first and most important one is being able to communicate design ideas quickly and accurately in free-hand sketches. For developing your design ideas in sketch form there are three simple approaches.

1. *Side or front* views allow you to explore, for example,
• comfortable sitting and working positions: length of reach, height of surface, position of support for seat and back, position of lighting (fig. 1);
• the most effective movement for a simple mechanism like a paper punch (fig. 2);

▼Fig. 1

▲Fig. 2

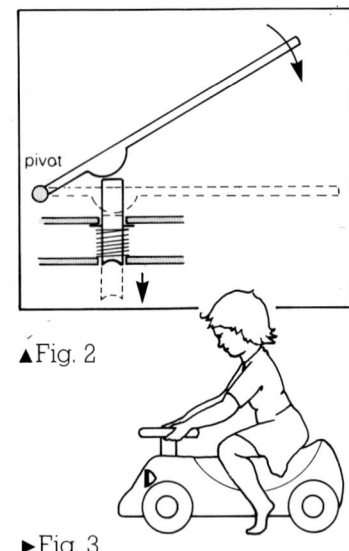

►Fig. 3

• the right sizes and positions for the parts of a toddler's push-along car (fig. 3).

2. *Plan views* are drawn looking down from above. They are specially useful for sketching *layouts*. For example, sketching a room plan helps to work out the best place for furniture (fig. 4). The keyboard layout in fig. 5 helps to position knobs and buttons in the best arrangement.

▼Fig. 4

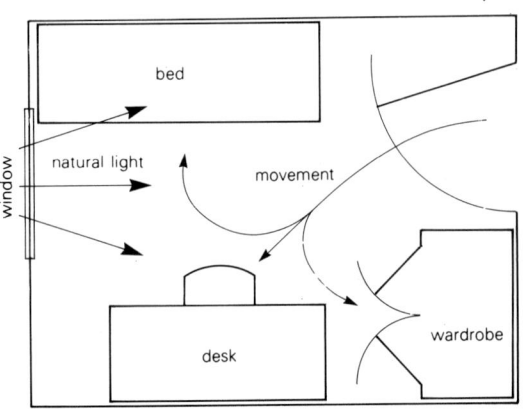

▼Fig. 5

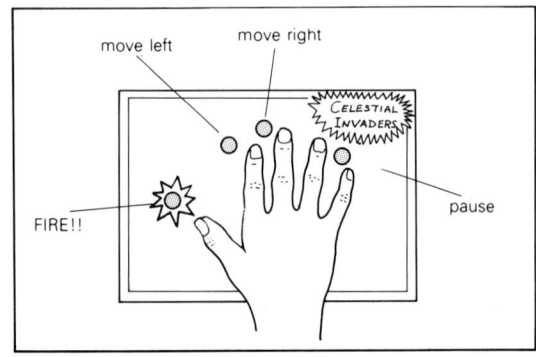

▼Fig. 6 Adjustable table leg

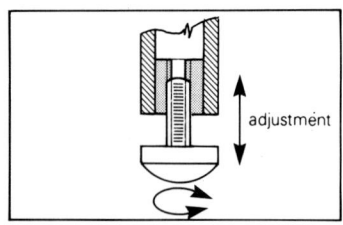

▼Fig. 7 A ball projector

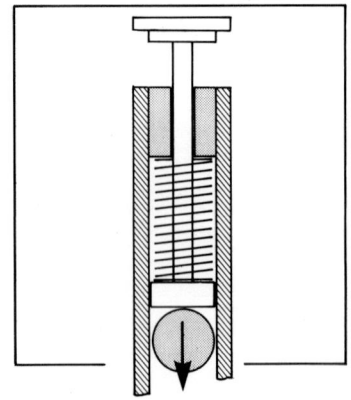

3. *Cut away* or *sectional* views make it possible to draw what is going on inside things. For example, to see how the adjustable foot on this table leg works you have to see inside (fig. 6).

The inside view of the ball projector (fig. 7) shows how the plunger is powered by a compression spring.

Questions

1 Draw a side view of a wheelbarrow when it is standing flat on the ground and when it is being wheeled along. Design the shape of the body of the barrow so that waste does not fall out in either position. **xo**

2 Draw a layout of your bedroom on squared paper. Make the drawing to a scale of 20:1. (A room 3 metres long is 3000 mm long. On the drawing it is 150 mm.) Draw in the furniture in its present position and then reorganise it on the plan to see if you can get a more efficient arrangement. You can use overlays or tracing paper to try out lots of different schemes. **xo**

3 Using front, side, plan and sectional views, illustrate simple domestic appliances: a door handle, mousetrap, can opener, etc. The drawings must explain how the article works. **xo**

DRAWING IT AS IT REALLY LOOKS

Side views and cut-away views are useful, but when you are designing there are lots of situations when it is much more useful to draw an object as it really looks. Any real object that you look at you will see in PERSPECTIVE, that is, it looks smaller the further away it is. If you trace the sight lines back far enough, they will all meet at vanishing points (VPs).

Cut out some photos from magazines, draw in the sight lines and find the vanishing points.

If you are straight in front of an object there will be only one vanishing point. If you are to one side of the object there will be two vanishing points.

For your own designing, if you start with a grid of sight lines it is easy to draw an object yourself as it really looks in perspective. Build up the drawing a stage at a time. Start with the base, then add the height and finally fill in the details. Try it out yourself with objects that you can see around you.

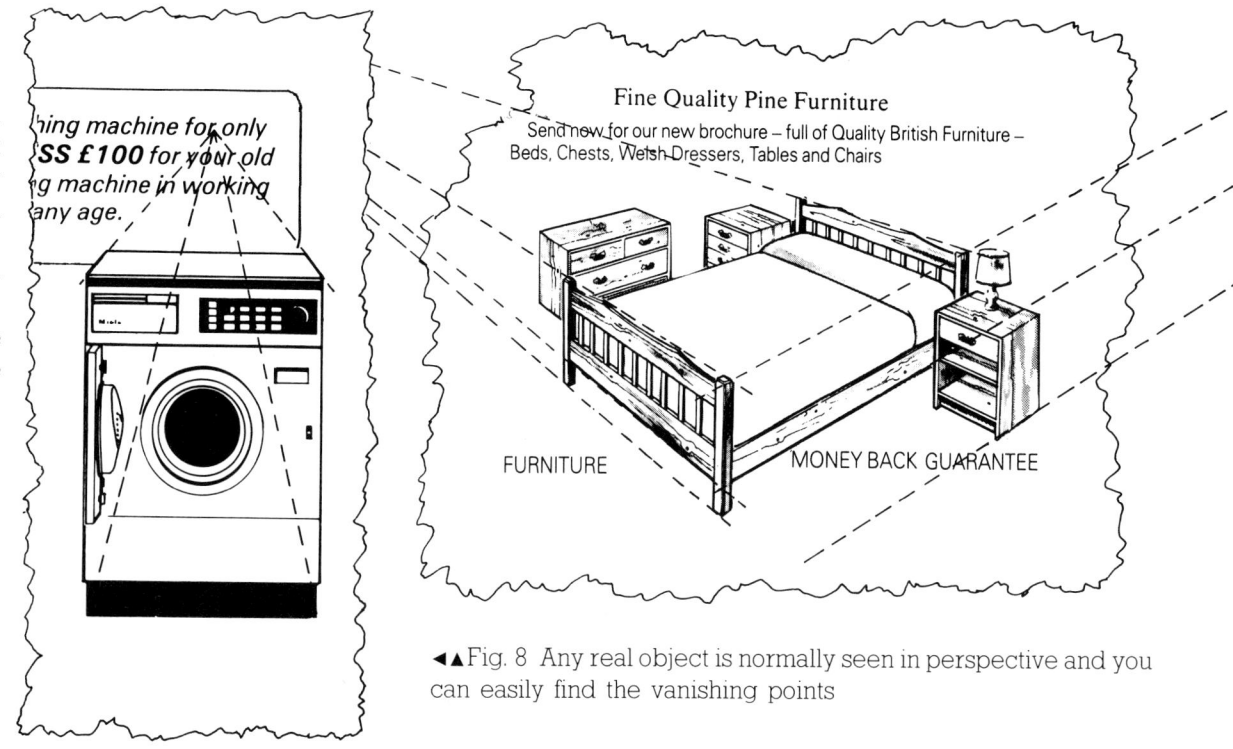

◀▲Fig. 8 Any real object is normally seen in perspective and you can easily find the vanishing points

▼Fig. 9 Starting with a grid, it is easy to draw real objects

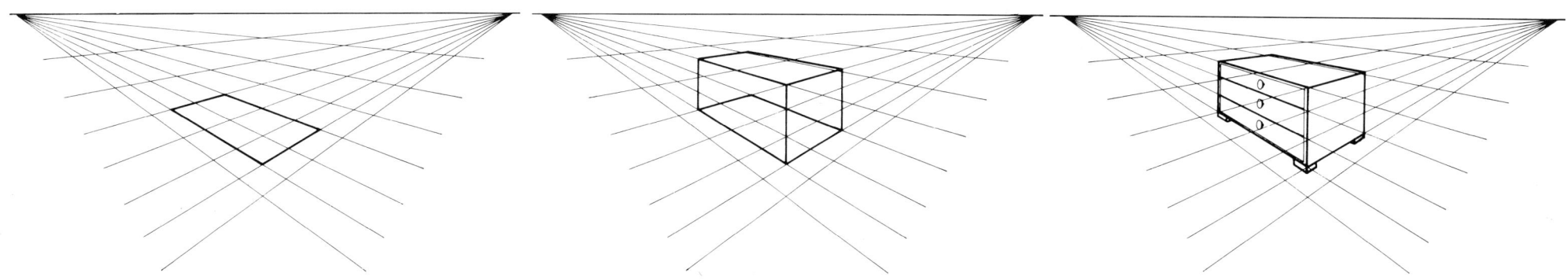

HAVING FUN WITH PERSPECTIVE SKETCHING

Notice how the perspective grid lets you see what you want to see. The lower you draw the object on the grid, the more you will see down on the top or down inside it. The higher it is on the grid the less you see of the top and the more you see of the front and side. It even lets you draw buildings as they really look. Above the eye line (which connects the VPs) you can see the underside of objects.

Notice also how shading makes the object more realistic. Imagine the light coming from one side, and then shade the surfaces that would be in shadow.

ISOMETRIC GRID PAPER also helps you to sketch objects which look realistic. It is a grid of lines set at 30° and is used in the same way as perspective grids. The disadvantages are that it can only show one position, and it is impossible to show tall objects realistically.

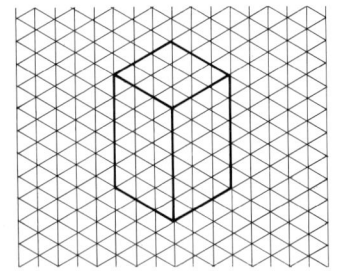

▶Fig. 10 Isometric grid drawings are not half so realistic

Questions

1 Using a perspective grid like the one in fig. 11, sketch a table or chair or similar object in three different positions on the grid. Shade the drawings. c

2 When you have finished, for each drawing position yourself so that the real object looks like that drawing. Note on the drawing how high your eyes are above the ground. o

3 On another perspective grid draw a building in two different positions – one as a pedestrian would see it, and the other as a helicopter pilot would see it. Try adding the garden and some trees around the building.

The more you practice drawing in perspective, the better you will get. Gradually you will be able to do without the grids, so keep drawing in a sketch book as much as you can.

▶Fig. 11 Any object can be drawn on a perspective grid – and they look real

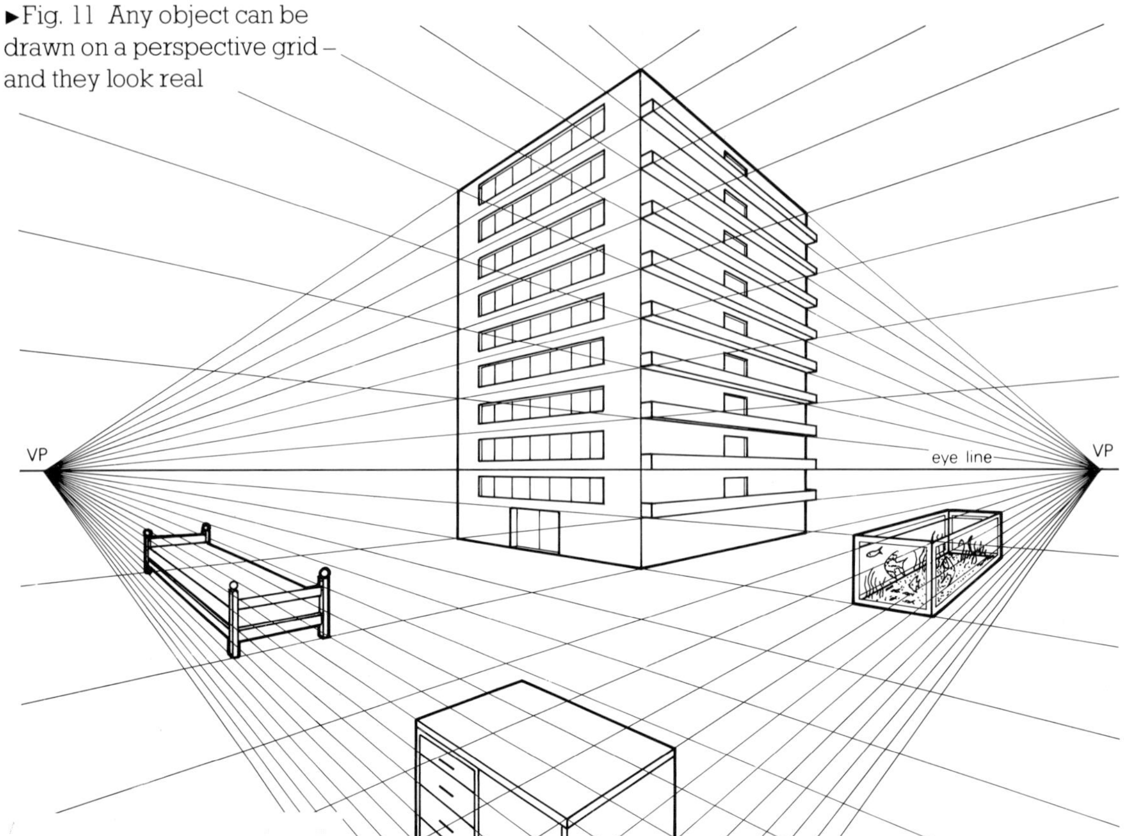

VP   eye line   VP

◀Fig. 12

PERSPECTIVE SKETCHING WITHOUT GRIDS

We have seen that perspective grids can be used to help create a realistic picture of an object. Also it lets us view the object from many different positions. However, if you don't have a grid handy, or if you are trying to get used to drawing without one, then try this exercise.

1. Draw a plan view of the object with you looking at it from almost straight in front. You must position yourself in line with the leading edge of the object.

▼Fig. 13

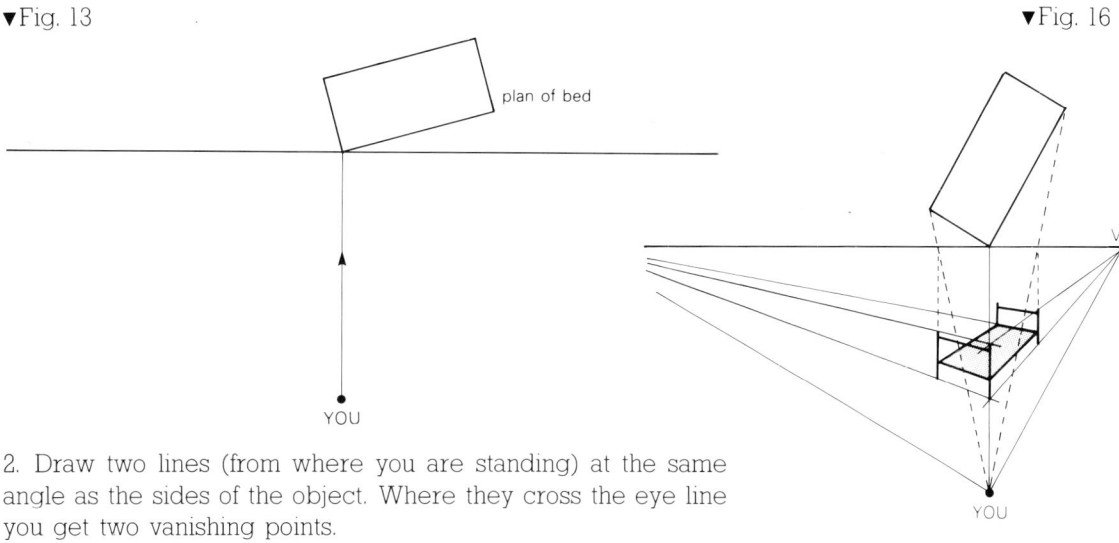

plan of bed

YOU

2. Draw two lines (from where you are standing) at the same angle as the sides of the object. Where they cross the eye line you get two vanishing points.

►Fig. 14

VP 75°   15°
                 VP

75°

15°

YOU

3. You can now draw in one or two grid lines and sketch in the object. Notice how much of the front you can see and how little of the end.

▼Fig. 15

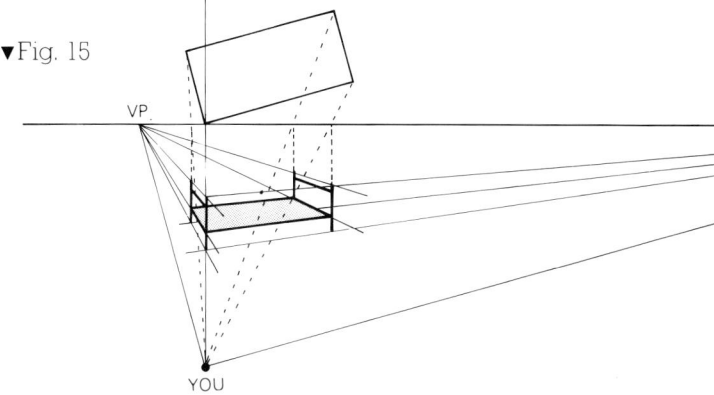

VP

YOU

▼Fig. 16

VP

YOU

4. If you want to see more of the end, just turn the plan of the object round a bit so you are looking more at the end of it. The VPs will now be in different places. The sketch will now show much more of the end and less of the front. Be careful to keep the sizes of the object in proportion.

5. Don't forget that you can also vary the height from which you look at the object. Above the eye line you will see the bottom. You can now draw flying bedsteads!

▼Fig. 17

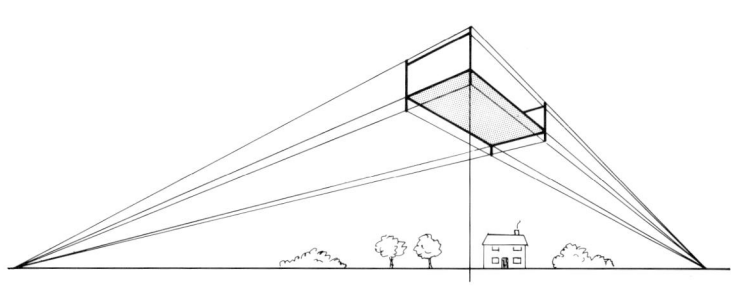

DESIGNING IN A ROOM

When you are designing furniture and domestic items it is very useful to draw the object in its proper setting. For this purpose you need to draw the *inside* of a room, and that can be done simply and accurately.

The starting point is to draw an accurate plan of the room and position an observer some distance away from the room. If the observer is too close to the plan view it distorts the picture. In the *picture* view, the observer must be in line with the observer in the *plan*, but can be at any height. A standing height of 5–6 feet is normal.

When you have tried drawing a few rooms like this you will see that you can vary the *picture* of the room by where you place the observer.

If the observer sits on the floor on the right hand side, the picture will show a lot of ceiling and left hand wall.

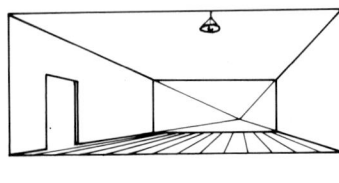

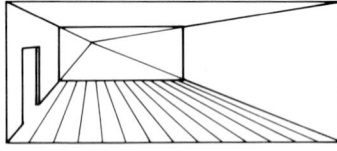

◄Fig. 18 You can control what you see by the position of the vanishing point

►Fig. 19

If the observer swings from the light fitting in the ceiling, the picture will show little ceiling and lots of floor.

The following stages 1–5 show you how to construct the picture accurately, but to make it work you must remember three rules:
1. All vertical lines and edges must stay vertical in the picture.
2. Lines parallel to the front of the room in the plan will always be horizontal lines in the picture.
3. All lines that go front to back in the plan of the room will go to the vanishing point in the picture.
Try drawing an accurate perspective view of part of your bedroom. Put the observer in different positions and see how it changes the picture. You will need to concentrate hard and follow the instructions carefully.

STAGE 1 Draw a plan of the room to scale and place the observer outside, looking in. Draw in the picture view of the room measuring the height to the same scale as the plan.

STAGE 2 The height of the observer in the picture must be drawn to the same scale as the room height. Draw lines joining the observer to the corners of the room in the plan and the picture.

STAGE 3 To find the position of the back wall. Join the observer to corner A of the plan. Where this line crosses the front edge of the room, project up onto the picture. Repeat the process on the right-hand wall. Draw in the walls, floor and ceiling.

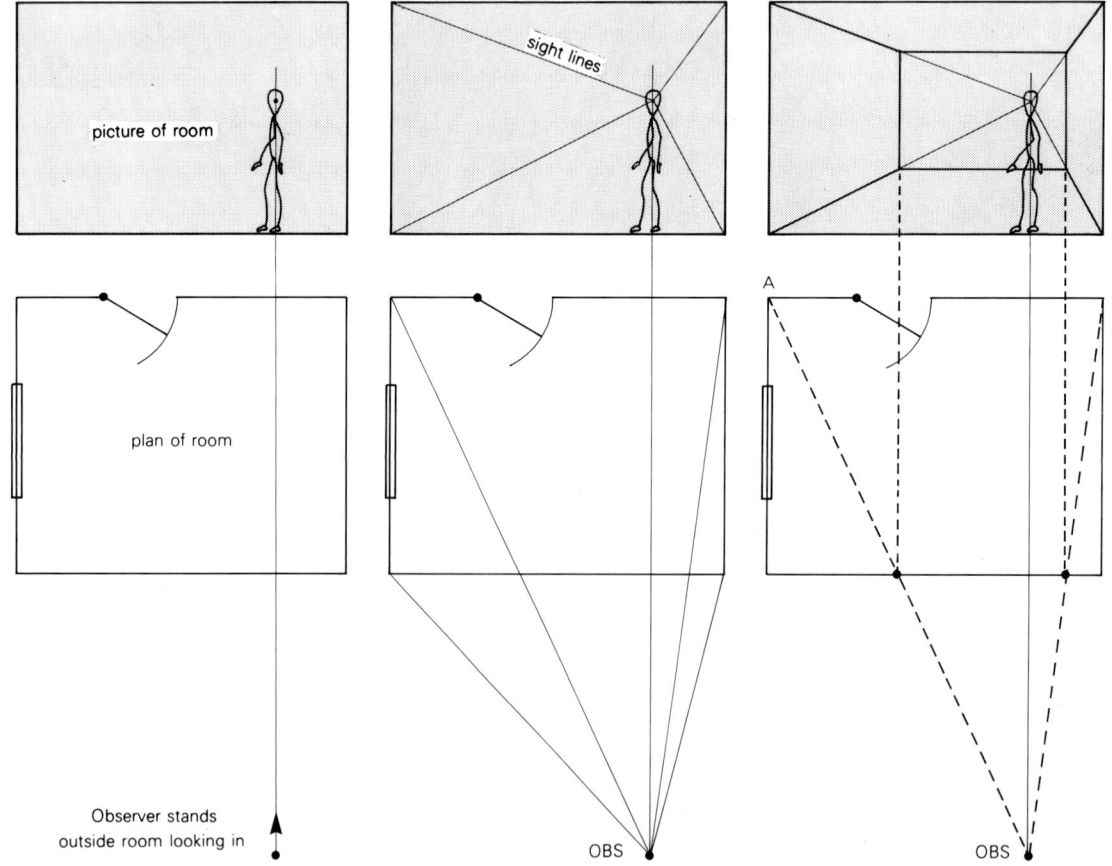

STAGE 4 To draw in the window. Join the corners in the plan to the observer. Where these lines cross the front edge of the room, project up onto the picture. Measure the height of the window and mark it up the left-hand edge of the picture to the same scale as the room. The top and bottom edges are found by joining the measured heights back to the observer.

STAGE 5 The position of the door is found in the same way and its height again measured up the left-hand edge of the picture and joined back to the observer. Objects can be drawn in the picture by finding their position from the plan. Their heights can be measured up the front edge of the picture and projected back to the observer in the picture.

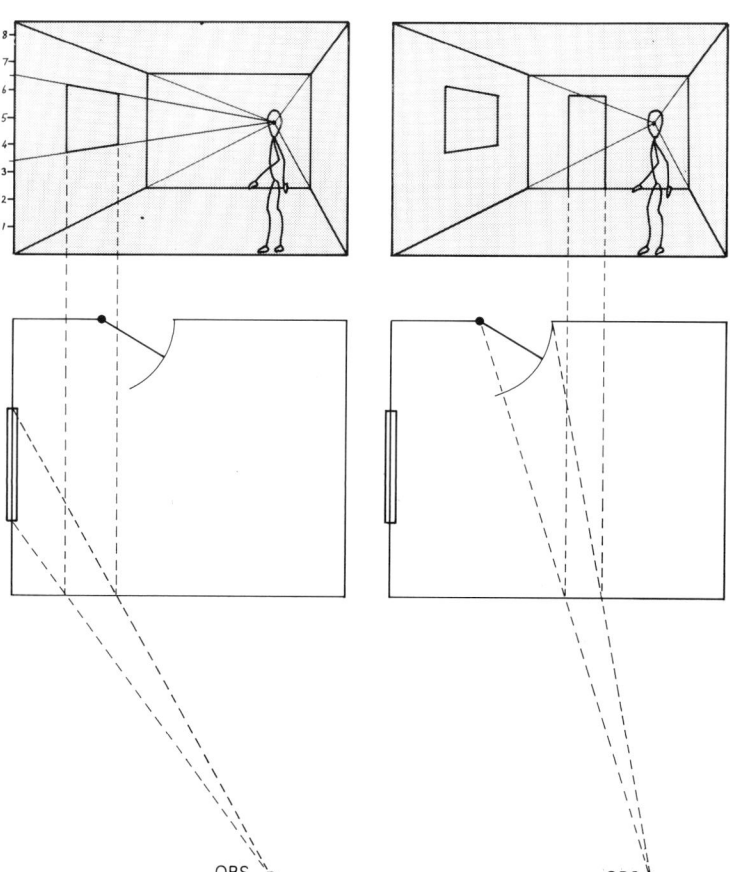

▶Fig. 20 Now you can draw your own interior designs

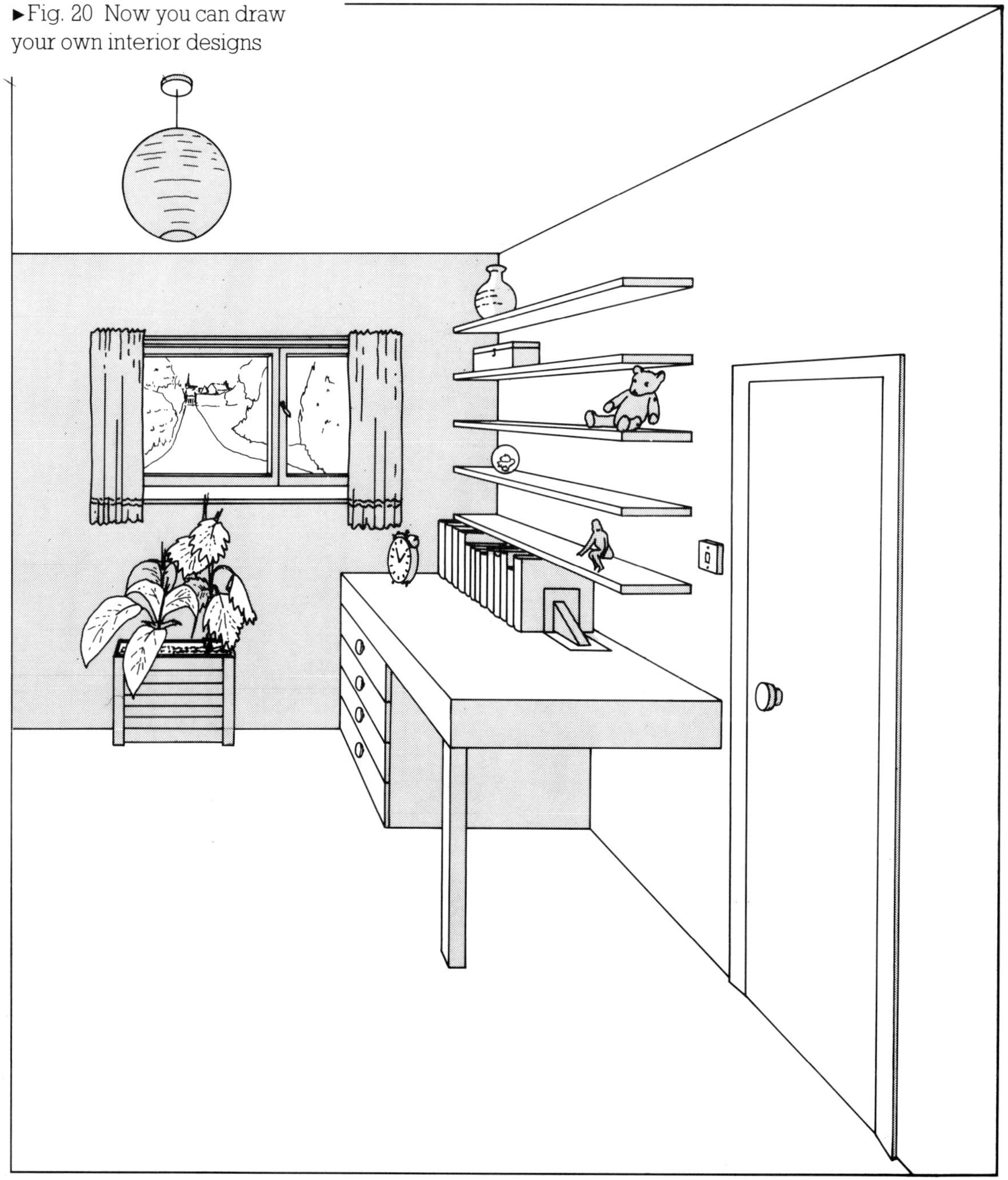

OBS

OBS

REFINING THE DESIGN BY MODELLING

At some point during the designing process you will need to try out your ideas in a more realistic way than is possible with just drawings. At this stage we use models to give a real impression of how the product might look or work when it is finished. What sort of model you make will depend on what you are trying to find out.

For example, in designing the post box two different sorts of models were used (pages 16–17). The first was simply to see how the design looked as a real object. Although it was very small, it could be photographed and blown up to look quite real. The second model was a much more detailed, full size, working model which was used to check out all the sizes, mechanisms and the general operation of the box.

The first sort of model has only to look like the final object. These *visual models* do not have to work. Their purpose is to check that the general form and proportion of the product is right. It is very important therefore that they look as realistic as possible. The models shown on this page are made mostly of wood.

Modelling to scale makes it possible to see what very big things will look like. The climbing frame shown in use in fig. 21 (left) is made of concrete and metal tube, but the wooden model fig. 21 (right) gives a realistic impression of how it will look.

If you are trying to model a copper necklace/pendant or bracelet, you can use copper coloured card to try out ideas. Metal and plastic products can be simulated by using spray paint finishes on wood.

◀Fig. 22 The radio model is very realistic – but made of wood and carefully finished

◀▼Fig. 21 A wooden model helps to visualise the details of the climbing frame.

Questions

1 Examine these sketches of different products. Decide what materials would be most suitable for modelling the forms, and produce realistic models. **x**

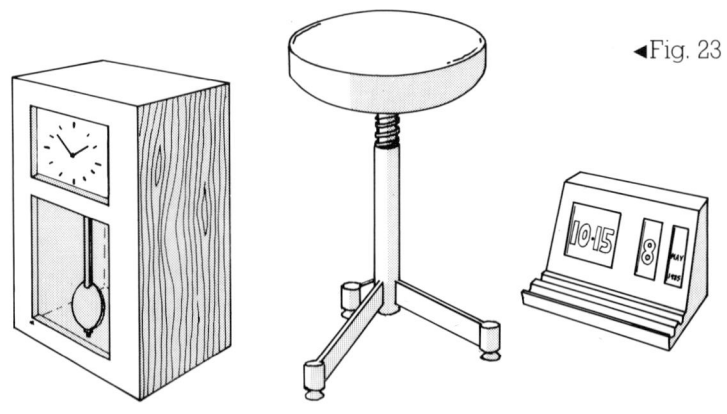

◀Fig. 23

2 What information will you be able to get from the models in addition to appearance?

MECHANICAL AND WORKING MODELS

When a product has moving or working parts, it is very important to make a model of the working parts to make sure that they function properly. It is often possible to make use of constructional kits like Meccano, Fischer Technic and Technical Lego, which have an enormous selection of axles, cog wheels, motors and other mechanisms. All of these can be simply clipped together to try out the design. The great advantage of these kits is that the design can be easily unclipped and reassembled in a slightly different way to modify a design if improvements are required.

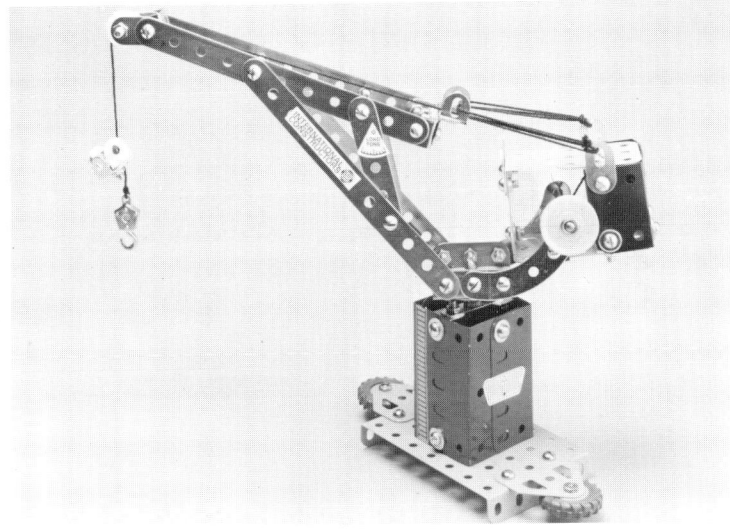

◀▲Fig. 24 Working models made from precision made kits (above) Meccano and (below) Technical Lego

▼Fig. 25 A full size precision model made of clay to test the aerodynamics of a car

Mechanical models are not the only type of working models that designers use however. The Ford Sierra was modelled for wind tunnel tests (see fig. 6 on page 28) to see how the form of the car affected the flow of air over the surface. A similar test is done on experimental boat hulls where models are tested in a water tank to see how the water flows around the model hull.

Questions

1 Figure 26 demonstrates the principle by which a typewriter key operates. Make up a rigid working model of this mechanism and use it to find out the following information.

▼Fig. 26 How the typewriter key works

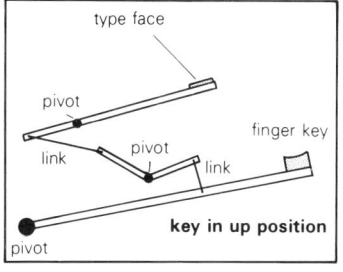 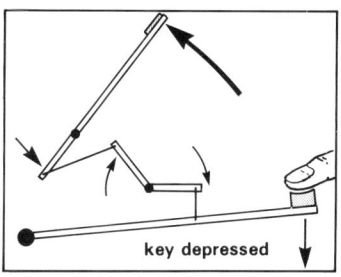

(a) How could you make the action operate with a lighter finger force? What effect does this have on the mechanism?
(b) Is it possible to make the action operate quicker or slower just by changing the length or position of some of the members?
(c) What is the relationship between the force applied at the key and the force of the letter on the paper?
(d) How can this relationship be varied? What effect would this have on the mechanism?

You could use one of the construction kits, or use strips of thin plywood mounted on fibreboard with drawing pins for the pivots. **x**
2 Make a similar working model for the action of a piano keyboard. What are the differences? **xo**
3 Examine the mechanism of an up-and-over garage door. Make a working model of it. **xo**

DEFINING THE DESIGN

When the design has been developed and refined to the point where the object is ready to be made, you need to put all the information into an accurate WORKING DRAWING. It must be possible for someone else to understand your design and make it using this drawing. The drawing must have all the sizes shown, all the materials specified, all the jointing systems detailed and all the finishes clearly marked. If you look back to page 18 you will see the overall working drawing (WD) of the post box. You can see there all the details that the designer had to include.

Designers and draughtsmen use a system known as ORTHO-GRAPHIC PROJECTION to present all this information. This merely means that the object is drawn from three different directions so that all the details can be seen and drawn accurately.

If you fold a flat piece of drawing paper in half, and in half again, you can cut along one crease to the middle of the paper and fold it up into a box. Any object can then be held in the box and viewed from above (A) to get a plan view, from the end (B) to get an end view, and from the front (C) to get a front view. It will help you to put it all in line if you use squared paper. When the paper is opened up again, you get the proper orthographic drawing.

◄Fig. 27

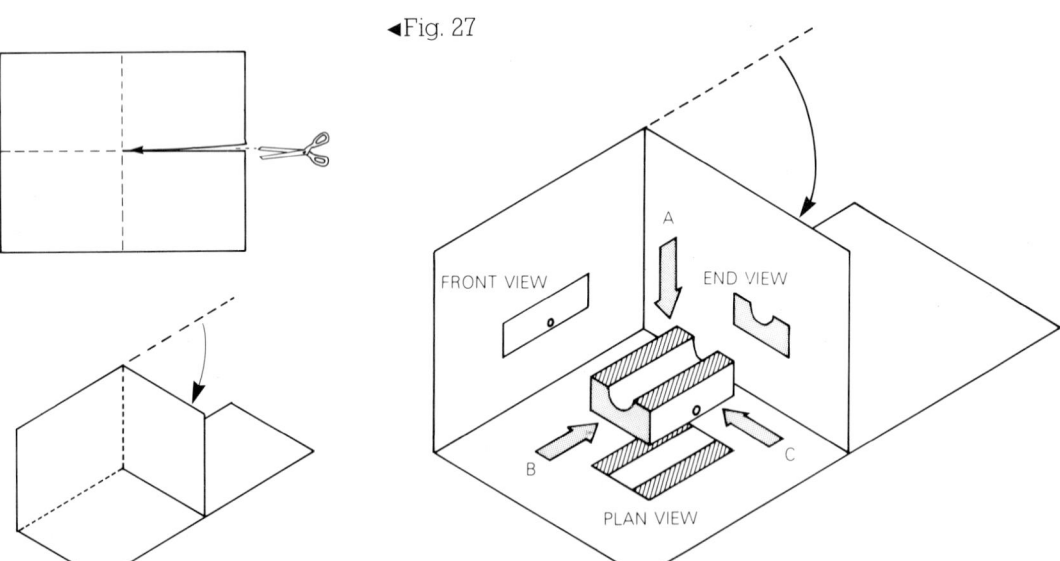

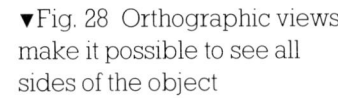

▼Fig. 28 Orthographic views make it possible to see all sides of the object

▶Fig. 29

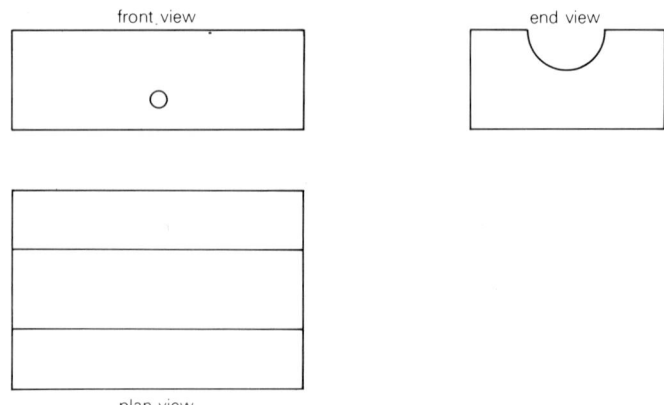

If you look carefully at the orthographic drawing of the block (fig. 28) and then try to make it, you will soon find that lots of information is still missing! There are no sizes, no materials are specified and the small hole in the front view does not appear on any other views – so it is impossible to see how deep it is.

In order to get all these sorts of information into working drawings we use shorthand systems or CONVENTIONS. Once you have learnt the conventions you can 'read' a detailed working drawing.

Here are some of the most common conventions that you must learn:

1. Sizes, or DIMENSIONS, are shown between limit lines, and are usually in millimetres (fig. 30).

▼Fig. 30   ▼Fig. 31

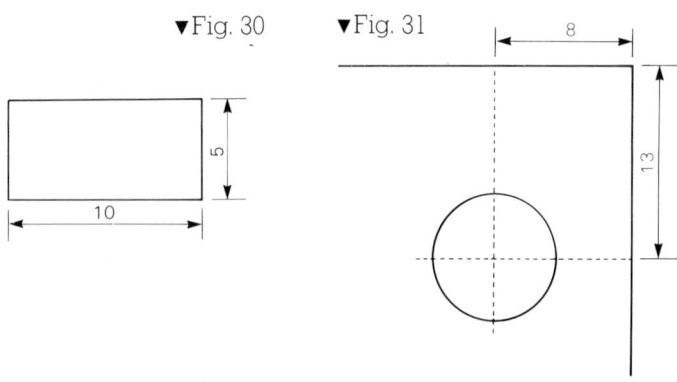

2. Holes always have dot–dash centre lines and their position can then be defined by dimensioning (fig. 31).

3. The size of the hole is usually shown as a DIAMETER (fig. 32).

▼Fig. 32   ►Fig. 33

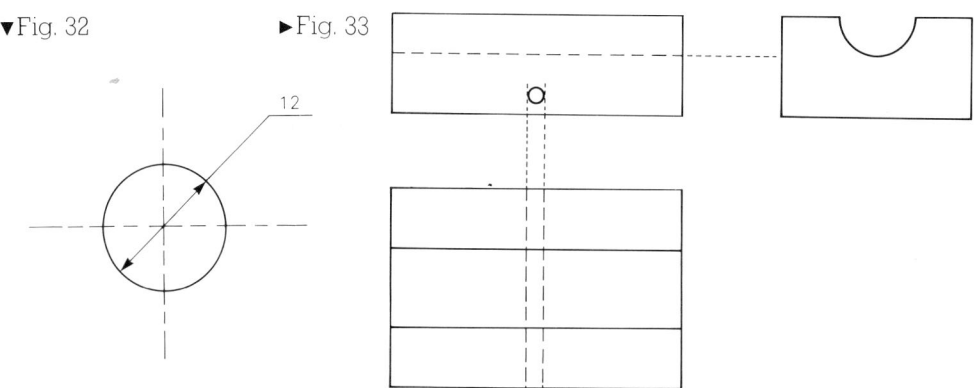

4. Hidden details can be shown by using dotted lines (fig. 33).
5. If you want to show what is happening in the middle of a piece of material you can cut it in half and draw a SECTIONAL view (fig. 34). Sectional views are always shaded – but when you cut through holes or spaces you don't shade those parts. Always show where the section is taken from.

▼Fig. 34   ▼Fig. 35

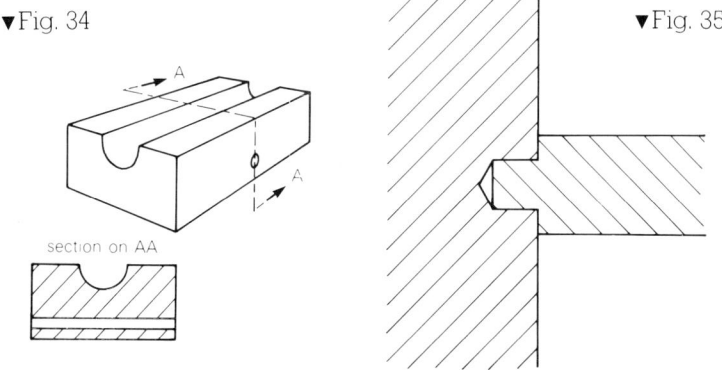

section on AA

6. If two pieces of material are touching and you want to do a sectional view, the shading must show them as different pieces (fig. 35).
7. Screw threads are shown as two sets of parallel lines that represent the top and bottom of the thread form (fig. 36).
8. A drawing must always have a title, a scale and your name clearly on it – and we usually put them all in a 'title block' (fig. 37). Also, working drawings often have lots of different parts in them,

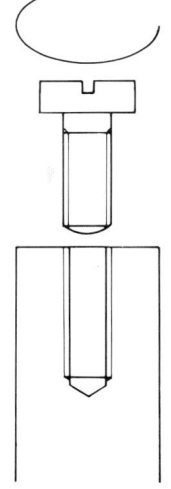

▲Fig. 36

and these are listed in a 'Parts List'. This list can contain information that will be important to anyone making the article.

►Fig. 37

7			
6			
5			
4			
3	Brass	Fixing bolts	1
2	Plywood	Baseboard	1
1	Mild steel	Central boss	1
Nº	MATERIAL	DESCRIPTION	Nº off

PARTS LIST

Title of drawing	
Scale of drawing	Dimensions in mm
Name	Date

9. You must also use a symbol on the drawing to show that the projection of the drawing is as described on the previous page. There are other ways of projecting views, but this form of projection is called FIRST ANGLE and is the most commonly used system (fig. 38).

►Fig. 38

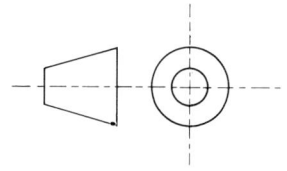

You now have enough information to 'read' quite complex drawings. Look at the drawing of a ping pong ball firer on the next page and try to sketch what it looks like in perspective.

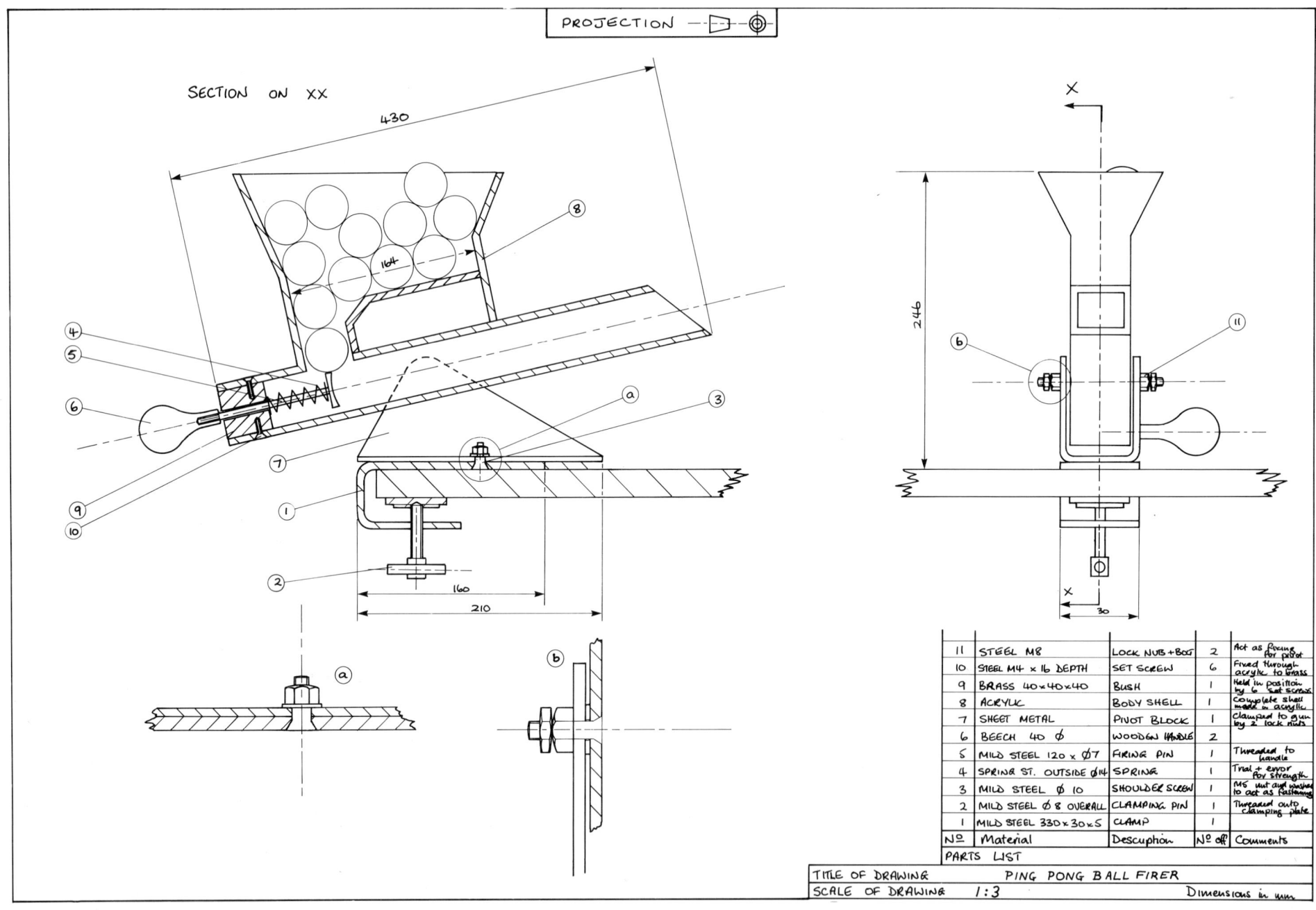

SECTION ON XX

PROJECTION

Nº	Material	Description	Nº off	Comments
11	STEEL M8	LOCK NUTS + BOLT	2	Act as fixing for pivot
10	STEEL M4 × 16 DEPTH	SET SCREW	6	Fixed through acrylic to brass
9	BRASS 40×40×40	BUSH	1	Held in position by 6 set screws
8	ACRYLIC	BODY SHELL	1	Complete shell made in acrylic
7	SHEET METAL	PIVOT BLOCK	1	Clamped to gun by 2 lock nuts
6	BEECH 40 ⌀	WOODEN HANDLE	2	
5	MILD STEEL 120 × ⌀7	FIRING PIN	1	Threaded to handle
4	SPRING ST. OUTSIDE ⌀14	SPRING	1	Trial + error for strength
3	MILD STEEL ⌀ 10	SHOULDER SCREW	1	M5 nut and washer to act as fastening
2	MILD STEEL ⌀ 8 OVERALL	CLAMPING PIN	1	Threaded onto clamping plate
1	MILD STEEL 330×30×5	CLAMP	1	

PARTS LIST

TITLE OF DRAWING	PING PONG BALL FIRER
SCALE OF DRAWING	1:3

Dimensions in mm

▲Fig. 39

It is often necessary to do a working drawing of an object that is far too big to go on a piece of paper, such as an armchair or a bed. In these cases we have to compress the article. This can be done by scaling it down and drawing it half, quarter or even 1/10 scale (depending on the size of the object and the size of the paper). Naturally, if you are drawing a very small object you can just as easily scale up the drawing and do it twice full size or bigger.

Another way of drawing large objects is to remove unnecessary parts altogether and thus squash the object down in size. The mirror shown here is a good example of this method. The drawing has to leave out quite a lot of the height of the mirror, but must still get in the parts that are needed to show how it is constructed. It is now *very* important to include the proper dimensions.

A different type of working drawing altogether is the EXPLODED DRAWING. This is a drawing in which all the parts of an object are 'exploded' apart, and it is usually used for showing how a complex article can be assembled (and disassembled). Examine the exploded drawing in fig. 42. It is still done on exactly the same system of orthographic projection, but all the main front views are shown in line so as to indicate how it all goes together. Try to draw an exploded drawing of an old ball point pen, or any other small article that will come apart simply.

▼Fig. 42 An exploded drawing can be used to show how a product fits together

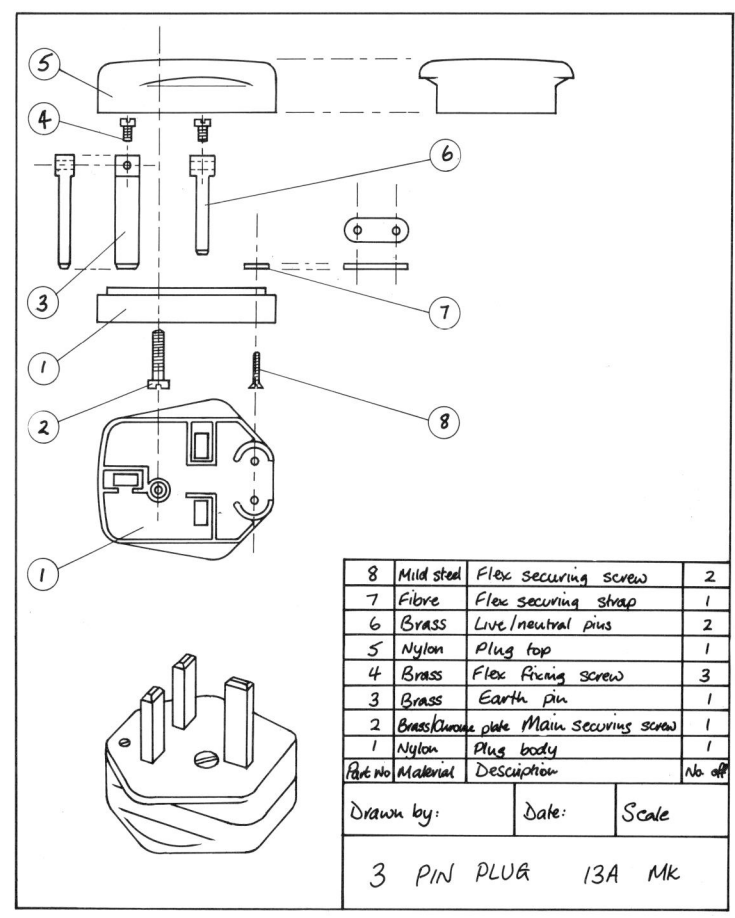

▲Fig. 40 A full length mirror can still be drawn onto one sheet of paper by removing sections that are not important

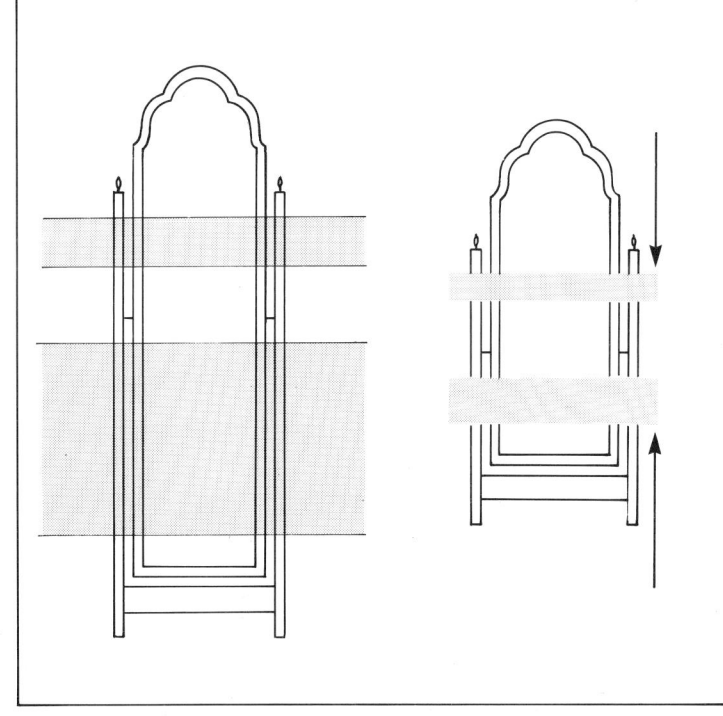

▲Fig. 41 Parts of the drawing can be removed if it doesn't lose important information

Part No	Material	Description	No off
8	Mild steel	Flex securing screw	2
7	Fibre	Flex securing strap	1
6	Brass	Live/neutral pins	2
5	Nylon	Plug top	1
4	Brass	Flex fixing screw	3
3	Brass	Earth pin	1
2	Brass/chrome plate	Main securing screw	1
1	Nylon	Plug body	1

Drawn by: | Date: | Scale

3 PIN PLUG 13A Mk

MAKING SKILLS

Before you make anything, you have to decide which materials you will use. The first part of this section is designed to help you make decisions in choosing materials. The rest of the section deals with how to handle a material once you have chosen it.

CHOOSING AND HANDLING MATERIALS

Each material that you or any other designer uses will have particular properties. It is these properties that govern what the material is like: whether it is hard or soft, flexible or stiff, heavy or light, shiny or dull, strong or weak. Any designer needs to know about the properties of a wide range of materials so that he/she can choose the best available materials for the job in hand. The scene in fig. 1 shows many different materials being used for a variety of purposes. We shall look at some of them and try to identify the properties the designers were exploiting when they chose the material.

The floodlights shining on the scene rely for their performance on several properties of the metal tungsten. This metal is used to make the filaments of the floodlights. Firstly, tungsten conducts electricity but has a fairly high resistance so that as the electricity passes the metal becomes very hot – so hot that it glows white hot. It is this white-hot glowing that produces the light. The temperature of the filament is 2800°C. The melting point of tungsten, which must be higher than this (why?), is 3377°C. At white heat tungsten reacts violently with air, so the filament has to be kept surrounded by an inert gas in a transparent container. As you know, a glass bulb is used. This reminds us of something we often take for granted: the optical properties of materials, that is, the way they reflect and/or transmit light. The appearance of all materials is dependent to a large extent upon their optical properties.

The loudspeakers which the announcer is using depend for their action on an electromagnetic effect. When an electric current flows through a wire, a magnetic field is produced.

Such a magnetic field plays an important part in the workings of a loudspeaker.

◄Fig. 1 Can you spot the different materials and explain why they are being used?

The riders are wearing quilted jackets. The quilting is made from polyester wadding. This material is an extremely good thermal insulator and is used in this case to prevent loss of body heat. The knee pads contain a foam rubber. The rubber and enclosed air bubbles are elastic. They deform on impact, absorbing the energy of the blow, and then return to their original shape. Can you find another example of elastic deformation in the scene?

The ramp the riders are climbing is made of plywood, in this case a 7-ply. Plywood consists of thin sheets of wood (veneer) glued together so that the grains in adjacent sheets are at right angles to one another. This laminating (sticking sheets together) results in a sheet material that does not warp or twist in damp conditions the way that solid timber does. Why is this important here? The glue used in plywood is waterproof but the veneers themselves can still be attacked by fungus if they are damp. This is called rotting and plywood for exterior use is always treated with a fungicide.

There are two structures in the scene: the one supporting the ramp is made of timber (probably pine) and the BMX frames are made of mild steel tubing. In both these frameworks the members will experience forces of tension or compression. The materials have been chosen and the members designed so that they will not break during use. The point at which a material breaks will depend on how strong it is. For mild steel the ultimate TENSILE STRENGTH is 400 MN/m². This means that it takes a pulling force of four hundred million newtons to break a piece of mild steel one square metre in cross section. It is quite easy to measure the tensile strength of a material (see later). It is much more tricky to find a value for the COMPRESSIVE STRENGTH. This will depend on the form the material is in as well as the nature of the material. If it is in the form of a thick short column, then it might squeeze out sideways like Plasticine when compression is applied. Or it might explode sideways if it is brittle. If the material is in the form of a rod or panel it might buckle. So values for the compressive strength of materials must always be used in conjunction with a knowledge of the form of the material. We can use information about tensile and compressive strengths to work out the loads at which pieces of material will fail. From this we can calculate what safety factors we need to build into our designs. Look back to chapter 1 and see how these ideas were used in the post box design.

The frames of the bikes in fig. 1 are made from tube, not solid rod. It would have been possible to make a solid-rod frame using the same amount of metal as is in the tubes, but the designer chose not to. Try to find out why. The pine wood used for the ramp frame has an ultimate compressive strength parallel to the grain of 15 MN/m². The ultimate compressive strength perpendicular to the grain is 2.5 MN/m². Can you explain why there is this big difference? The ultimate tensile strength of pine parallel to the grain is 18 MN/m². How big do you think the ultimate tensile strength of pine perpendicular to the grain will be? How can you check your estimate?

The timber is much less strong than the steel and its strength depends on whether loading is parallel or perpendicular to the grain. Steel has the same strength in all directions and is therefore called an ISOTROPIC MATERIAL. Timber does not, and is called an ANISOTROPIC MATERIAL. The density of mild steel is thirteen times greater than that of pine wood. So, on a weight for weight basis, how does the strength of pine compare with that of mild steel?

To make the right choice of materials we also have to look at how materials behave when they are stretched. This is measured on a tensile tester. A simple one is shown in fig. 2. It stretches the material at a constant rate and measures the force needed to do this. The two readings of extension (the amount the material is stretched) and force can be plotted on a graph as shown in fig. 3.

▼Fig. 3 A graph of force vs. extension

▼Fig. 2 A simple tensile tester

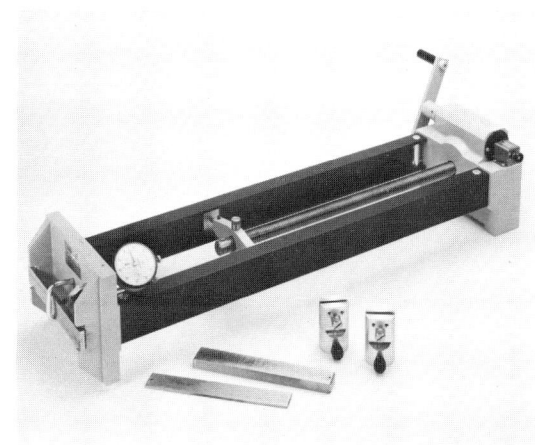

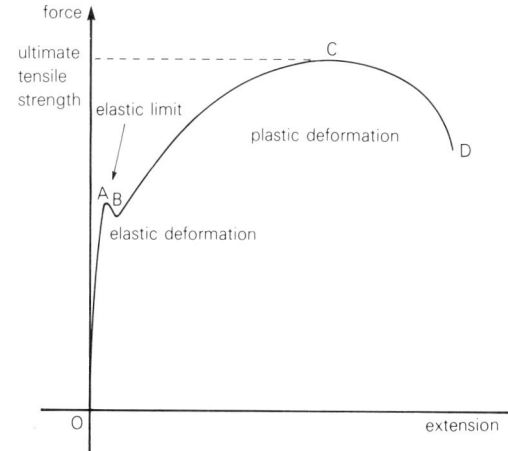

Imagine that you are the piece of material under test. Between O and A the stretching is reversible. If the load is removed you return to your original size. You have been deformed elastically and can spring back again. Point A on the graph marks your elastic limit. Between A and B the force required to stretch you decreases as you begin to stretch non-reversibly. This is called YIELDING and marks the beginning of plastic deformation. Any stretching you now undergo is permanent. When the load is removed you will not return to your original size. This happens between B and C on the graph. At C your ultimate tensile strength is reached. This is the highest force you will be able to take before you break. Between C and D you start to get thinner, your cross-sectional area decreases. This is called NECKING. At D you break!

Designers and engineers have found it more useful to compare STRESS and STRAIN rather than force and extension. The stress in a piece of material is the load applied to that material divided by the cross-sectional area of the material. So we may write:

$$\text{stress} = \frac{\text{load (N)}}{\text{cross-sectional area (m}^2)}$$

The units of stress are N/m^2 (or kN/m^2 or MN/m^2). It is usually a very large number. The strain in a piece of material is the relationship between the change in length (caused by the stress) and the original length of the piece of material. So we may write:

$$\text{strain} = \frac{\text{change in length}}{\text{original length}}.$$

As strain is a ratio of two lengths it has no units. A graph showing what happens to the strain in a mild steel specimen as it is gradually loaded (stressed) is shown in fig. 4. Between O and A the stress is proportional to the strain so the graph is a straight line. During this part of the graph the specimen is deforming elastically. On removal of the load it will return to its original size. If loading is increased beyond the elastic limit, plastic deformation takes place until the peak of the graph is reached at B. The stress value at this point is called the ultimate tensile stress. Further loading causes the specimen to break at C. Can you explain why the curve slopes downward between B and C?

We find the STIFFNESS of the mild steel by looking at the slope

of the line OA. This is called the MODULUS OF ELASTICITY of mild steel or YOUNG'S MODULUS for mild steel and is usually given the symbol E. Each material has its own particular value for its modulus of elasticity. It is a property just like any other property, but it is very important that you don't confuse it with the property of *strength*. The following examples should help:

biscuit – stiff (high E) but weak (low tensile strength),
steel – stiff (high E) and strong (high tensile strength),
nylon – flexible (low E) and strong (high tensile strength),
strawberry jelly – flexible (low E) and weak (low tensile strength).

When engineers and designers use a material they never use it at the limit of its strength. This is because conditions over which they have no control can cause stress on the material greater than it can bear. Examples of such conditions are (a) overloading, (b) freak weather, (c) corrosion effects, (d) vibrations. So engineers and designers use materials in conditions where the elastic limit is not even approached. Imagine the problems if a bridge (or a BMX bike) was designed so that plastic deformation took place on loading!

To allow for this in their calculations, designers use SAFETY FACTORS. The safety factor is the ratio of ultimate stress to working stress. The value of the safety factor depends on circumstances but a ratio of 4 to 1 is commonly used. So if a part of a structure has a safety factor of 4, it will take four times the normal allowable load to break that part.

The metal used for the gear wheels in BMX bikes must be strong and stiff. What problems might arise if a gear wheel had flexible teeth? The gear teeth must also be hard. Can you think why? Steel is used to make the gears and their surface is hardened by heating in a carbon-rich material. This 'case hardening' produces a very hard skin without affecting the strength and stiffness of the body of the metal.

The helmets used by the riders are made from glass reinforced plastic (GRP). Table 1 summarises the properties of GRP and the constituent materials. Try to explain why GRP is so different from glass and plastic.

DECIDING WHICH MATERIALS TO USE

The following list of questions will help you to make decisions on choosing materials when you are designing and making.

▼Fig. 4 A graph of stress vs. strain for mild steel

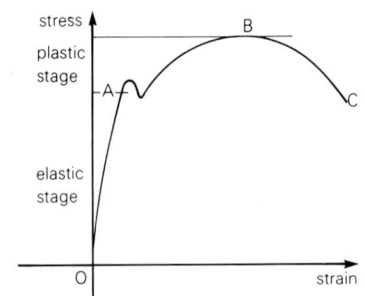

For a particular part or component ask:

▶Fig. 5

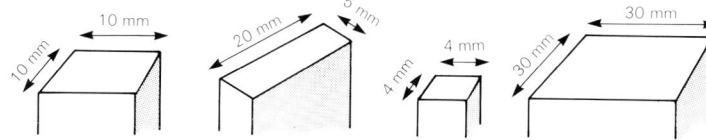

1. What are the functions of that part?
2. What properties should I be looking for in the material that I choose to do the job?
3. What materials have these properties?
4. Of those materials that have the necessary properties, which can I afford?
5. Of those materials with the necessary properties that I can afford, which am I able to work most successfully?
6. What conditions will the material be used in? Can the material withstand these conditions without treatment or is it necessary to apply a surface finish?
7. Of the surface finishes available, which can I afford?

8 A round steel tie bar in a roof truss has to take a load of 20 kN. The ultimate stress for steel is 440 MN/m². Assuming a safety factor of 4, calculate (a) the cross-sectional area of the tie bar and (b) the diameter of the tie bar. x

9 If the slates on the roof in question 8 are replaced by heavier tiles, then the load taken by the tie bar becomes 60 kN. What alterations, if any, should be made to the tie bar? x

10 For each of the materials listed in Table 2, choose items that include that material in their construction. Use the data in the table plus the questions in the 'Deciding which materials to use' section to justify the use of that material. c

11 The helmets have a head band inside which fits on the rider's head and there is a gap between the head band and the helmet. Try to find out why the helmet is constructed in this way. o

TABLE 1

	TENSILE STRENGTH	MODULUS OF ELASTICITY
Glass	160 MN/m²	77 000 MN/m²
Plastic	35 MN/m²	3 000 MN/m²
GRP	350 MN/m²	6 000 MN/m²

Questions

1 Suggest two reasons why the tungsten filament in a lamp is in the form of a coil.

2 Find out how the electromagnetic effect is used in a loudspeaker. x

3 Polyester wadding is a good thermal insulator. Use a data book to find a value for the thermal conductivity of polyester. Try to state very clearly exactly what this value means. Explain clearly why it is used as a wadding for insulation purposes. x

4 Find out the constructional details of a pneumatic tyre and try to explain why each of the materials used is chosen. o

5 Find out the important properties of the following man-made boards:
  chipboard, hardboard, blockboard, plywood. x

6 The ultimate tensile strength of mild steel is 440 MN/m². What tension load is required to break the steel members shown in fig. 5?

7 Explain clearly why it was unnecessary to specify the length of the steel members in question 6.

TABLE 2   PROPERTIES OF SOME MATERIALS

Material	Density (kg/m³)	Modulus of elasticity (MN/m²)	Tensile strength (MN/m²)
High tensile steel	7700	210 000	1550
Mild steel	7700	200 000	440
Carbon fibre composite	?	200 000	350–1050
Titanium	4540	120 000	700–1400
Copper	8940	96 000	140
Aluminium alloys	2800	73 000	140–600
Glass	2460	70 000	160
Magnesium alloys	1760	42 000	200–300
Brick	1500–1800	21 000	5.5
Concrete	2200–2400	15 000	4.1
Spruce	600	13 000	10
Plywood	600–700	4000–10 000	8 perpendicular to face grain 16 parallel to face grain
Hardboard	800–1000	4000–6000	25–55
Chipboard	450–1300	2000–4000	2–10
Polystyrene	1050	3400	48
Nylon	1120–1170	2400	60
Polythene (low density)	920	700	20–30
Acrylic	1200	3000	60

SHAPING LIQUIDS INTO SOLIDS

As you know, solids have their own shape but liquids take the shape of anything they are poured into. FLUID FORMING is what we call the process of pouring a fluid material into a mould, making it set hard and removing it (like ice cubes). The process is used to make complex forms that would be far too difficult to create in any other way. Obviously it can be done only with materials that can be made fluid. Metals change from solids to liquids when heated above their melting point. Plastics can be made in a mould from liquid chemicals that set hard by chemical action.

METALS

Metals usually have very high melting points. Steel melts at 1550°C, aluminium at 659°C and brass at 900°C and a furnace has to be used to get the solid metal up to this temperature. The ingots are melted in a crucible supported in the furnace. The crucible is usually made of a ceramic material that will not melt.

Once the metal is fully melted (molten) it can be poured into a mould and left to cool. When it cools to below its melting point, it

▼Fig. 6 A steel furnace

solidifies back into a block. It can then be removed from the mould, cleaned up and put to use.

CASTING METALS There are many different sorts of metal casting but they all have some things in common. The most important part of casting metal is to make a mould that will not burn or be damaged when you pour very hot metal into it.

Moulds can be fairly simple if you only want to produce a simple shape, but they can be extremely complicated if you want to produce more intricate shapes.

SAND CASTING Sand is the basic moulding material used when casting metals, because it is very heat resistant and it can be moulded into very intricate forms. There are two sorts of sand: *greensand*, which holds the shape of the moulding by being damp (like sandcastles on the beach), and *petrobond*, which is impregnated with oil to hold it into the moulded shape. The sand is rammed into steel boxes around a *pattern* which is made to exactly the same shape as the required finished object. Patterns are usually made of wood and are therefore quite simple to cut into the desired form.

Obviously this moulding process will work only if the pattern can be removed from the sand. Once it is removed molten metal can be poured into the hole that remains. When it cools and solidifies you can remove the metal, which will have the exact shape of the pattern. This very simple sort of moulding has two major drawbacks:

1. As the metal is poured in, the surface of the shape in the sand may be washed away or disturbed.
2. The top surface of the metal will be rough when it solidifies. It will also be sucked in a bit by the contraction of the metal. The casting therefore has only one good surface, where it has been in contact with the mould.

For some articles this may not matter so it can be a useful simple technique, but for more important castings you must overcome these problems. It is done by using two moulding boxes, a top box (called a cope), and a bottom box (a drag), and completely enclosing the pattern. Once the sand is properly 'rammed up' the boxes can be separated and the pattern removed. When they are reassembled, the metal can be poured in through the big hole (the runner) and as the mould fills up it comes up the air vent. Notice that the metal is not poured directly into the mould cavity, but into a well which then feeds into the cavity through a

▼Fig. 7 Making a simple sand mould

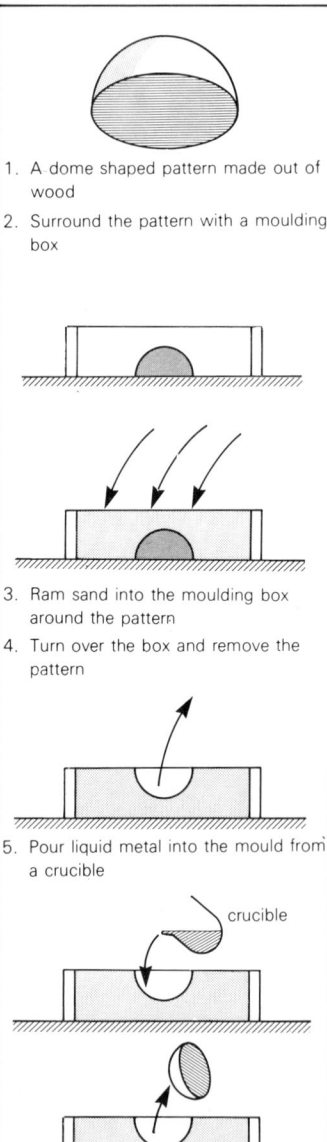

1. A dome shaped pattern made out of wood
2. Surround the pattern with a moulding box

3. Ram sand into the moulding box around the pattern
4. Turn over the box and remove the pattern

5. Pour liquid metal into the mould from a crucible

crucible

6. The casting is an exact copy of the pattern

▼Fig. 8 Sand casting using two moulding boxes to give a good surface finish all over

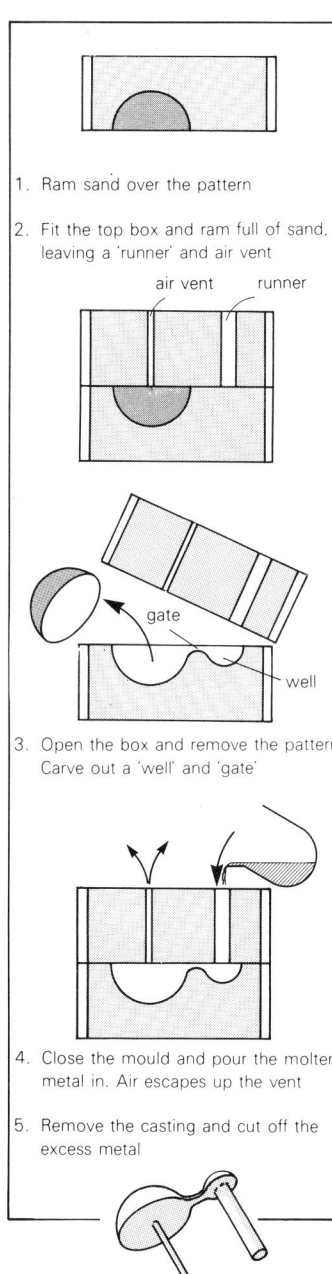

1. Ram sand over the pattern

2. Fit the top box and ram full of sand, leaving a 'runner' and air vent

air vent   runner

3. Open the box and remove the pattern Carve out a 'well' and 'gate'

gate

well

4. Close the mould and pour the molten metal in. Air escapes up the vent

5. Remove the casting and cut off the excess metal

little 'gate'. When cool, the moulding can be cut from the runner and vent and it will have a good surface all over, with no shrinkage.

In the example shown in fig. 8, the top box just made a flat surface on the casting, but we can also design a pattern that uses the top box as well as the bottom box to make a two-sided casting.

One of the biggest problems with sand casting is that, as the metal is poured in, it burns the surface of the sand and when it cools again the cast product will not lift cleanly out of the sand. Some of the sand will stick to it and the whole mould will have to be broken up. You can of course use the pattern to make another mould. Sand casting is a 'one off' process, and the mould making is a repetitive and laborious process.

The post box described in chapter 1 (pages 6–25) was made by the sand casting process.

DIE CASTING In industry, where many items of the same form need to be cast (e.g., many car components), sand casting is too slow and a mould has to be made that can be used rapidly over and over again. This process is called DIE CASTING, as the moulds are called dies. They are machined very accurately from special steels that can resist the high temperature of the molten metal.

Die casting is usually restricted to the relatively low melting point metals (aluminium, brass, zinc etc.). Why can't you cast steel into a steel die? Using this process it is possible to produce one component every minute, instead of every half hour with sand casting. However, it is very expensive to produce the dies and therefore only worthwhile if you need a very large number. (See page 14 and the casting of the post box.)

LOST WAX CASTING Both sand and die casting processes use the idea of a split mould or die which allows the cast object to be removed once it has cooled. A different method of casting is LOST WAX CASTING, which uses the idea of a pattern made of wax (fig. 9). The advantage of this is that a mould can be cast around the wax pattern (it is usually made of Plaster of Paris), and once it has set, the whole lot is heated until the wax pattern melts and runs out of a small hole. This leaves the mould with a hole in the middle which is exactly the size and shape of the original wax pattern. Metal can now be poured into the hole and when it cools the plaster mould is broken up to remove the metal casting. Not only is this a 'one off' process for the mould, but also the pattern

▼Fig. 9 The lost wax casting process is a very ancient one, but is still used for intricate 'one off' castings

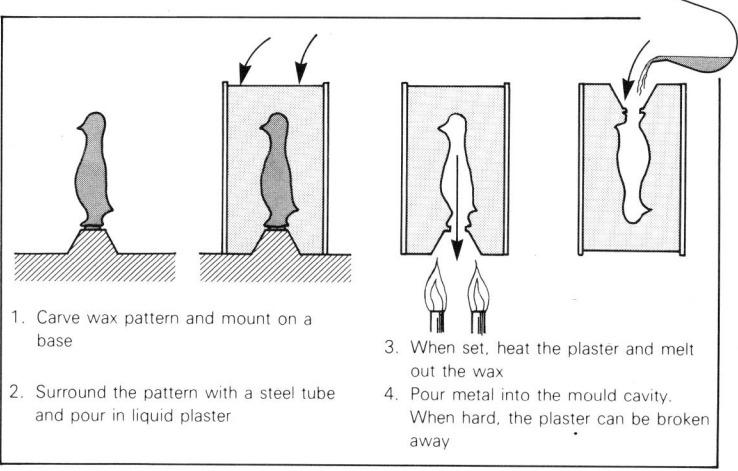

1. Carve wax pattern and mount on a base

2. Surround the pattern with a steel tube and pour in liquid plaster

3. When set, heat the plaster and melt out the wax

4. Pour metal into the mould cavity. When hard, the plaster can be broken away

has been lost. It is a process that is used only for small castings in fine silversmithing and jewellery.

Questions

1 When you make a sand mould using damp greensand, what would you expect to happen if the sand was (a) too dry? (b) too wet? Which of these is the most dangerous and why?

2 When petrobond is used the sand often bursts into flames. Why is that, and what should you do about it?

3 List the possible dangers of sand casting in a school workshop. What precautions do you take in your school to guard against these dangers?

4 Any die cast product has been mass produced in a split die. Try to find such a product (aluminium alloy car wheels is one example). Examine the moulding, spot the 'flash' lines and see how the die was split.   o

5 How would you tell the difference between a product that had been die cast and one that had been cast by the lost wax process?

6 Look at page 21 and see how the post box is cast with the hole in the middle. Cores are used to do this. See if you can find some other examples of hollow castings. Can you work out how the cores were used?   c

PLASTICS

There are two classes of plastics: THERMOPLASTICS which will melt if heated to a suitable temperature, and THERMOSETTING PLASTICS which will not melt at all but will burn if heated sufficiently. Both of these classes of plastics can be formed in the liquid state. Thermoplastics such as PVC, acrylic, polyethylene and polystyrene can be melted and moulded. Thermosetting plastics can be bought as liquid resins (polyester or epoxy) and made to harden in a mould by chemical action.

▲Fig. 10 Thermoplastics are used for a wide range of household objects

THERMOPLASTICS Injection moulding of thermoplastics is very similar to the die casting of metals. In this process plastics are heated until they melt and are then injected under pressure into a split mould. Once the plastic cools it can be removed by opening the mould. The mould is closed again for the next injection. Moulds are usually made of steel and have to be *very* accurate as they have to fit together well and every detail will show up on the final plastic moulding.

Industrial injection moulding machines are very large, powerful and expensive; products as big as sailing dinghies can be moulded in seconds. In schools, injection moulding is done on small hand-powered machines. The process is limited by the difficulty of making accurate split moulds. It is, however, quite possible to produce simple mouldings up to about the size of a golf ball.

THERMOSETTING PLASTICS The fluid forming of thermosetting plastics in schools can be divided into two parts: (i) the casting of liquid resins into suitable moulds, which produces solid castings; (ii) the use of liquid resins with a reinforcement of glass fibres to 'lay up' forms on an open mould, which produces 'hollow shell' mouldings.

CASTING THERMOSETTING RESINS Casting resins is very much like casting metals, but without all the problems of high temperature. Moulds can therefore be made of wood instead of sand. However, instead of the temperature problems you get the problems of removing the cast object from the mould once it has hardened. It will tend to stick to the surface of the mould and can be very difficult to remove. Successful castings usually result from a simple form and a well-made mould. Wood and plaster can be used to make moulds for most simple resin castings. In both cases it is essential to prevent the liquid resin from sinking into the surface of the mould. As both wood and plaster are POROUS materials the surface must be thoroughly sealed. In addition to this careful sealing of the surface of the mould you must also paint or spray on a special 'releasing agent'. This also helps to prevent the resin from sticking in the mould.

To make a mould for casting a resin hemisphere you can:
1. Turn the shape out of wood on the lathe. This gives you a female mould to pour the resin into.
2. Turn a wooden male mould, and use it to cast a plaster female mould to pour the resin into.

It is usually easier to make male moulds than female moulds from wood, even though it involves an extra process. The casting process is very simple once the mould is properly prepared. 1. Clean, seal and apply release agent. 2. Mix resin and colour pigment and chemical hardener. 3. Pour the mix into the mould. 4. When it has hardened (12 hours) remove it from the mould.

One of the major problems of removing the casting is that both the mould and the cast object are hard, inflexible materials. It would of course be possible to break up the plaster mould and thereby remove the casting, but if several castings are needed it would be very wasteful. *Vinamould* is a flexible silicone rubber moulding compound that gets over this problem. With it you can make a mould that is strong enough to take a resin casting, but still flexible enough to be 'peeled' off afterwards. It also releases well from the surface of the resin. When you have finished with the mould it can be remelted and used again for another mould.

▼Fig. 11 Two ways to make a simple mould for resin casting

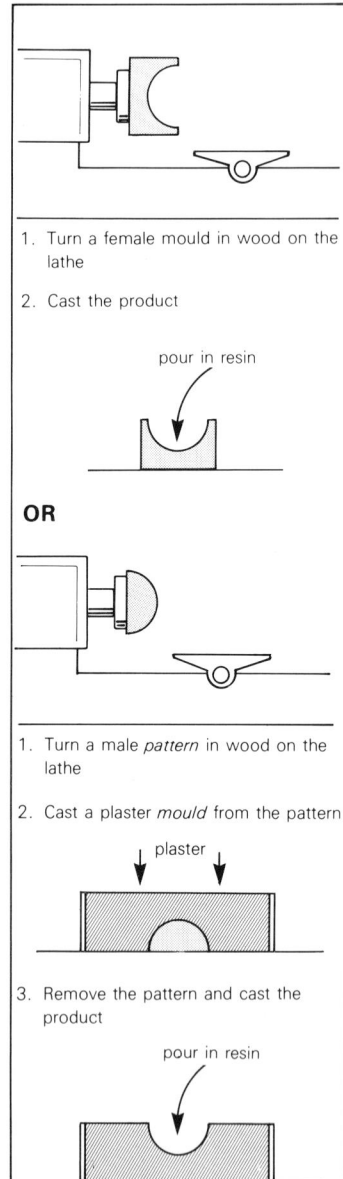

1. Turn a female mould in wood on the lathe
2. Cast the product

pour in resin

OR

1. Turn a male *pattern* in wood on the lathe
2. Cast a plaster *mould* from the pattern

plaster

3. Remove the pattern and cast the product

pour in resin

▼Fig. 12 Vinamould is a flexible and re-usable moulding rubber

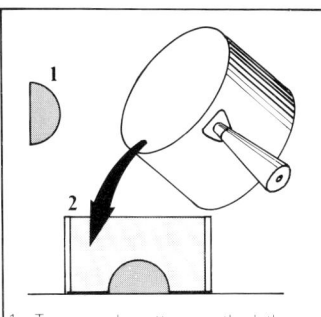

1. Turn a male pattern on the lathe
2. Heat up the vinamould and pour over the pattern
3. Cast resin into the vinamould

pour in resin

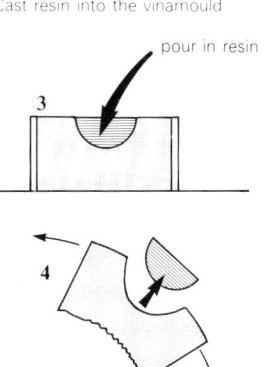

4. Peel the vinamould off the cast resin product
5. When finished with, the vinamould can be remelted and used for another mould

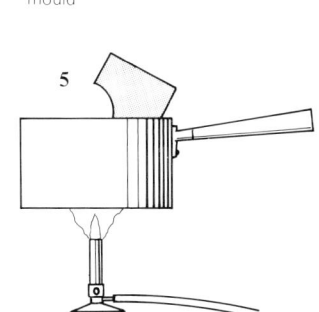

SHELL MOULDING IN GLASS REINFORCED PLASTIC Using liquid resins with a glass fibre reinforcement makes it possible to produce quite complex hollow shell mouldings. This is done on a rigid mould, usually made of wood or plaster, and the surface finish of the mould is again very important. The process is quite similar to the papier maché technique (fig. 13).

▼Fig. 13 Making a glass-fibre shell

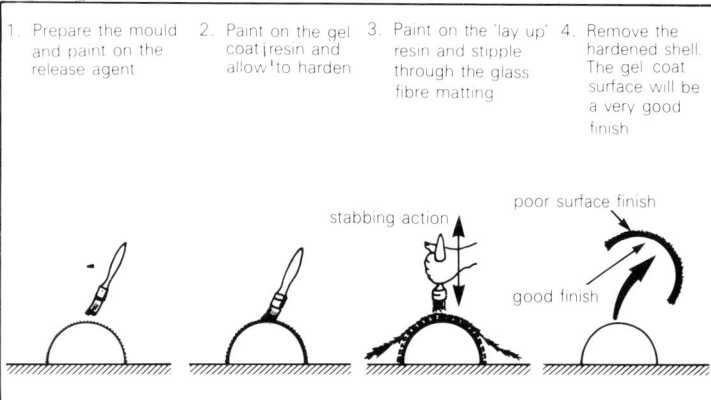

1. Prepare the mould and paint on the release agent
2. Paint on the gel coat resin and allow to harden
3. Paint on the 'lay up' resin and stipple through the glass fibre matting
4. Remove the hardened shell. The gel coat surface will be a very good finish

stabbing action

poor surface finish

good finish

Several points in this process are of considerable importance.
1. The mould can only put a good surface finish on *one side* of the shell. The reverse side will be rough and uneven. So you need to think where you want the good surface *before* you make the mould.
2. It is possible to make a fibreglass female mould from a wooden male mould (fig. 14).

▼Fig. 14 A female GRP mould from a wooden male mould

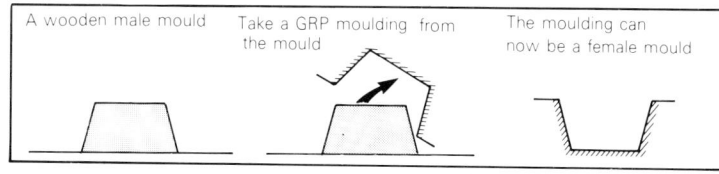

A wooden male mould | Take a GRP moulding from the mould | The moulding can now be a female mould

3. The thickness of the shell can be increased by using more layers of resin and glass fibre.
4. The colour of the product is not just skin deep. All the resin layers can be dyed the colour you want the final product to be.

Industrially this process is used to make products as varied as Formula 1 racing cars, crash helmets and the hulls of naval warships. It has the benefits of being very tough (because of the reinforcing glass fibre) and also hard on the surface (because of the thermosetting resin). Resins should always be stored in a cold outside store, and should only be used indoors in a proper fume cupboard. There is always a fire risk with the chemicals and the chemical reaction gives off noxious fumes.

◀Fig. 15 Very high quality products can be produced in GRP

Questions

1 Lots of domestic plastic products have been injection moulded. Look at a plastic dustbin and see if you can work out where the mould was split to allow the removal of the bin. The flash lines on these products usually show how the mould was constructed.   o
2 See if you can find a product that was made from a mould with *more* than two parts.   o
3 Why is it so important that split moulds for injection moulding should fit together *very* accurately?
4 When the plastic is injected, where does all the air go that previously filled the mould? What would happen if a mould was airtight?
5 How can you speed up or slow down the rate of hardening of a resin casting?   c
6 When mixing the resin/colour/hardener, why do you put the hardener in last?   c
7 Vinamould comes in several different grades of hardness and each grade has a different colour. Why might you need different grades, and why are they given different colours? Draw up a chart which lists the grades in order of hardness.   x
8 Why is it easier to make male moulds in wood, rather than female moulds?
9 Find out what fumes are given off in the reaction of thermosetting resins. What are they, and why are they harmful?   x

BENDING AND FORMING SHEET MATERIALS

Sheet materials are very widely used in industry because it is possible to bend and form them into three-dimensional objects. Bending and forming are not the same thing. It is much easier to bend sheet than to form it. BENDING sheet material is simply like folding a sheet of paper. You can do it with a sharp crease or with a gentle curve. They are both quite easy to do. FORMING sheet is much more difficult. Try making a flat sheet of paper into a dome shape and you will see the problem. You can't do it without creasing and buckling the sheet, and even then it won't be a good dome.

This section is concerned with the making processes that use force to bend and form flat sheet materials into three-dimensional objects. Metal, plastic and wood can all be made in sheet form and they all have different properties and uses.

METAL SHEET

Metals are divided into two classes. Ferrous metals like cast iron and mild steel contain *iron*. Non-ferrous metals like copper and aluminium do not contain any iron. The simplest way to tell the difference is with a magnet. All ferrous metals are magnetic, and none of the common non-ferrous metals are (except nickel). It is important to be able to tell the difference because they behave differently when you try to bend or form them.

FERROUS METALS The two sorts of ferrous metal sheet normally used in industry or in schools are mild steel sheet and tinplate. MILD STEEL SHEET is rolled out at white heat from an ingot or a

▼Fig. 16 Forming is far more difficult than bending

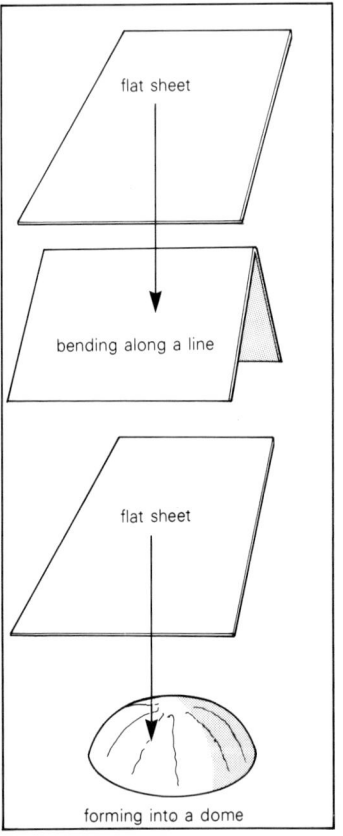

flat sheet

bending along a line

flat sheet

forming into a dome

block and can be bought in big sheets in many different thicknesses down to as little as $\frac{1}{2}$ mm. It has many uses such as in the body panels of motor cars and central heating radiator panels. TINPLATE is made from mild steel sheet coated in tin. The tin fuses onto the surface of the mild steel and prevents it from rusting or corroding. Tinplate (which is more properly called 'tinned plate') is used mainly in food and drink canning.

Because both of these sheets are made of the same basic material, steel, their bending and forming properties are very similar. They look very different because of the silvery tin coating on tinplate, but they are both equally difficult to bend and form. The huge presses in car body factories make it possible to press mild steel sheet into quite complex curved forms, but in schools it is impossible to do this. Because of the toughness and hardness of steel the use of both mild steel sheet and tinplate is restricted in schools to simple bending and folding along one edge or round a simple curve.

To make three-dimensional forms, you must find out what shape the materials used will make when laid flat. This shape can then be cut out and folded up (fig. 18).

▼Fig. 18 Bending up a 3D box in ferrous metal sheet

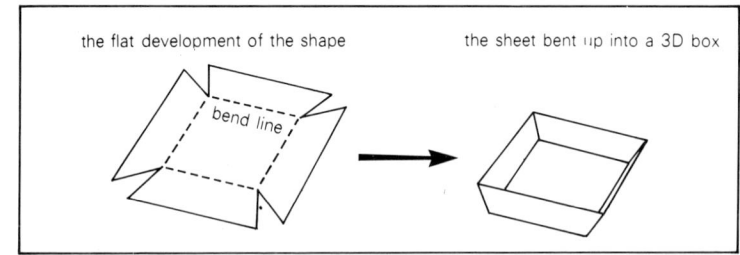

the flat development of the shape   the sheet bent up into a 3D box

bend line

▼Fig. 17 The making of sheet steel and tin plate

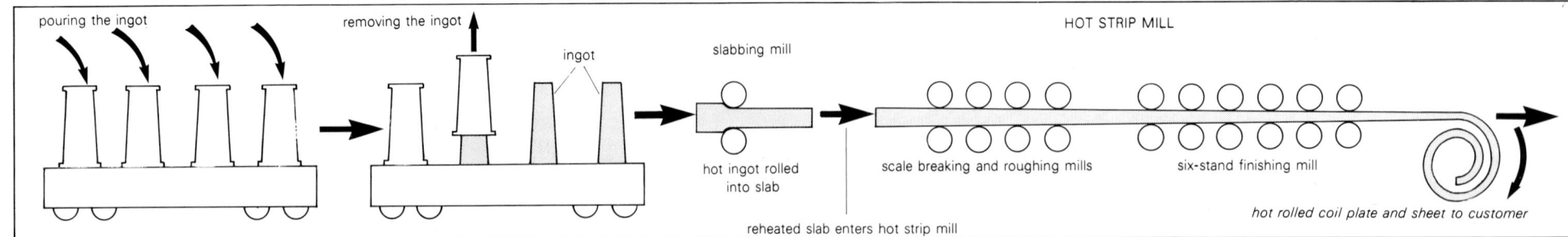

pouring the ingot   removing the ingot   ingot   slabbing mill   HOT STRIP MILL

hot ingot rolled into slab   scale breaking and roughing mills   six-stand finishing mill

reheated slab enters hot strip mill   hot rolled coil plate and sheet to customer

NON-FERROUS METALS Non-ferrous metals have a very different structure to ferrous metals. They are generally softer and more malleable (less resistant to shaping). As a result it is possible to *form* them as well as to *bend* them. Softness and malleability are *not* the same thing. Soft metals are easily scratched or dented; malleable metals are easily bent or stretched.

To make a flat sheet into a dome, you must stretch the material, making it thinner at the edges than in the middle. As it stretches, the 'extra' size that results can be shaped by hammering into the dome. Hammering stretches and shapes the sheet metal. Most of the techniques of silversmithing are based on hammering non-ferrous sheet to 'raise' or 'hollow' a three-dimensional form. The cup section of a copper goblet (fig. 19) can be raised from a flat sheet by hammering, first on a former and then on a 'stake' of the right shape (fig. 20). Once the form is produced it can be hammered or 'planished' to a very smooth finish by using different hammers. All malleable metal sheet can be formed in this way.

To achieve this rather extreme amount of stretching, the copper has to be softened (annealed) at regular intervals as the hammering process tends to WORK HARDEN the material. Work hardening occurs when excessive hammering distorts the crystal structure of the metal and prevents further bending. ANNEALING is a heating process, and at the right temperature the crystal structure of the metal returns to its original condition. The metal will then be just as malleable as it was originally.

Three-dimensional forming is also achieved industrially by pressing metal and by spinning on a lathe. Pressing is done rapidly in powerful presses with the metal sheet pressed between matched formers. The same principle of changing the thickness of the sheet applies, but it is done almost instantaneously. Spinning is done around a former on a lathe, and the force is applied

▼Fig. 19 A goblet form

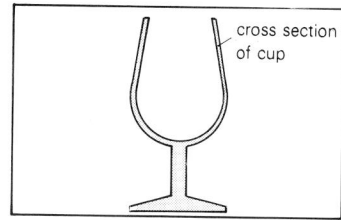
cross section of cup

▼Fig. 20 'Raising' the cup section from a flat sheet of copper

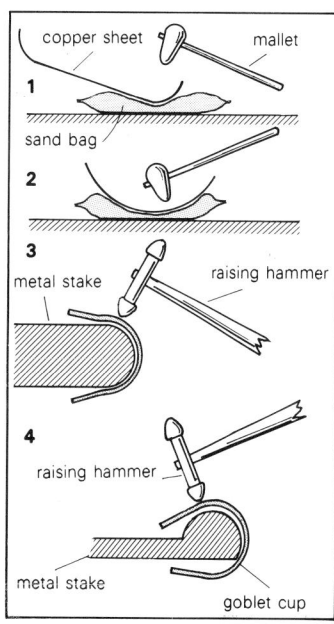
copper sheet   mallet
1
sand bag
2
3
metal stake   raising hammer
4
raising hammer
metal stake
goblet cup

by a heavy steel bar rolled around the former as it and the metal sheet spin. The steel bar forces the sheet to curl around the former.

Questions

1 Some fizzy drink cans are made of tinplate and some of aluminium. How would you tell which is which? Examine some of each and see which type has the most joins or seams. Why do you think this is? o

2 All ferrous metals are liable to rust and this is always a problem with motor cars. What metals (other than mild steel) could a car manufacturer use for the body panels of a car? What would be the advantages and disadvantages of each alternative?

3 It is often necessary to work out the flat shape of a folded up 3D object. These flat shapes are called 'developments' and are often used in technical graphics. How would you work out the flat shape of the 3D forms in fig. 21? x

▼Fig. 21

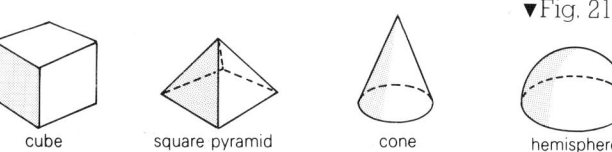
cube   square pyramid   cone   hemisphere

4 Malleable metals are easiest to form as they stretch and deform relatively easily, but they must also be fully annealed. Get samples of a range of non-ferrous metal sheet (copper, aluminium, brass, lead) and anneal them all. Design a simple test to find the most and the least malleable. Remember that malleability is not the same as softness. Design another simple test to put the samples in order of hardness or softness. x

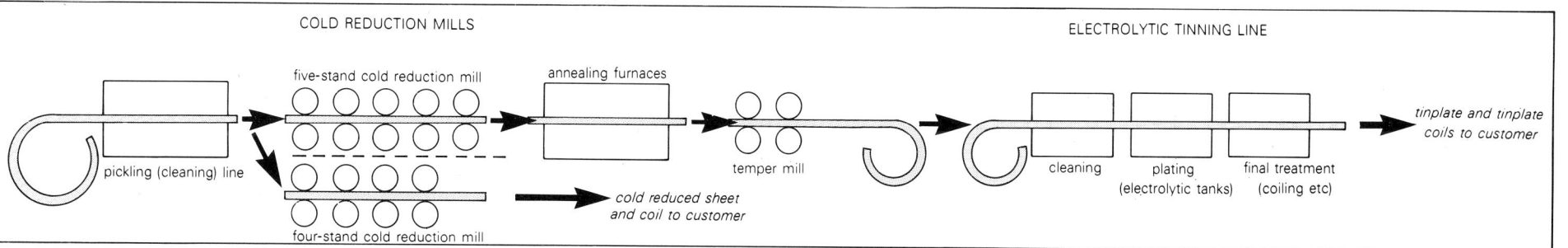
COLD REDUCTION MILLS   ELECTROLYTIC TINNING LINE
five-stand cold reduction mill   annealing furnaces
pickling (cleaning) line
                                                              temper mill
cold reduced sheet and coil to customer
four-stand cold reduction mill
cleaning   plating (electrolytic tanks)   final treatment (coiling etc)
tinplate and tinplate coils to customer

PLASTIC SHEET

Most plastic sheet in its normal condition tends to be hard and non-malleable. As a result it cannot be formed. However, thermoplastics (which soften and become malleable when they get hot) can be formed if they are first heated to the right forming temperature. Most thermoplastics become formable between 150 and 200°C. To control the bending of thermoplastic sheet, it is therefore essential to control the way you heat it.

To put a fold in a flat sheet of acrylic or PVC, the sheet must be heated just along the line of the required fold. The narrower the heated line is, the sharper the bend will be. Accurate bending should always be done on a jig or former, but remember that the plastic will be soft and the surface will be easily damaged and deformed by a rough or badly made former.

It is also possible, however, to form the same thermoplastic sheets (acrylic and PVC) into three-dimensional forms. In this case the whole sheet has to be heated up, and when soft it can be forced into a 3D form through a variety of processes.

1. Pressing plastic sheet is almost exactly the same as pressing metal sheet except that when it is sufficiently hot the plastic sheet needs very little force to squeeze it between the formers. Wood and plywood moulds are quite strong enough to cope with this process. Even complex shapes can be produced in this way. If the male and female halves of the mould are matched carefully, the pressing is simple (fig. 23).

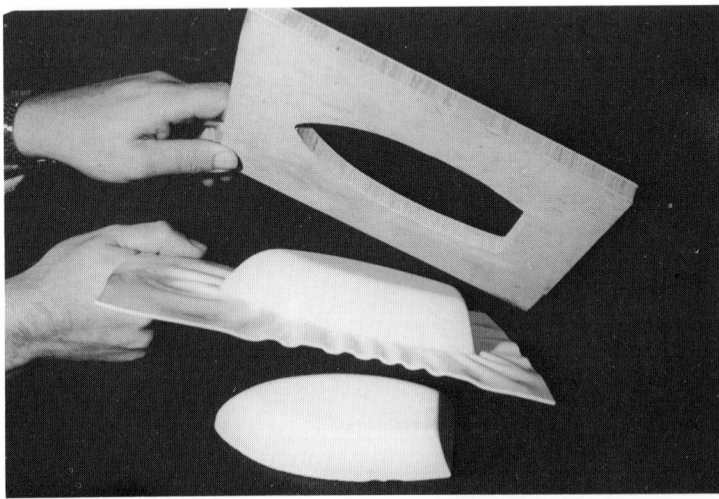

Fig. 22 To control the bending of thermoplastic sheet, you must control how the heat is applied

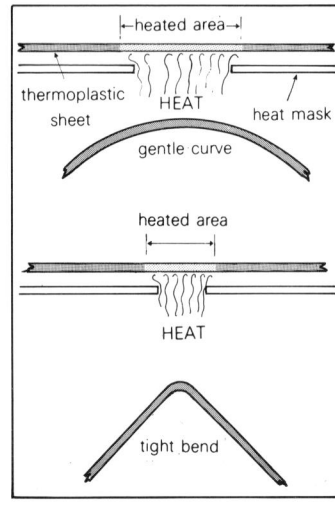

Fig. 25 The sheet thins as it stretches

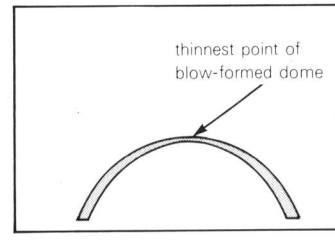

◀Fig. 23 Complex forms can be pressed in very simple formers

2. Blow forming is in many ways an even simpler process as it requires only one half of a mould. The forming force is supplied by compressed air. The moulding ring (which may have any shape cut out) has to be clamped hard down onto the forming table to avoid air leaks under the heated plastic sheet. If you cut through the middle of the dome formed in this way, you will see how the thickness of the material has been changed. It is like blowing up a balloon: as it gets bigger the plastic has to stretch, and as it does so it has to get thinner.

▼Fig. 24 Blowforming can be done through almost any shape of moulding ring

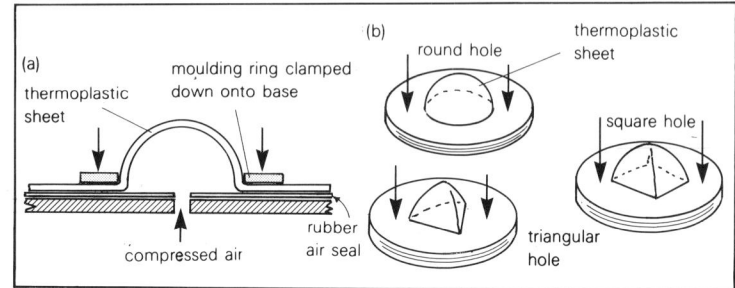

3. Vacuum forming is another forming process that uses a relatively simple mould and the forming force is provided by atmospheric pressure. A mould is placed in an airtight box and a plastic sheet clamped over it. When the sheet is heated sufficiently, the valve to a vacuum pump can be opened and the air under the plastic sheet sucked out. As the vacuum begins to form under the sheet, atmospheric pressure forces the sheet down onto the mould. As it cools it will harden and it can be removed from the mould. A number of technical points have to be remembered if successful mouldings are to be obtained:

▼Fig. 26 In vacuum forming, atmospheric pressure forces the softened sheet over the mould

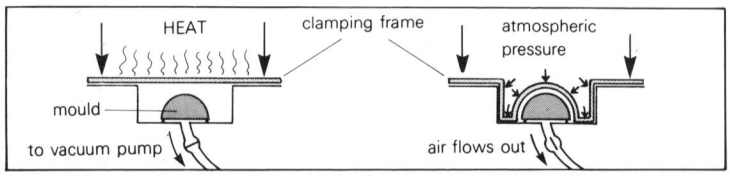

▼Fig. 27 Any air pockets have to be vented if the plastic is to pull down into them

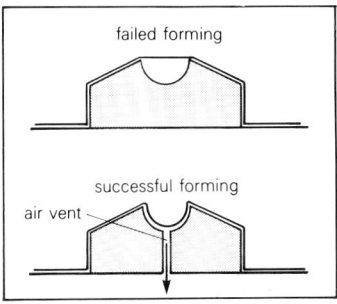

(i) The mould must not have any pockets that will trap air, or the plastic will not pull down into them.

(ii) The mould must have a release angle so that the moulding will pull off when it has cooled.

(iii) As with blow forming, the plastic gets thinner wherever it is stretched. So the final moulding will have a varying wall thickness. The rule that governs this thinning is that as the plastic pulls down over the mould, the first point to touch will end up thickest and the last point of the mould to be touched by the plastic will have the thinnest layer.

WOOD SHEET

Wood sheet comes in a number of different types, plywood blockboard and chipboard being the most common. However, these wood sheets are designed to be used as rigid flat panels. In this section we are concerned only with how these sheets can be bent and formed. Wood is not at all malleable, so it cannot be formed in the same ways as metals and plastics. However, wood is flexible and it is possible to use this flexibility to produce curved forms in wood by the process of lamination.

Thin sheets of plywood can be bent quite easily, but under normal conditions they would just spring back flat as soon as the bending force was removed. Laminating is the process of forcing several thin layers of wood to bend over a mould and gluing them together in this bent condition. Once the glue has hardened, the wood is unable to spring back because it is held rigidly by the glue. Remember, though, that the wood is constantly trying to spring back, so the strength of the glue used for laminating is just as important as the strength of the wood. A glue that remains even a little bit rubbery (impact glues and PVA woodworking glue) will not be suitable, as the wood will eventually force itself back to a straight line.

Laminating can be done on a small scale with little strips of wood bent in simple wood formers. It can also be done on a large scale with sheets of thin plywood formed over a mould in a flexible neoprene rubber bag press.

Questions

1 When doing simple line bending in plastic, why is it more accurate to use a former to create the bend?

2 When press forming, it is quite usual to find the plastic product sticking tightly to the male mould. It never sticks in the female half of the mould. Can you explain why?

3 When press forming, the male and female halves of the mould are not the same size. Why is that, and by how much are they different?

4 When vacuum forming simple containers like seed trays, you could form into a female mould or over a male mould. In each case show exactly where the plastic will be thinnest and thickest. Now think where the product needs the most strength and decide which mould you would use.

5 To get the plastic to form down into a female mould, the air has to be vented out through little holes (vents) in the corners. Why are the vents in the corners and not in the middle? Why are they made so small (1 mm diameter) when bigger holes would allow the trapped air to escape much more quickly?

6 When laminating wood strips it is very important to clean, seal *and wax* the faces of the former. Why is that?

7 When using thin plywood as a laminate, it bends more easily in one direction than in the other. This is specially true when there are only three layers in the plywood. Look carefully at the layers of wood that make up the plywood and explain why it is more difficult to bend one way. You should now be able to tell just by looking at a sheet of plywood which way it will flex most. **x**

8 Bent forms in wood, metal or plastic are always more rigid than flat sheets of the same thickness. Corrugated iron or plastic sheets show how the corrugations give strength to the material. Where else can you see this principle in use? **x**

▼Fig. 28 The mould must have release angles at the sides

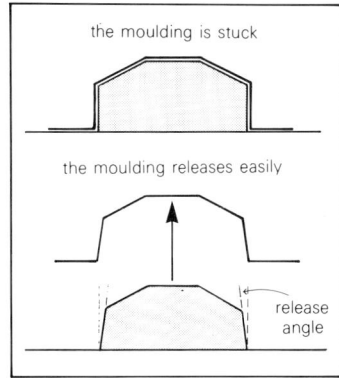

▼Fig. 29 When the glue has hardened the lamination will stay in the shape of the mould

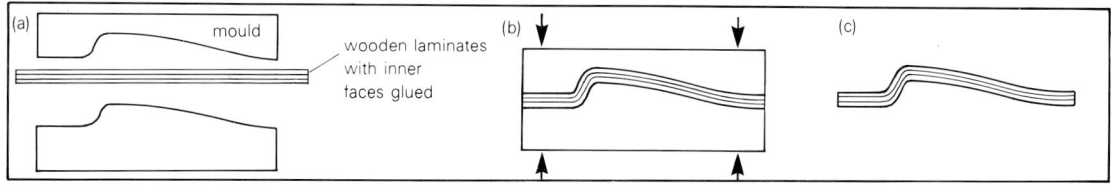

CUTTING AND SHAPING

WHAT IS CUTTING?

Saws, chisels, planes and files all work on the same principles of cutting. They all have hard, wedge-shaped cutting edges. Sometimes it is a single cutting edge (like a plane, chisel or lathe tool) and sometimes it is a row of cutting edges (like a saw or a file). In all cases, however, the cutting edge must be *harder* than the material it is trying to cut and it must be *wedge-shaped* to force the material apart. Based on these principles, each tool has been developed for a particular type of cutting or for use with a particular material. We will examine how the saw has been adapted to different materials and circumstances.

CUTTING WOOD Examine a piece of wood and you will see that it has many fibres running along its length, and this mass of fibres is what we call the GRAIN of a piece of wood. It is because of its fibrous nature that wood is so much stronger in one direction and this is why we use it in *lengths* with the fibres running along the length.

If you want to cut off a length of wood, you have to cut across the fibres, and that is more difficult than cutting along them. Generally, the harder a material is to cut, the smaller the 'bite' that you can take out at one go.

Consequently, harder cutting jobs need saws with more small teeth and easy cutting jobs can be done with fewer, bigger teeth. So in cutting across the grain we use a CROSS CUT SAW which has more and smaller teeth than a saw designed for cutting along the length of wood, a RIP SAW. In addition, the teeth must remove enough material so that the saw will not jam in the cut. Once again, because of the fibres the cross cut saw has to remove a wider slot that gives the saw enough CLEARANCE to move freely. This clearance is achieved by kinking (called *setting*) the teeth alternately right and left. Look down the length of a saw and see the set of the teeth. A rip saw will have very little set and a cross cut saw will have far more.

Most wood saws are made from a solid sheet of steel with the teeth cut into one edge. They are known as BACK SAWS because they have a solid back, and when they get blunted the teeth can be resharpened by being cut further up into the steel back. This is a difficult and time consuming process, but fortunately does not have to be done too often.

CUTTING METAL The problem with cutting metal is that most

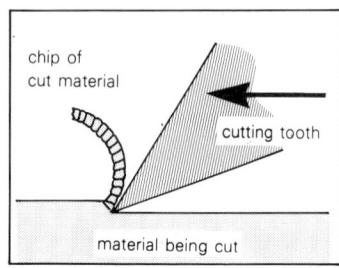

▼Fig. 30 Cutting edges must be wedge shaped and harder than the material being cut

▼Fig. 31 Cutting *across* the fibres is harder work than cutting *along* them

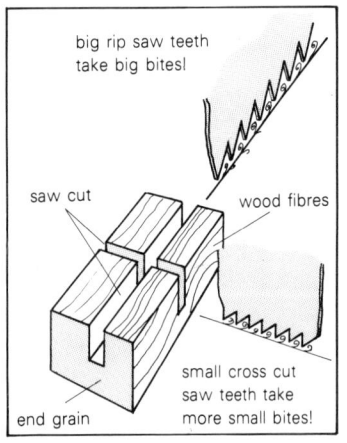

▼Fig. 32 Back saws have teeth cut into a solid sheet of steel

▼Fig. 33 Frame saws have a thin blade of teeth held in a frame

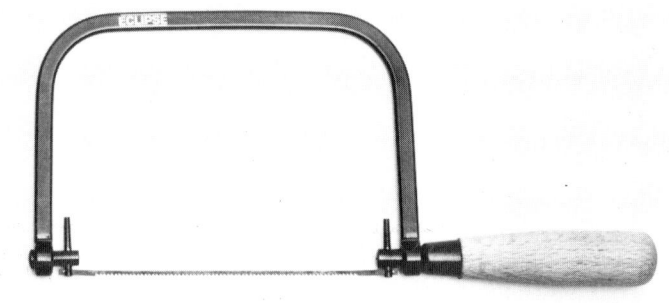

metals are much harder than wood. Consequently metal saws get blunt much more quickly than wood saws. Metal saws are usually designed as thin saw blades held in a frame. The blades are specially hardened, but when they get blunt they can be thrown away and replaced with a new one. The most common frame saw for metal is the hacksaw. Hacksaw blades still need some clearance to avoid jamming. The teeth are too small to be 'set' individually, so the clearance is achieved by stamping a wavy edge onto the blade. The width of the cut slot is therefore greater than the thickness of the blade. Because the hacksaw is a frame with interchangeable blades, it is a universal saw for metals and each new situation or material can be handled by choosing and

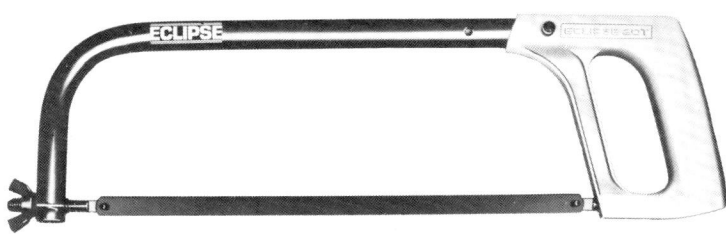

fitting an appropriate blade. The same rule about the *hardness* of the cut material and the *size* of the cutting tooth applies as in wood. Very soft metals like copper or aluminium need very coarse blades with very few teeth per inch (TPI) (fig. 36). Fine blades would soon clog up and cease to work. However, it is also important – and particularly with metals – to make sure that several teeth are in contact with the metal at all times. If you cut fine tube with a coarse blade there might be only one tooth cutting at a time, and this will damage the tooth and spoil the tube. For thin sections of metal you must use a blade with lots of fine teeth (many TPI) (fig. 37).

CUTTING PLASTICS There are very few tools designed specifically for cutting plastics, and mostly we use wood or metal saws as appropriate. However, the same principles apply. Some plastics are much harder than others and they often come in very thin sections of sheet or tube. So, for example, to cut acrylic sheet (which is quite hard and brittle) you would *not* use a back saw such as a tenon saw because, even if it had the right TPI, the saw would blunt very quickly and back saws are not easy to re-sharpen. A frame saw (like a hacksaw) allows you to fit a blade with the appropriate TPI and when it gets blunt it is easy to replace the blade.

Softer plastics like PVC, and certainly polythene which is very soft indeed, may well be cut with a suitable tenon saw. Remember to check that the TPI is suitable for the thickness of material you are cutting. If the plastic splits or chips or shatters you probably have too few TPI (the teeth are too big). However, if the plastic tends to melt around the blade then either it is blunt and generating too much frictional heat or there are too many small teeth getting clogged up and thereby generating the frictional heat. THINK before you cut.

It is not only saws that conform to these simple principles of cutting. They apply equally to all other cutting tools.

◄Fig. 34 A metal cutting hacksaw is a frame saw with interchangeable blades

▼Fig. 35 A wavy cutting edge to the hacksaw blade gives clearance for the blade

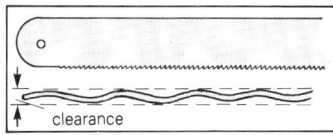

▼Fig. 36 A coarse blade with 5 TPI

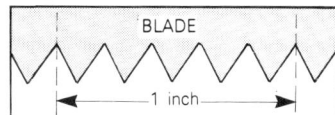

▼Fig. 37 A coarse blade must *not* be used on fine wall tubing. Several teeth must always be in contact with the metal

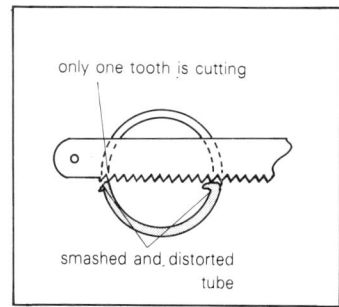

• A file is like lots of hacksaw blades side by side, and it cuts a flat surface. Files (like saws) have to have the right TPI, and if you use a fine file on aluminium it will soon clog up.
• A plane is like a file with one adjustable and resharpenable tooth. When used properly it can generate very fine flat surfaces.
• A lathe tool can peel off metal shavings in a very similar way to a plane peeling off wood shavings. The tool will need to be harder and the angles will vary, but the principle is the same.
• A circular saw will need a cross cut blade and a ripping blade just like the hand saws, and the 'set' of each will vary.
• A milling cutter is like a circular saw blade but with a few large teeth. As with a drill, you can buy cutters of different hardness.
• A chisel is exactly like a plane blade, except that it is designed to be held by hand instead of in a rigid body. It is a very versatile cutting tool.

Questions

1 When using frame saws like hacksaws, coping saws and piercing saws it is very easy to fit blades the wrong way round. Explain how you make sure that they are the right way round. If they do get reversed what is the effect on the cutting operation and on the workpiece?

2 If you cut through a piece of thin wall mild steel tube using a hacksaw with a low TPI blade, it cuts quite well to start with but then the cutting action gets very rough and jagged. Try it out and explain why it happens. **x**

3 One of the essential requirements of a frame saw is that the frame must hold the blade under tension to keep it straight. Explain how this tensioning is done with:
(a) a hacksaw,
(b) a coping saw,
(c) a piercing saw,
(d) a bow saw. **x**

4 Frame saws with disposable blades are far more convenient for keeping sharp, but are not so good as back saws in other respects. In what ways is a back saw better?

5 As well as tensioning the blade, the blade fixings on frame saws often have an angle adjustment. Why is this adjustment necessary?

SHAPING BY CUTTING

We have already seen how materials can be shaped by forming them from the fluid state and by bending and forming them using heat and pressure. We shall now look at the other major means of shaping materials: by cutting them and removing some parts.

Some shaping operations are quite simple, some are more tricky to get right and some are impossibly difficult and time consuming. When you design something you have to be aware of how you might make it simply and quickly. To help you, this section will divide shaping by cutting into four stages. These stages progressively get more difficult, more time consuming and require more skill.

STAGE ONE: Flat shapes (shaping in two dimensions)
Cutting out flat shapes uses relatively simple cutting operations, in wood, metal or plastic. The parrot in fig. 38 illustrates the simplicity of two-dimensional shaping. The cutting may be in straight lines with saws and planes; it may be curved using a coping saw, band saw, piercing saw and sanding disc; or it may be done with drills, fly cutters or tank cutters. Once the cut is made it merely requires the edges to be finished. This can be done with files and glasspaper. It is much easier to finish outside curves (convex curves) than inside ones (concave curves), but neither is particularly difficult or time consuming (fig. 39).

▼Fig. 39 It's easier to get at convex surfaces to clean them up

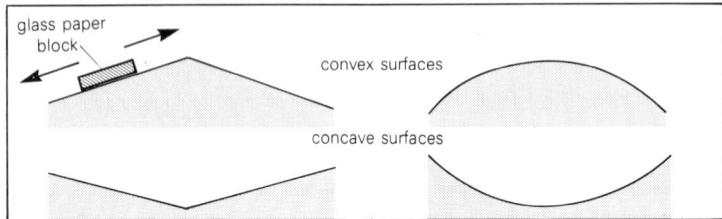

STAGE TWO: Round shapes (2D shapes in rotation)
Shaping material on a lathe is an extension of two-dimensional shaping. It is like cutting a flat shape and rotating it into a three-dimensional form.

The main problem with this shaping is holding the workpiece securely whilst the cutting operation is carried out. There are two ways of doing this and they have a considerable effect on the sort of three-dimensional forms that you can produce. These two

▼Fig. 38 Even complicated shapes are easy to cut from flat sheet

▼Fig. 40 Shaping on the lathe – 2-dimensional shapes in rotation

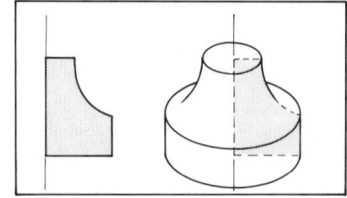

methods apply equally to wood and metal lathes.
1. Holding work between centres A block of material can be supported at both ends on 'centres', one of which provides a spinning force for the block. The other centre merely supports the block and spins freely. The ends of the wooden workpiece have to be left intact for the centre supports, but the middle of the block can be cut to almost any shape that is a regular rotational shape. The ends can be trimmed off last, when the shaping is complete.

▼Fig. 41 Turning between centres is used for long thin forms

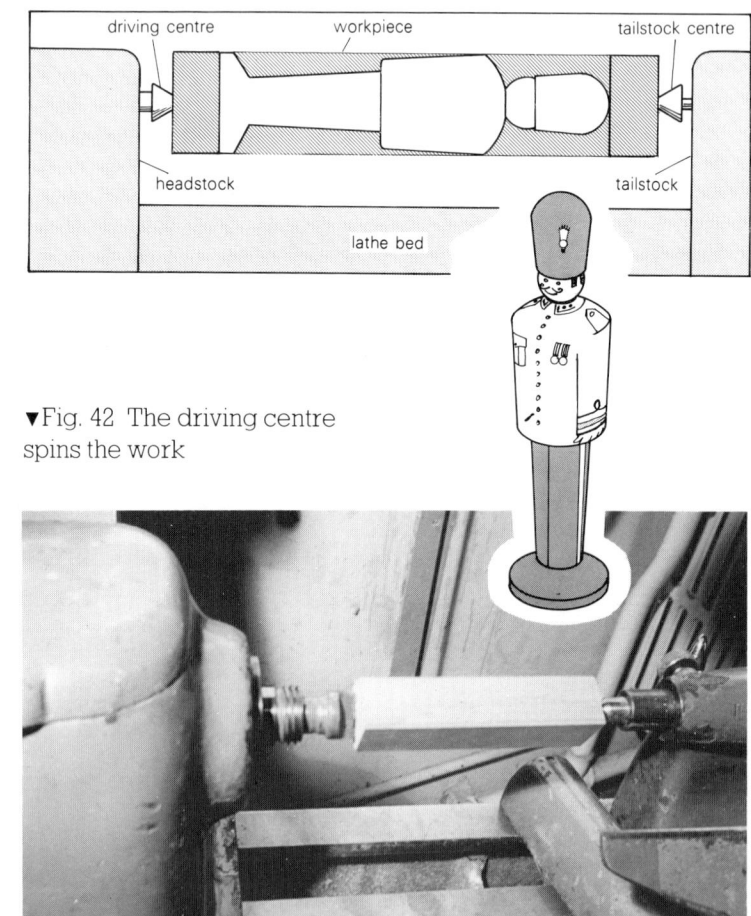

▼Fig. 42 The driving centre spins the work

2. Holding work in a chuck or on a face plate With this arrangement the work is held at the end, and you can get at the sides *and* the end of the block. It is possible to produce some complex forms with internal as well as external shaping.

▼Fig. 43 Chuck turning allows you to work on the *end* of the work piece

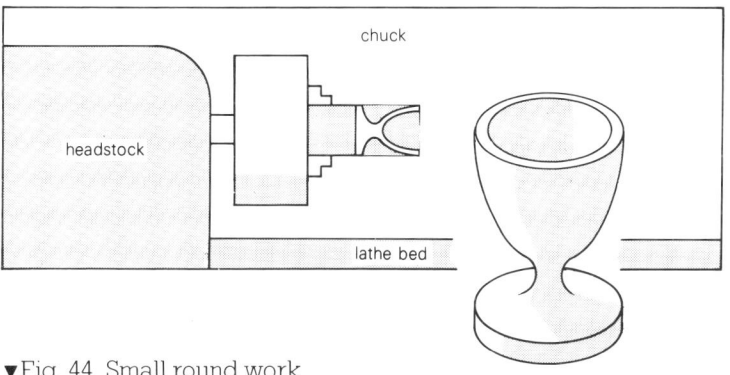

▼Fig. 44 Small round work can be turned using a 3-jaw chuck

◄Fig. 45 Large work can be held on a faceplate

Whilst both of these arrangements are equally possible with wood and metal lathes, free curves can only be achieved on a wood lathe where the cutting gouge is held by hand. Metal lathes can only cut straight lines unless the tool movement is computer controlled.

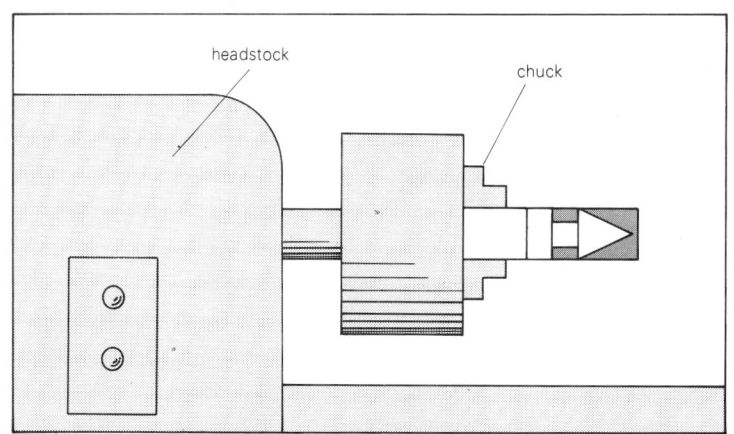

◄Fig. 46 Metal lathes can only cut in straight lines

STAGE THREE: 3D shaping – regular geometric forms. Three-dimensional forms that are not simple rotational lathe forms are more difficult and time consuming. However, regular geometric forms are much easier than free sculptural forms because a greater selection of tools and machinery is available for use. All materials come in standard stock sizes and you can save an enormous amount of time by choosing the right stock form to start with. The two basic forms are cuboid forms (using square or rectangular stock) and cylinders (using round stock).

▼Fig. 47 Boxes based on simple geometric forms using circles and straight lines

These two basic stock forms may then be shaped by sawing, drilling, filing, chiselling, planing or milling. All these cutting tools do basically two things: they either cut slots, holes and recesses or they flatten surfaces. When cutting slots and recesses in wood,

▼Fig. 49 Cutting flat surfaces in wood and metal

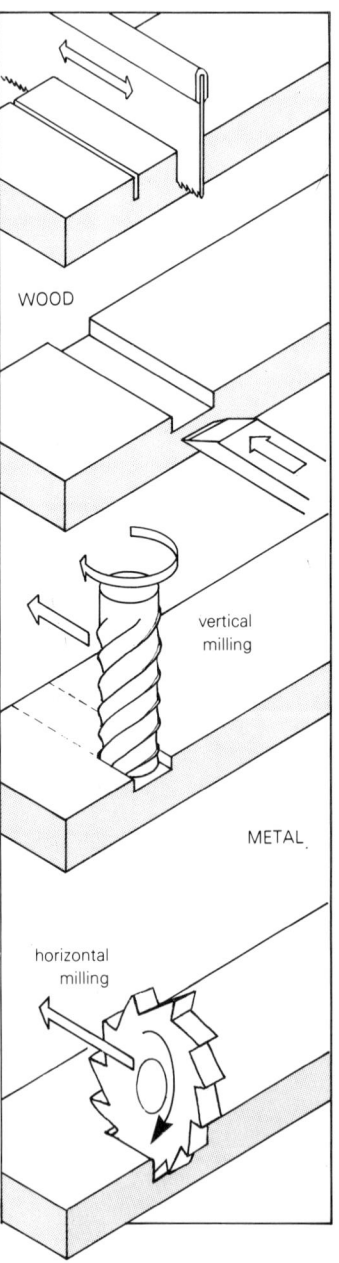

▼Fig. 48 Cutting slots and recesses in wood and metal

WOOD

vertical milling

METAL

horizontal milling

we use saws and chisels, and in metal we use the vertical or horizontal milling machines. To flatten surfaces in wood we use planes, and in metal we use files (or sometimes wide milling cutters if it has to be very accurate). You can get all sorts of different planes (for wood) and milling cutters (for metal) so that you can cut some very complex forms.

When you are deciding on a cutting operation, you will find it helpful to think carefully through a few simple rules.

1. When you start a MACHINING operation like milling, it takes far longer to set up the cutter and the workpiece than it does to do the actual cutting. It may be quicker as a hand operation.

2. There is *always* more than one way of doing the job. Make sure that you choose the simplest.

▼Fig. 50 Which way would you do it?

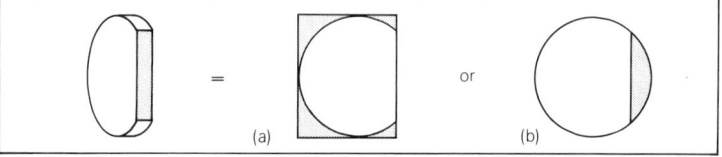

(a)   or   (b)

3. Don't always assume that it *has* to be a cutting operation.

▼Fig. 51 Think about which will be quickest – easiest – and best

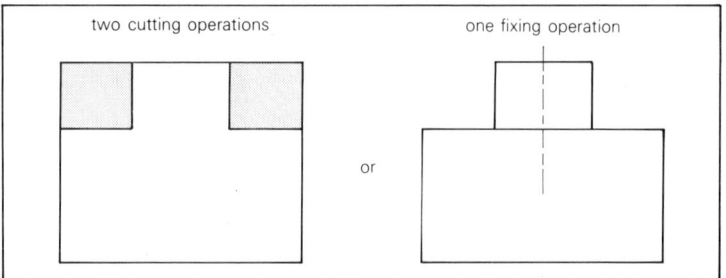

two cutting operations   one fixing operation

or

4. If you have more than one cutting operation to do on a piece of material, make sure that you do them in the right order.

Both these objects need two separate cutting operations. Which order would you do them in?

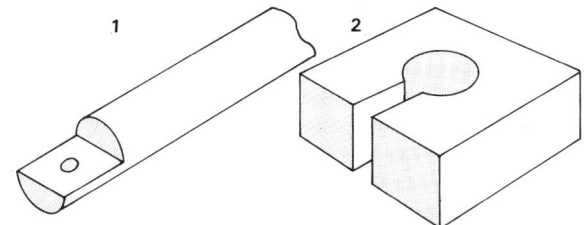

Item 1	(a) Cut recess	OR	(a) Drill hole
	(b) Drill hole		(b) Cut recess
Item 2	(a) Drill hole	OR	(a) Cut slot
	(b) Cut slot		(b) Drill hole

Explain your decisions.

For each job, write out a *procedure sheet* that covers all the marking out and cutting operations. (See how procedure sheets have been used on pages 43 and 84).

STAGE FOUR: 3D shaping – non-geometric forms.
Three-dimensional non-geometric forms are the sort of 'free' forms that we see in carving and sculpture. These forms cannot be machined as they do not have regular surfaces and if the shaping is to be done by cutting, it all has to be done by hand. With metals and plastics this would be a silly waste of time and effort because it is much easier to use a different forming process, such as casting or pressing (see pages 106–113).

In wood however, we do use carving techniques to produce complex three-dimensional forms. Wood is usually carved with *gouges* which come in many different forms, but it can also be carved with *surforms*, *rasps* and *spokeshaves*. The finishing of the surface will be dealt with on page 126.

►Fig. 52 Sculptural forms can be cut only by hand

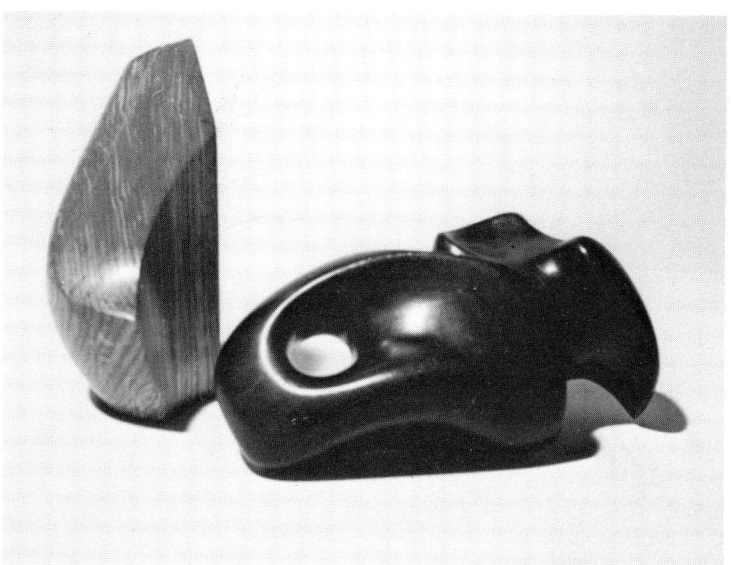

Questions

1 Why is it easier to clean up the edges of convex shapes than the edges of concave shapes?

2 When you are cutting and cleaning up shapes in plywood, the sheet tends to split and chip out at the back. What causes this damage and how can it be reduced?

3 When turning wood between centres, the work is clamped between the driving centre and the tailstock centre. The tail-stock centre must be regularly tightened to keep the workpiece secure. What causes it to get slack? When preparing the workpiece to be mounted between centres, why do we plane the corners off? Wouldn't it be easier to cut them off with the lathe tool when it is on the lathe?

4 If you want to turn down a piece of metal accurately and you only have $\frac{1}{2}$ mm more to take off the diameter, how far do you move the tool in? Explain your answer.

5 If you want to cut a cone with an included angle of 30° on a metal lathe, at what angle do you set the compound slide? Explain this answer. **x**

6 Assume you have to produce an accurate cube from a length of 50 mm square aluminium bar. Draw up a procedure sheet for doing this job on a vertical or horizontal milling machine. **c**

JOINTS AND FIXINGS

There are all sorts of ways of joining materials together and this section will help you make the right choice for your particular needs. Materials can be fixed together mechanically (with nails, nuts and bolts, etc.), or chemically (with glues and cements) or by heat (soldering, welding, etc.). Some of these systems are suitable for any material and some for only one material. We shall take these systems in turn.

	MECHANICAL FIXINGS			CHEMICAL FIXINGS	HEAT FIXINGS
	PERMANENT	TEMPORARY	FLEXIBLE		

WOOD	nails
	joints for gluing
		screws
		KD fixings
		wedge
			pin hinge	with mechanical joints =
				   natural
				   casein
				   synthetic
				   impact	

METAL	rivet	nut/bolt/screw KD fixings spring clips	pin hinge ball joint	epoxy resins 'super' glues	weld braze solder
PLASTIC	rivet	nut/bolt/screw KD fixings	pin hinge flexing strip	solvents cements superglues	weld

MECHANICAL FIXINGS

There are three types of mechanical fixings. *Permanent fixings* are designed to hold the materials together permanently. *Temporary fixings* are designed to hold materials together tightly, but they are removable. *Flexible fixings* are designed to hold materials together but to allow them to move in relation to each other. PERMANENT MECHANICAL FIXINGS The permanent mechanical joining of wood is usually done by nailing or pinning. This process relies solely on the frictional grip of the wood fibres on the sides of the nail (fig. 53). It is possible to rip apart a nailed joint or to pull out the nail. However, it is classed as a permanent joint as it is not *intended* to be removable and the material may be damaged by attempting it (fig. 54).

Metals and plastics are *not* fibrous materials so it is not possible to use nails. However, rivets are commonly used. Instead of

▼Fig. 53 The wood fibres grip the nail

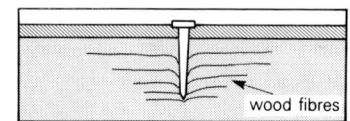

▼Fig. 54 The wood can be seriously damaged by the pincers

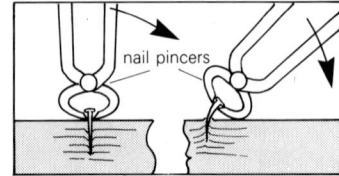

relying on the friction of the fibres to hold the nail down, rivets squeeze the material between two heads. The hole must be pre-drilled to allow the rivet to be pushed through the metal and the squeezing force is created by hammering over the plain end into a second head (fig. 55). There are several different styles of rivet head, the most common being the round 'snap' head and the countersunk head (fig. 56). This latter one is used to give a smooth surface after the joint is finished. Aircraft bodies are made from aluminium alloy sheet riveted together with countersunk rivets.

▼Fig. 55 Four stages of riveting

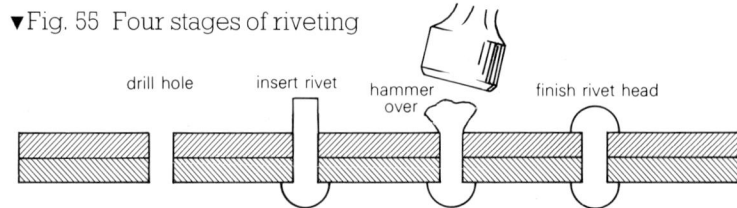

drill hole   insert rivet   hammer over   finish rivet head

▼Fig. 56 Countersunk head rivets give a smooth surface

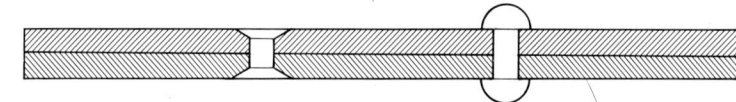

Until recently, it was impossible to rivet materials together if you couldn't get to both sides of the joint. Now we can use 'pop' rivets which make it possible to rivet into the sides of tubes and in other inaccessible places. Stage 1 of fig. 57 shows a normal pop rivet form. The sleeve that surrounds the central pin is usually a soft metal, such as aluminium. The pop rivet is placed in the drilled hole through the two pieces to be joined. The pop rivet gun holds the rivet in place whilst gripping the central pin and pulling it (stage 2). The bulbous end causes the soft metal sleeve to pucker up and create a sort of rivet head on the underside (stage 3). Further pressure applied by the pop rivet gun breaks the central pin off, leaving the rivet in place (and usually the bulbous end imprisoned) (stage 4).

▼Fig. 57 Pop rivets are quick to use and need access to one side only

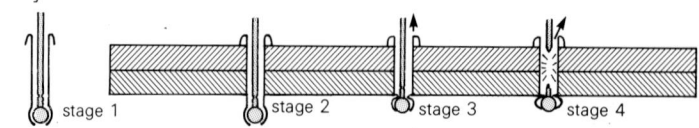

stage 1   stage 2   stage 3   stage 4

One of the valuable qualities of riveting as a joining technique is that it is one of the few ways of permanently fixing different materials together, such as plywood to metal tubing or plastic sheet to metal strip. Mechanical wood joints that are designed to be glued together (like dovetail joints) will be dealt with under chemical joining.

TEMPORARY MECHANICAL JOINTS These joints are designed to be assembled and disassembled at will. The most common ones are based on screw threads. Wood screws rely for the strength of their grip on the fibres of the wood (just like the nails do). As the screw thread is forced into the wood, the sides of the thread grip into the fibres and prevent it being pulled out. To be successful in holding two pieces of wood together, the screw has only to grip into *one* of the pieces. The two pieces are then squeezed between the grip of the screw thread and the head of the screw. That is why the head end of the screw does not have any thread on it.

▼Fig. 58 Wood screws are a clearance fit through one piece and screw into the other

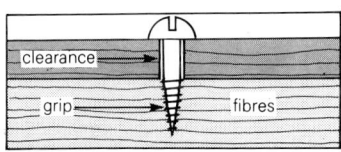

▼Fig. 59 The important sizes of a screw

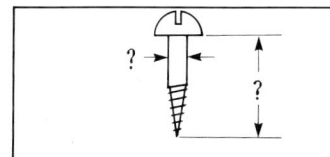

To choose the right wood screw you must make four decisions: what length, what thickness, what type of head (roundhead or countersunk) and what material (steel or brass) is needed? Because of the need to grip into the fibres, screws will not work in the end grain of wood. If you have to screw into end grain, insert a piece of dowel rod first (across the grain) and then screw into that (fig. 60).

▼Fig. 60 The only way to screw into end grain

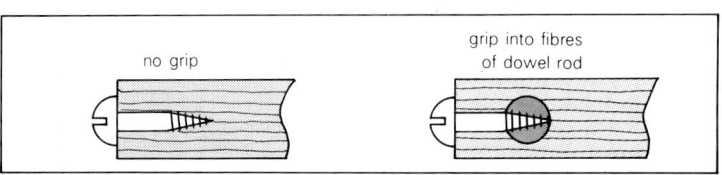

▼Fig. 61 Two systems for screwing metal components together

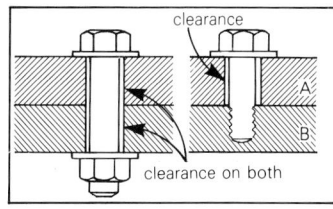

▼Fig. 62 The three most common types of screw head for metal

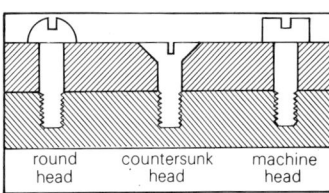

The screws that hold metals and plastics together have to be very different because the materials are not fibrous. A bolt can be put into a pre-drilled hole and the squeezing effect created by a nut on the blank end. Because of the turning/tightening action of the nut (using a spanner), it is normal to protect the metal surfaces with washers under the heads. It is also possible to make much neater screw joints by cutting a screw thread actually in the pre-drilled hole. The bolt then need not come out the far side. This arrangement is very similar to the wood screw, with a free running hole through part A and the screw in part B (fig. 61). A still neater arrangement is to use metal screws with heads like wood screws: either round head, countersunk or machine head (fig. 62). Metal screws are defined by length, diameter and head form. The diameter refers to the non-threaded part of the screw.

Another class of temporary mechanical joints that can be used with wood, metal and plastics is the 'knock down' (KD) joint. This is seen most frequently in 'flat pack' self-assembly furniture like kitchen units. These KD fittings usually take the form of plastic corner blocks that can be cross screwed into both pieces to be joined (fig. 63). A more sophisticated type is the two-part block. Each piece of wood has a part of the block screwed to it, and then it clips, slots or screws together.

▼Fig. 63 K.D. fittings are very common in chipboard furniture such as kitchen units

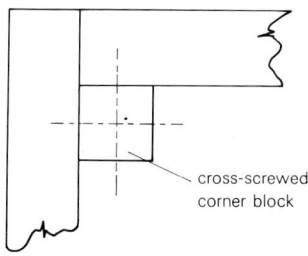

A number of less common temporary mechanical joints have been designed for special purposes. Circlips are often used to hold revolving shafts in place in engineering components. They can be sprung on and off the shaft to remove and refix components. Simple wedges can be used to lock furniture (usually benches and tables) together.

▼Fig. 65 Can you work out the difference between (a) and (b)? How does the screw design affect the behaviour of the hinge?

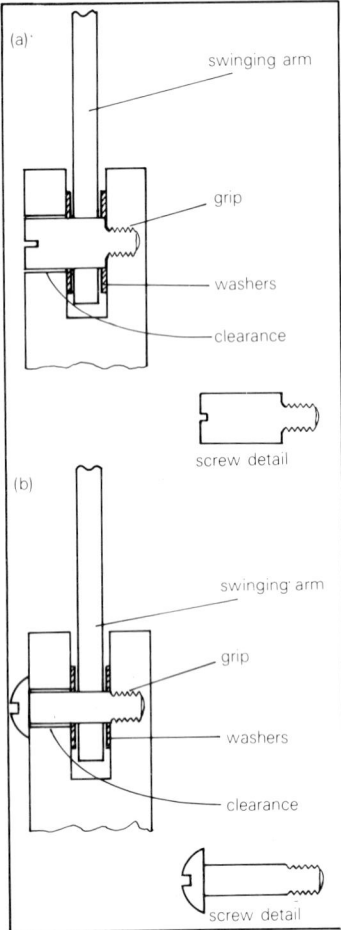

(a)

swinging arm

grip

washers

clearance

screw detail

(b)

swinging arm

grip

washers

clearance

screw detail

FLEXIBLE MECHANICAL JOINTS In its simplest form a flexible mechanical joint is simply a PIN JOINT in which the two parts pivot on a central pin (fig. 64). It is in fact a simple hinge. To make this work with repeated use, it is important to get the fixings right. The pivot pin screws into one side of the forked piece and must have a free running 'clearance hole' through the swinging arm (fig. 65). This sort of joint is used in adjustable desk lamps and even in adjustable try-squares.

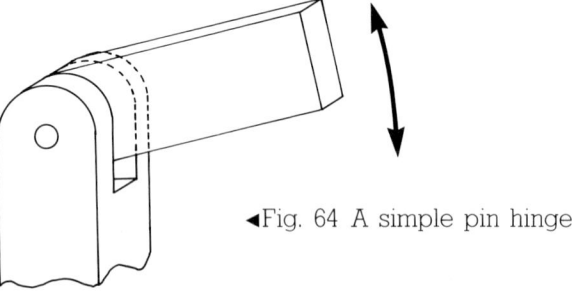

◄Fig. 64 A simple pin hinge

This pin joint can only be pivoted back and forth. A more sophisticated flexible joint, the BALL JOINT, is capable of total three-dimensional movement. It consists of a metal ball rolling in a metal (or sometimes plastic) casing. The casing is designed to hold the ball enclosed but not clamped tight. It can then swing around in any direction until the arm hits the top of the casing. It is used in any situation where total angular adjustment is important, such as the unit that clamps a camera to the top of a tripod. Both the simple pin hinge and the ball joint can be made to lock.

▼Fig. 66 A ball and socket has three-dimensional movement

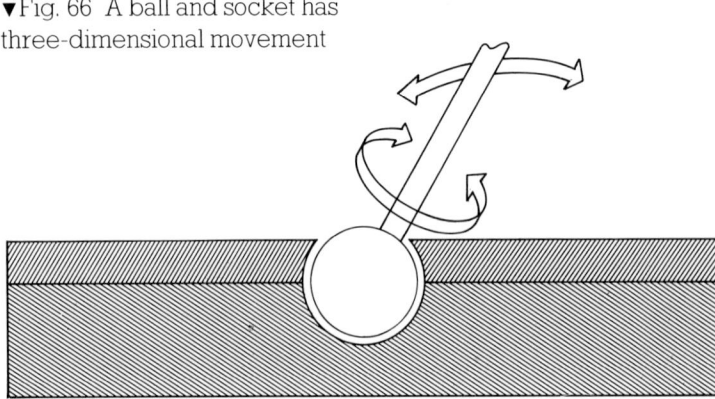

A third way to make a flexible joint is to join two pieces of material with a third piece which is flexible. Some plastics are particularly good to use for flexing strips. Often drawing instrument cases are moulded in plastic (polypropylene) with a 'live' hinge made in the moulding as a tiny piece of flexing plastic. They are surprisingly strong and durable.

Questions

1 If you have to remove nails or pins from a piece of wood, why is it better to use pincers rather than ordinary pliers?

2 In shipbuilding, rivets were commonly used to hold the metal hull plates together. They were always put in red hot. What are the two main advantages of using red hot rivets?

3 The diameter of wood screws is defined by a number (2, 3, 4, etc.) and the higher the number, the thicker the screw. Draw up a table that gives the diameter in millimetres for each size and note what *clearance* drill you would use for each one. **x**

4 When you measure the length of round head and countersunk screws, where do you measure from at the head end?

5 When drilling a clearance hole through wood you sometimes have to drill a slightly larger hole than for a clearance hole for the same screw in metal. Try it out and explain why. **x**

6 Examine a 'pop rivet' gun carefully. Draw a diagram to explain how the squeezing force applied on the handles is converted into a pulling force on the rivet shaft. **x**

7 Nuts and bolts are often used to fix pieces of machinery that are constantly vibrating. This vibration tends to undo the nuts and so they have to be 'locked' on. Look around your workshop and see how many different systems you can find for locking a nut in place. **x**

8 Knock down (KD) fixings were specially developed for mass produced chipboard furniture like kitchen units. List some of the advantages of these KD fixings over conventional carcase joints.

9 Where else, other than on camera tripods, do you find ball and socket joints?

10 Figure 66 shows one design for a ball and socket joint. How else could it be designed? As the ball or the socket begin to wear down, how can you prevent the fit becoming sloppy? How can the joint be made to lock? **c**

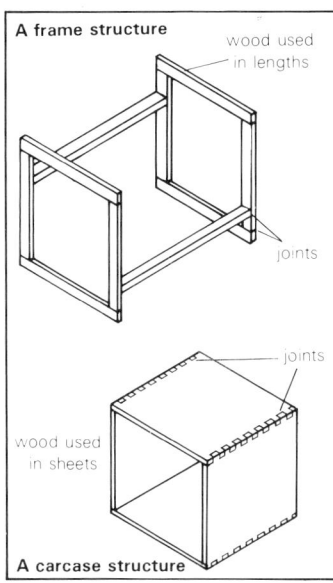

▼Fig. 67 The difference between frame and carcase structures

A frame structure
wood used in lengths
joints

A carcase structure
joints
wood used in sheets

▼Fig. 68 The strength of a joint is related to the glueing area between the two parts of the joint

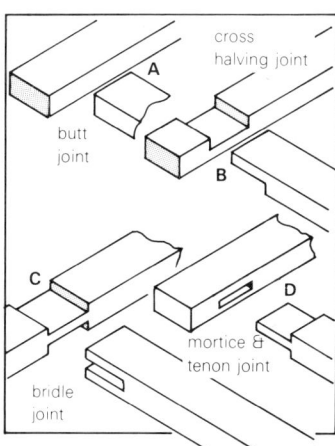

cross halving joint
butt joint
A
B
C
D
mortice & tenon joint
bridle joint

CHEMICAL JOINING

This section is concerned with the use of adhesives and cements that fix materials together chemically. They are permanent and irreversible.

When joining two pieces of wood together with a glued joint, the strength of the joint comes both from the mechanical linking of the two pieces and from the strength of the glue. Wood constructions are of two types: FRAMES (open structures) and CARCASES (box structures).

Framing is much the easiest, and uses wood in lengths joined with 'L', 'T', and 'X' joints. Joints should be designed to give the maximum possible gluing area. A 'T' joint can be made in several ways. In fig. 68 you can see that both C and D have double the joint area of B and are therefore much stronger. Gluing the end grain of wood is never very effective, so joint A is virtually useless. As well as having a large gluing area, it is important not to weaken the two parts by removing too much of either. In fig. 69, (1) and (2) are normal joints, but in both (3) and (4) one of the parts is very weak. Look at the direction of the grain and see if you can work out the mistakes.

▼Fig. 69 The joint must be designed to weaken each part equally. Which parts of 3 and 4 are too weak?

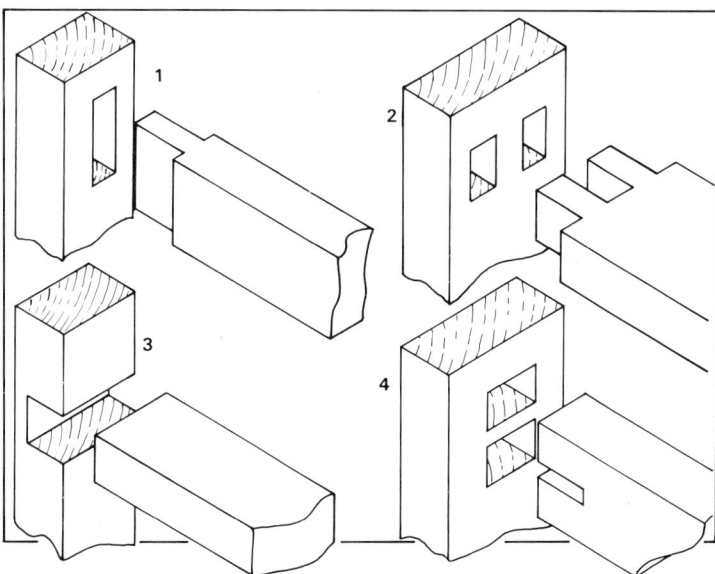

1
2
3
4

Carcase jointing is used to join wide boards of wood into boxes. The corners should never be just butted together. Slotting will give a little more strength, but finger and dovetail joints are very strong because of the large gluing area they give. Grooves and rebates can also be used to join panels into the box structure.

▼Fig. 70 Even when it is pinned, the butt joint is by far the weakest carcase joint

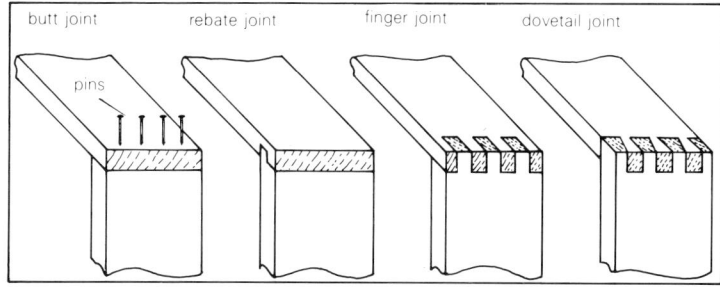

butt joint   rebate joint   finger joint   dovetail joint
pins

When the joints are cut and ready to glue, you have to select the right glue. For example, if the joint is to work out of doors, then the glue must be waterproof. There are three classes of glue that can be used for frame and carcase gluing.

1. *Animal glues* – made from the boiled up skin and bones of animals. They are difficult to use and are badly affected by heat and water.

2. *Casein glues* – based on milk (the most common trade name is Cascamite). This is a white powder that has to be mixed with water to a creamy paste. It gives a strong joint that sets in 6 hours and is both heat and waterproof.

3. *Synthetic resin glues* – (a) Urea formaldehyde glues (trade name Aerolite) come in two parts, a resin and a hardener, and the glue only starts to set as they are mixed. It is therefore possible to control the setting time and it can be very fast indeed (15 minutes). It gives a very strong joint. (b) Polyvinyl Acetate (PVA) (trade name Evo-Stick Resin W) is a ready mixed white creamy glue. It sets fast (in about $\frac{1}{2}$ hour) but never gets totally hard so does not give a very strong joint. It is easy to use but is *not* waterproof.

All these glues are used specifically for wood, but there is another class of glues – the IMPACT glues – that can be used for gluing different materials together, e.g. cloth to plywood, or wood

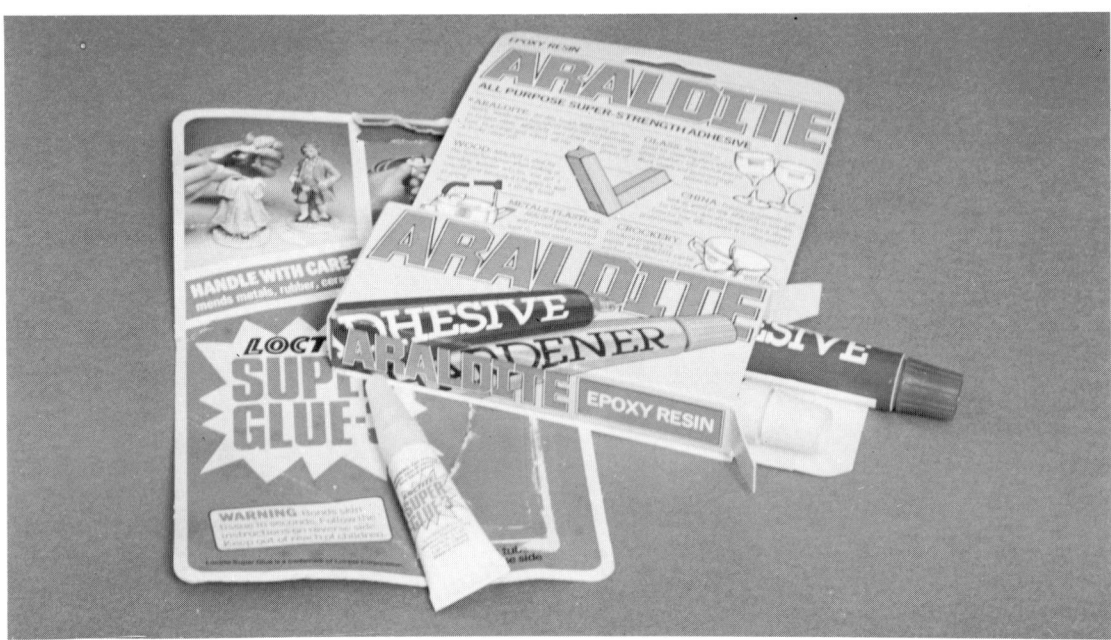

▲Fig. 71 The new chemical adhesives have to be used very carefully – READ THE INSTRUCTIONS

to metal. These impact glues (trade name Evo-Stick or Bostik Impact) are very useful for giving an instant grip between two unlike materials. However, they will always remain slightly rubbery and will never harden into a very strong joint.

As the chemical industry develops new plastic materials, the range of glues for special purposes steadily increases. Epoxy resin glues (trade name Araldite) were the first to enable the gluing of unlike materials into a hard and rigid bond. Metals could be stuck to each other and to other materials for the first time. More recently, a range of cyano acrylate glues (trade name Loctite Super Glue) have resulted in even stronger and quicker-setting joints between unlike materials. We can expect further developments in this field in the near future. With all these synthetic chemical adhesives it is *very important* to read the instruction on the packet carefully. If you do it wrong they will probably not stick at all, and it might be dangerous.

These special synthetic adhesives can be used with plastics as well as metals, but often it is better to stick plastics to each other by SOLVENT BONDING. Most plastics can be dissolved in a suitable solvent. Chloroform will dissolve many plastics, but it has to be used very carefully as the fumes are dangerous. If two plastic surfaces are put together and a suitable solvent run between them, the surfaces will dissolve into each other. This fuses the two pieces together, creating a rigid join. The disadvantage of solvent bonding is that the solvent evaporates so quickly that it does not have time to dissolve much depth of material. The joint is therefore very shallow and quite weak. To overcome this you can use solvent CEMENTS, which are a mixture of the solvent and a small amount of the plastic already in solution in it. These syrupy cements evaporate more slowly than the pure solvents and therefore allow the joint to develop much more strength. Tensol Cement is the cement developed by ICI for use with acrylics.

HEAT JOINTING

Heat joints are used on metals and to a small extent on plastics. Metal heat joints are of two sorts.

WELDING, in which two pieces of the same metal are heated to their melting temperature. As they melt they flow into each other and then solidify into one piece. Welding is usually done on mild steel. It is a very strong joint as the final piece is one solid bar of steel. The joint is as strong as the original metal.

BRAZING and **SOLDERING**, in which the two pieces of metal are heated up to the (lower) melting point of a different metal (a brass alloy for brazing; a lead alloy for soldering). As the pieces to be joined reach the right temperature, the lower melting point metal is touched onto the joint. It then runs through the joint, bonding to both pieces and holding them together. The strength of all heat joints is controlled by the strength of the metal that melts into the joint.

Brazing is again usually done on mild steel, but the metal that melts through the joint is a *brass* alloy. Brass is significantly weaker than mild steel so when stressed it will break on the brazed joint.

Soldering can be done on mild steel, but a *lead* alloy is the metal that runs through the joint. This is a very soft and weak metal which gives a very weak joint. It is also possible to solder with harder (higher temperature) solders based on silver alloys. They are stronger but very expensive.

Silver solders come in a range of grades that all melt at different temperatures, 'Easy Flo' being the lowest temperature and weakest, and 'Hard' being the highest temperature and strongest. It is important to have all these grades so that when you are

	Mild steel constructions	Silversmithing with copper/brass etc.	Temperature (°C)	Strength	
Welding			1600	high	
Brazing			900		
Silver solders:					
hard			765		
medium			745		
easy			720		
easy flo			630		
Lead soldering			220	low	

making a small silversmithing item with several joins in it, the first one does not melt when you do the second one. Each joint can have a different solder which melts at a slightly lower temperature.

As a general guideline, heat joints get weaker as the jointing temperature gets lower. However, it is possible to do very delicate silversmithing joints with silver solders and lead solders. Because they are at a lower temperature, the metal distorts less, gets less spoiled and is therefore easier to clean up afterwards.

PLASTICS The only heat jointing that is possible with plastics is welding – and it is only possible with some thermoplastics. PVC is the most commonly welded plastic. Instead of using a gas torch you have to use a hot air torch (heated electrically) to heat the joint. A flame would burn the surface of the plastic. Once the joint is at the right temperature, the two parts can be made to fuse together in almost exactly the same way as welding metals.

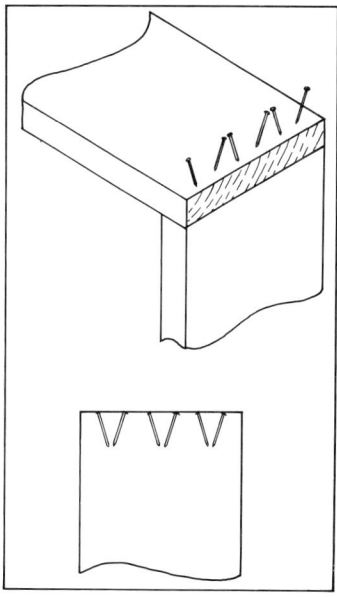

▲Fig. 73

Questions

1 Most carcase structures are now made of chipboard covered with a veneer of wood or plastic. How would you tell if a piece was made of chipboard? Look carefully at the edges and see how the chipboard edge has been covered. **x**

2 Remembering the rules about the design of framing joints, design strong joints for the following situations (fig. 72). For both of them, explain the reasons for your design. All the pieces are solid wood of 60 × 30 mm cross section. **c**

▼Fig. 72

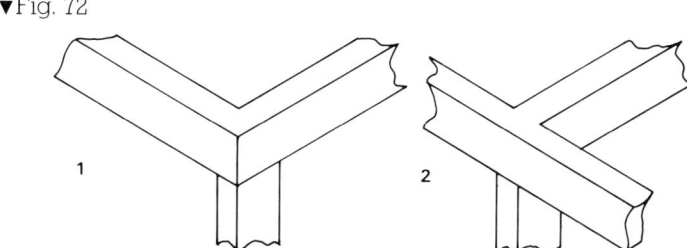

3 A very quick way of joining wide boards is to use dovetail nailing. This is just ordinary nails driven in at angles to imitate the dovetail angles (fig. 73). Why is it stronger than ordinary nailing?

4 We very seldom use animal glues any longer. Why is that?

5 PVA woodworking glue is very simple to use as it comes ready mixed and ready to use. What are the *disadvantages* of buying ready mixed glues?

6 Describe clearly the *proper* procedure for using impact glues. What are the dangers of using this type of glue?

7 Each solvent cement tends to be useful for only a small range of plastics. Tensol cement is designed for use on acrylics, and 'Airfix' modelling cement is intended only for polystyrene models. Why is each of these cements for such a small range of plastics? How many other cements can you identify in the shops? Note down the materials they work on. Which cement works with PVC? Can you find one that sticks polythene? If not, why do you think that is?

8 List the normal circumstances that will prevent you from getting a good solder joint between two pieces of copper.

CHOOSING THE RIGHT FINISH

Choosing the surface finish for a product is a decision that has to be made at the design stage. When you decide what material you are going to use to make the product, you automatically limit the range of finishes that are possible. It would be foolish to design something in one material and then at the last stage decide that you wanted a finish that could not be achieved in the material.

The first and critical decision, therefore, in thinking out the right surface finish, is to clarify the *function* or purpose of the finish. A kitchen work surface needs to be hard, scratch resistant, heat resistant and waterproof. No natural wood finishes can give this range of properties.

Selecting the right *material* is therefore the first task in getting the right surface finish for the product. However, the *type* of surface is also important. A smooth metal bar can be very slippery, but by putting a rough texture on it (for example by knurling) it can be made *non* slippery. Texture can easily be moulded into glass fibre surfaces or pressed into metal surfaces. Once the material and the type of surface has been selected there will still be an enormous range of possible surface finishes that can affect significantly the surface properties.

WOOD FINISHES

	VISUAL PROPERTIES				PHYSICAL PROPERTIES			
	NATURAL FEEL AND APPEARANCE	NATURAL APPEARANCE	COLOURING	APPLIED DESIGN	WATERPROOF	HEATPROOF	SCRATCH AND KNOCK RESISTANCE	
							LOW	HIGH
Seal and polish	▓							
Varnish		▓	▓		▓		▓	
Stain/dye			▓					
Paint			▓					
Cover completely (e.g. with plastic laminate)					▓	▓		▓

PREPARING THE SURFACE A sharp smoothing plane will give a flat, smooth surface to wood, which should then require very little further preparation. If the surface does need further smoothing, use a suitable grade of glasspaper wrapped around a cork block.

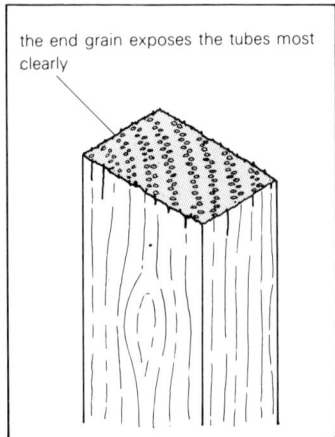

▼Fig. 74 The structure of wood is like a mass of tubes that must be sealed before any finish can be applied

the end grain exposes the tubes most clearly

Always glasspaper *with the grain*, as cross-grain scratches will be very difficult to remove. There is a range of grades of glasspaper: 0–1–1½–f2–M2. 0 is very fine and M2 is quite coarse. Normal wood can be finished satisfactorily with grades 1 and 1½.

SEALING THE GRAIN Wood is a natural material that reacts dramatically to its environment. In damp conditions it takes in moisture and swells up. In dry conditions it gives up this moisture and shrinks. This natural movement in wood is very difficult to stop but it can be reduced by preventing moisture from getting into the surface. This is called 'sealing the grain' of wood and it is an essential first step in most wood finishes. It is done in two ways:

1. By painting on a liquid cellulose sealer. In this liquid state the cellulose is dissolved in acetone. As the acetone evaporates away, the solid cellulose is left filling the pores of the surface.
2. By painting on a liquid that slowly turns into a solid plastic coating, for example, polyurethane varnishes.

A cellulose sealer is usually used as a base for wax polishes. It will not be waterproof, but it does bring out the natural beauty of the wood. Polyurethane varnishes do give a hard and waterproof surface, and as they can also be transparent they are very useful as a natural finish on wood that will receive hard treatment. Polyurethanes come in 'matt' or 'gloss' finishes and in ready mixed pots or two-part mixes.

COLOURING WOOD Wood can be coloured using dyes and paints. A dye is applied before the grain is sealed. It soaks into the grain, colouring the surface of the wood without hiding the grain. The surface of the wood must be sealed after the dye has been applied.

Paints completely hide the natural appearance of the wood. They are applied in at least two layers. The first layer is called a PRIMER paint. It seals the grain and provides a surface on which the next paint layer can grip. Further layers give hardness and colour to the surface. Most paints 'dry' by turning into plastic films through reaction with the air. Emulsion paints can be thinned with water and although they dry quickly they do not give a very hard surface. They give a matt or silk finish. Oil and polyurethane based paints cannot be thinned with water. They require special chemical thinners. They dry much more slowly but they do give a hard and tough surface in either a matt or gloss finish.

METAL FINISHES

	VISUAL PROPERTIES				PHYSICAL PROPERTIES			
	NATURAL APPEARANCE	SURFACE REACTION COLOURING	APPLIED COLOURING	APPLIED DESIGN	OXIDISING RESISTANCE LOW	HIGH	SCRATCH RESISTANCE (LOW)	(HIGH)
Polish	█							
Lacquer	█				█			
Chemical colouring		█						
Paint			█			█	█	
Plastic coat			█			█		█
Enamel			█			█		█
Electroplating						█		
Etching				█				
Anodizing (Al)			█	█		█		
Blueing (steel)		█			█			
Sand-blasting	█			█				

PREPARING THE SURFACE As with wood, the first stage of the finishing process is to give a smooth surface to the metal, removing scratches, dents and file marks. With steel this usually involves fine filing and the use of various grades of emery cloth. With non-ferrous metals (like copper and brass) fine files can be followed by wet or dry waterproof abrasive paper, which gives a very smooth and even surface.

Once the surface is properly prepared there are five different approaches that you can use to finish it.

1. Bring out the natural colour by polishing.
2. Paint or lacquer the surface.
3. Remove parts of the surface either physically (by sandblasting) or chemically (by etching).
4. Chemical colouring.
5. Coat the surface with solids (by electroplating, enamelling etc.).

▼Fig. 75 In which direction does the wood swell and shrink most?

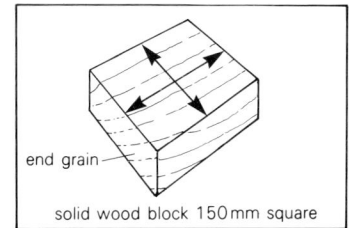

end grain

solid wood block 150 mm square

1. **POLISHING** can be done by hand or on a buffing wheel. The principle is the same in either case. Polishes contain grades of abrasive grit either in a liquid (for hand use) or in a wax block (for buffing wheels). By rubbing the metal with progressively finer grits you gradually get a highly polished and shiny finish.

2. Transparent **LACQUERS** can be used to preserve the high finish on metal surfaces. They are usually a solution of cellulose and they dry very quickly. They can be brushed or sprayed on the metal. They do give some protection from oxidation of the surface (rusting or tarnishing) but very little scratch resistance. PAINTS completely hide the natural appearance of the metal but do give good protection both from oxidation and from scratching. They give a wide variety of colours and can be brushed or sprayed on. The first paint layer must be a primer to give good surface grip to the later layers.

Questions

1 When trying to get a smooth, flat surface with glasspaper, why do we wrap the glasspaper round a cork block instead of just using it with our fingers? Why is the block made of cork?

2 Wood does not swell up and shrink equally in all directions. Design a simple experiment to find out in which direction most of the movement occurs. Is it along the grain or across the grain? Can you work out the percentage increase or decrease in size? Try your experiment on a similar piece of wood that has been properly varnished. Do you get the same amount of movement? **x**

3 It is the intake of moisture that causes the swelling. Which room in your house would you expect to cause most movement in natural wood?

4 What finish would you use for the following products:
(a) a baby's wooden building bricks,
(b) a front door for a house,
(c) a wooden desk top,
(d) a hanging mobile made of thin plywood pieces?
In each case explain the function of the finish and all the reasons for your final choice of finish.

5 Why do wood dyes not 'seal' the grain when they are applied to timber?

3. **ETCHING** uses chemicals to attack a metal surface. Copper can be etched by dipping it in a bath of dilute nitric acid or ferric chloride solution. The value of etching is in the patterns or pictures that can be etched into a highly polished surface. It can only be effective if the etching can be done in carefully defined areas. This is done by coating the whole surface in an acid resistant material (usually a wax or bitumen) and then scratching through the wax where you want the acid to eat into the surface. The longer you leave the metal in the acid, the deeper it will eat into the metal. Don't forget that it will eat in from *both* sides, so coat the back of the metal with wax as well.

Etching leaves a slightly textured surface which will allow the pattern or picture to stand out against a highly polished surface. It is also possible to eat away the surface by SANDBLASTING it, that is by spraying the surface with a blast of fine sand. The sand cuts into the surface leaving a fine textured finish. It is important to start with a well polished surface all over, then some areas can be masked off with masking tape. If you blast the whole surface, when the tape is removed the pattern will be cut into the polished surface. With both etching and sandblasting the surface must be protected by lacquering.

4. **CHEMICAL REACTIONS** can be used to colour highly polished metal surfaces. When polished steel is heated in air, the steel reacts with oxygen to form an oxide film. This film goes through a range of colours from pale yellow to bluey-purple. The hotter the metal gets, the thicker the oxide gets. Thin films appear yellow and thick films appear blue. It is possible to hold the blue colour on the surface by quenching the metal in cold water as the colour appears. This is called 'blueing' and it gives a little protection from rusting. Highly polished copper can be coloured by dipping into certain solutions. For example, hot copper sulphate solution gives copper a matt, purple-brown coating and a hot solution containing iron nitrate and sodium thiosulphate gives copper a semi-gloss black coating. These coatings require lacquering to protect them.

Aluminium can be very brightly coloured by a process called ANODISING. When a direct electric current is passed through dilute sulphuric acid, oxygen is produced at the anode and hydrogen at the cathode. If an aluminium object is made the anode in such a set up, the oxygen given off combines with the aluminium to give a tough aluminium oxide film that is firmly attached to the aluminium. This oxide film is white and porous. It

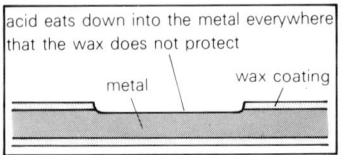

▼Fig. 76 By using the wax coating you can etch patterns into the surface of the metal

▼Fig. 77 'Anodising' aluminium can make it possible to colour the metal very brightly

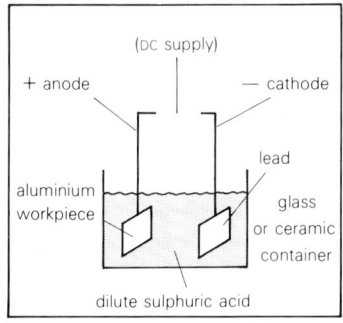

▼Fig. 78 Copper plating can be done simply in the workshops

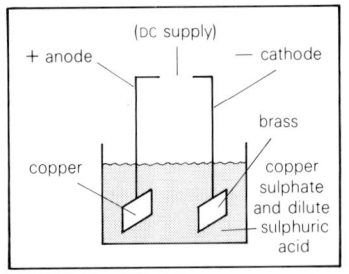

will absorb coloured dye, so the aluminium object may be coloured by placing it in a boiling dye solution. Once again, the coloured surface will need lacquering.

5. **ELECTROPLATING** involves covering one metal with a thin film of another metal. You can electroplate copper onto brass using the apparatus in fig. 78. When a direct current flows between the electrodes, copper comes off the positive electrode (anode) and into the solution and from the solution onto the negative electrode (cathode), the brass. The copper skin is chemically bonded onto the brass. In a similar way, copper and brass can be silver plated to make them look better and more expensive. Unfortunately the solutions used are too poisonous to be used in schools.

▼Fig. 79 Silver containers can be decorated by etching and by enamelling

ENAMELLING is a process of fusing coloured glass onto the surface of metal. In schools this is a purely decorative technique. The coloured glass can be bought in powder form. It is sprinkled on the prepared metal and placed in an oven. At about 750°C the powder will melt and flow over the surface. When cool, the metal will have a smooth, hard, glass coating. The range of colours is enormous. To create patterns in enamel it is necessary to create small reservoirs on the surface so that different colours of the melting glass can be contained in particular areas. This is done in two ways:

(a) by *etching* a reservoir down into the surface (the champlevé technique),

(b) by soldering wire onto the surface (the cloisonné technique).

COATING METALS WITH PLASTIC can be useful for several reasons. It protects the metal from oxidation and gives it a much softer feel – useful, for example, in making handles. Industrially it can be used to give a very scratch resistant coating, but this protection will of course depend on what plastic is used. Whilst nylon or epoxy coats can be used industrially to give very resistant properties, in schools it is normal to have only polyethylene coating facilities. This is a soft thermoplastic material which melts at about 160°C. The process involves dipping the heated metal (180°C) into a pot of polythene powder. The powder melts on and sticks to the metal. To make sure that the coating is even all over, it is best to 'fluidise' the powder by passing air through it. This will create a cloud of powder into which the hot metal workpiece can be dipped (fig. 82). The process is often called 'dip-coating'.

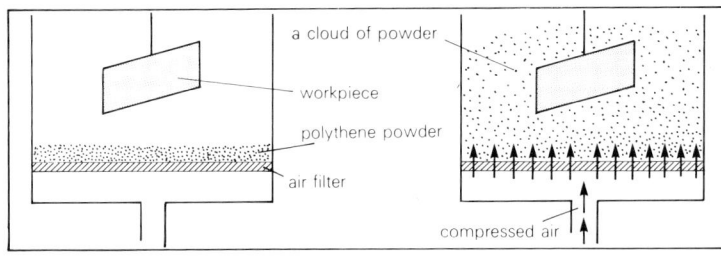

PLASTIC FINISHES

	VISUAL PROPERTIES			PHYSICAL PROPERTIES
	NATURAL APPEARANCE	APPLIED COLOUR	APPLIED DESIGN	SCRATCH RESISTANCE (LOW)
Polish	▓			
Dye		▓		
Paint		▓	▓	
Sandblasting	▓		▓	

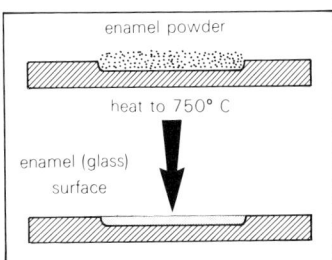

▼Fig. 80 The champlevé technique

enamel powder

heat to 750° C

enamel (glass) surface

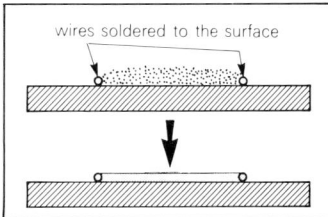

▼Fig. 81 The cloisonné technique

wires soldered to the surface

◄Fig. 82 The compressed air 'fluidises' the powder into a fine cloud

The range of finishes available for plastics is very much more limited. The finishes that can be used are identical to some of the metal finishes, that is, polishing, painting and sandblasting. The procedures are exactly the same as for metal. It is also possible however, to dye transparent plastic sheet (acrylics or polystyrenes) with water-based dyes. If a piece of transparent sheet is left in a strong mix of dye for a few minutes, the dye will penetrate minutely into the surface. The effect will be to give a delicate shade of that colour to the sheet. It will be transparent, but will be like looking through tinted glass.

Questions

1 Suggest a reason why steel or copper cannot be anodised.   x

2 Use the tables on pages 126, 127 and 129 to decide on finishes for the following items. State clearly the reasons for your choice of finish.

(a) Brass handle on a chest of drawers.

(b) Aluminium handles on a wardrobe door.

(c) Wooden bannister rail.

(d) Collapsable picnic table top made of plywood.

(e) Softwood wheels on a pull-along toy.   c

3 How does lacquer on a shiny metal surface prevent corrosion?

4 What might happen if a metal is left in etching solution for too long?

5 Why can't copper be blued in the same way as steel?

6 Explain the difference between anodising and electroplating.   c

7 When you sandblast metal surfaces you get an even textured finish. What happens if you sandblast a wooden surface? Try it on a small sample and then explain the result.   x

8 Why is the process of colouring aluminium (by dyeing the oxide film) called anodising?

9 When you enamel copper, you put a fine layer of coloured glass over the surface. What would you expect to happen if you then bent the copper?

10 Use the chart on page 127 to answer the following questions.

(a) What choices do you have if you want to apply a design to some aluminium earings cut out of an aluminium sheet?

(b) What can you do to give high oxidising resistance (i.e. good non-rusting properties) to a piece of mild steel? What choices do you have if you want to keep a metallic surface?   c

EVALUATION

There are three areas that must be investigated when evaluating something that has been designed and made. Firstly, we have to find out if it works well and if it can be made to work better. This is called FUNCTION EVALUATION. Secondly, we have to find out if it has a pleasing appearance and if its appearance can be improved. This is called AESTHETIC EVALUATION. Thirdly, we have to find out if it meets any economic requirements that were present in the design brief, for example, it must not cost more than a certain amount to produce, or it must be produced in a certain time. This is called ECONOMIC EVALUATION. It is very difficult to separate these three from one another.

FUNCTION EVALUATION

One way to find out if something works well or not is to ask the people who use it. It is easy to get confused about exactly who to ask. Looking at fig. 1 should help you to sort this out. In part A the designer, maker, client and user are all the same person. This is the case when you design and make something for yourself. So you can ask yourself a range of questions about whatever you have designed and made. Questions about how well something works usually lead on to questions about whether the item can be altered in any way to make it work better. This second stage of

questioning is very important if any improvements are to be built into future versions of the design.

It is quite possible that you will design and make something for somebody else. This is the case in parts B and C of fig. 1. In part B the person who asks you to do the designing, the client, is also the person who uses the item when it is made, the user. Another example would be if you designed and made an aid for a handicapped friend. In such a case you can ask the user what he or she thinks of the item and the way it works. Of course, they may just be being polite when they tell you it works well, so it is important to check this by observing them using it. If they don't ever seem to use what you have made this could be a strong hint about how good it is!

In category C of fig. 1, the client and the user are not the same person. It is sometimes easy to forget this and ask the client what he thinks of the design instead of asking the user. (Remember the warden of the swimming pool in chapter 2?) Again, observation of the item in use is an important way of finding out if it works and could be improved.

The final category in fig. 1 describes the situation where the designer, maker, client and user are completely different people. This is usually the case for items that are mass produced, for example, 'off-the-peg' clothes, items that are used by the general public such as telephone kiosks and items that are extremely complex such as television sets. As with all the other categories, observation of the item in use as well as questioning the users is an important way of evaluating how well the item works and if it

▼Fig. 1 Designer – maker – client – user. Which is which?

A Designer, Maker, Client, User are all the same person – Sue

B John is the Designer-Maker Gran is the Client-User

C Alison is the Designer–Maker The vicar is the Client The congregation is the User

D Designer, Maker, Client and User are all different people

can be improved.

When lots of people use an item it is important to get more than one opinion about how good it is. It is very time consuming and difficult to question a lot of people personally, so questionnaires have to be used. It is important that such questionnaires are written clearly and the results they give are analysed carefully if the information they provide is to be valid.

AESTHETIC EVALUATION

We all see things around us everyday that do not seem to have a great deal of practical use, such as fashion accessories, or have no practical use at all, such as jewellery. Things like this are designed primarily to have visual appeal, and although the wearer will be conscious of how the objects look, it is other people on whom they will have maximum impact. It is very difficult to draw up a list of criteria by which to judge the appearance of something, especially items like those just listed. Whether they appear ugly or beautiful is governed not only by their actual appearance but also by the values of taste and fashion prevailing at the time. So when you try to evaluate the appearance of something you will be attempting to do something that depends on many variables.

Perhaps the first thing to establish is that the decorative features in the design do not in any way interfere with the function. For example, imagine that it is possible to carve chess pieces from a material that comes in two distinct and beautiful colours, but that on ageing the material becomes so slippery that the pieces are impossible to hold. The beautiful colour of the pieces cannot be denied, but the slippery nature of the material makes it useless for items that have to be handled with precision.

Once you have established that the appearance of an item does not impair its proper functioning, then you should be able to say whether you like its appearance or not *and give reasons*. Look at the photographs of two chairs in fig. 2. Surrounding the chairs is a range of adjectives. For each chair, pick at least five words which you think describe the chair. Now use your lists of words to explain why you like or dislike each chair. For any object you should be able to think up lists of words to describe the shape or form and the appearance of the surface – its texture, pattern and colour. You can then use these lists to explain your likes and dislikes.

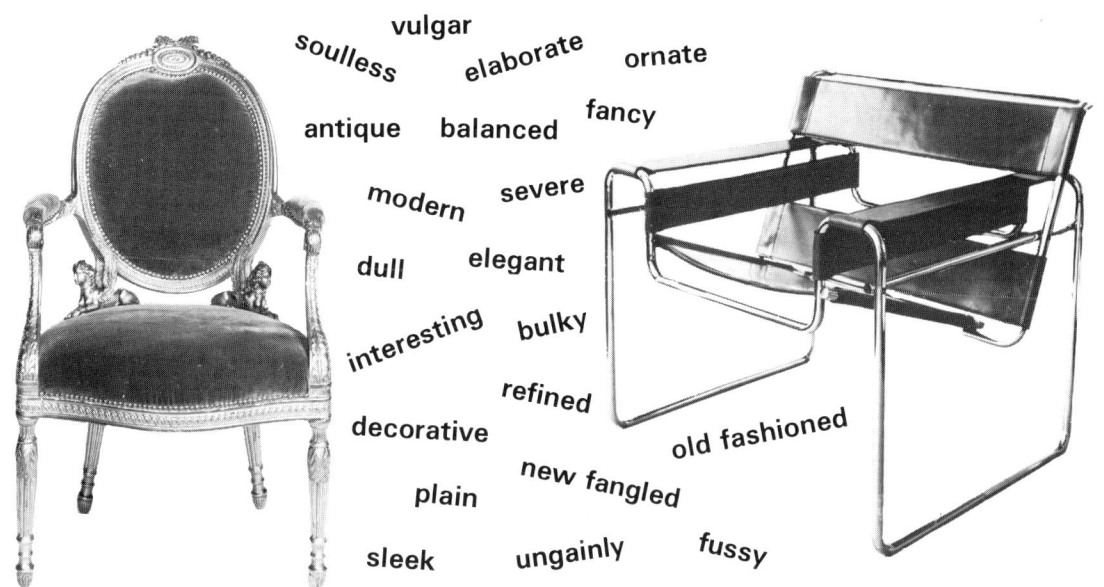

▲Fig. 2 Which words will you use to describe the chairs?

ECONOMIC EVALUATION

In all design briefs there will be cost requirements to be met. So it is important to think about costing from the beginning of the design process. If you are designing and making something for yourself, you will have to take into account your own financial resources. Remember you may have to buy more than just materials; you may need services. Any process you can't carry out yourself you will have to pay someone else to do for you – sandblasting a pattern onto the surface of a glass topped table for instance. If you are designing and making something for somebody else, you will have to be clear on the amount of money available for the design. This money will have to cover all parts of the design process; you can spend quite a lot on materials for models and mock-ups before you decide upon and purchase materials with which to build the chosen solution. Again, you will have to take into account any services you are forced to buy in.

Professional designers may work as individual freelance designers or as part of a design consultancy group. A breakdown of the fees charged by a design consultancy for developing the design of a hairdryer is shown in fig. 3. A large firm will have its own design department and the financial directors of the firm will allocate a budget to the design department, within which it will have to operate. A breakdown of the funding received by the design department of a large chain store is shown in fig. 4.

▼Fig. 3 Fees charged by a design consultancy for developing the design of a hairdryer

These will depend on the size of the consultancy, where it is based and which staff are involved in developing the design.

A large London-based consultancy fee for developing the design of a hairdryer might look like this:

Time spent	By whom	Chargeable hourly rate	Cost
10 hours	Senior Designer	£33.00	£330.00
40 hours	Designer	£24.00	£1060.00
10 hours	Junior Designer	£14.00	£140.00
		TOTAL COST	£1530.00

The fees charged by a small out-of-London consultancy for developing the same design might look like this:

Time spent	By whom	Chargeable hourly rate	Cost
10 hours	Senior Designer	£18.00	£180.00
50 hours	Designer	£12.00	£600.00
		TOTAL COST	£780.00

In some situations there is the added complication that the design, once agreed with the client, has to be produced within a specified time. This is usually negotiated by the client with who-ever is responsible for making the design. In some cases, for example, a small furniture manufacturer, the designer may be directly involved in the making, but in most cases a manufacturer

▼Fig. 4 A design department's budget

The example taken here refers to a medium sized design department of a large chain store. The department is concerned mainly with designing packaging and signs.

Position	Annual Salary	Annual Cost
Senior Designer	One at £13 000	£13 000
Designers	Two at £10 000	£20 000
Junior Designers	Three at £7000	£21 000
Assistants	Two at £4500	£9000
Consummable budget		£4000
Specialist services bought in as required		£3000
	TOTAL	£70 000

agrees with the client the time by which the items must be produced. Failure to meet these agreed deadlines can result in large losses if the agreement included a clause stating 'genuine pre-estimate of losses'. For example, a manufacturer might agree to supply swimwear for the summer season to a large chain store by the beginning of May. The agreement could read, 'The manu-facturer shall pay £300 per day for each day the order is overdue, this sum being a genuine pre-estimate of the loss incurred and not by way of a penalty'. How does the client, in this case the chain store, calculate the pre-estimate of loss?

In situations where very complex projects are being under-taken, for example, the development of an oil rig, there will be many thousands of complex design projects. To support such ventures the clients must make large amounts of money available to designers and manufacturers well in advance of any possible return. This amount of investment in advance is only possible through loans from governments and large banks to the client. Such loans are always at certain interest rates; that means the borrower has to pay back what he borrowed plus a percentage. The financial arrangements are very complex and it may take several years before a client is in a position to start paying back the initial loan. (In the design and manufacture of an oil rig, who is the client and who is the user?) Small businesses too, often need investment capital monies and in Great Britain there are government schemes to provide such loans.

Any improvements indicated by function and aesthetic evaluation must be viewed in the light of their possible economic consequences. For example, it might be possible to improve the sensitivity of the control and the appearance of a gas cooker by changing the design of the control knobs. The capital cost of acquiring the machinery to produce new knobs might be so great that the cost of the cooker becomes greater than most people are prepared to pay. In this case it would be unwise to carry out the functional and aesthetic improvements recommended by the evaluation.

▼Fig. 5 Telephone receivers – which do you think looks best?

Questions

1 For each of the following items, write down which person or groups of people are likely to be the maker, designer, client and user:
(a) a homemade kitchen cabinet,
(b) a 'one-off' piece of expensive jewellery,
(c) off-the-peg clothes,
(d) an electronic calculator.

2 Draw up a questionnaire that you would use to evaluate the functioning of a post box, a TV set and a house.

3 For the following items, list those functions that decorative features must not interfere with: chess pieces, lamp shade, skirt, trousers, bed, cutlery, chair, chest of drawers.

4 Look at the photographs of telephone receivers in fig. 5. They all work extremely well. The electromagnetic devices within them, the microphone and the receiver, are identical. Put them in order of visual appearance, from best to worst. List the ways in which their appearance might interfere with their function. **c**

5 What could the manufacturers of gas cookers (see above) do to make the inclusion of the new design of control knobs possible? **c**

6 The government runs schemes to help small businesses, providing both money and expert design assistance. Find out more about these from The Design Council, The Department of Industry and the Local Chamber of Commerce. **o**

FIVE

SOLVING THE EXAMINATION PROBLEM

Examinations in design are different from most other examinations. There are no right or wrong answers to design problems, only better or less good solutions. So taking a design examination is very like doing a design project, but in a very limited time.

It is essential to use the same overall approach in the design examination as you would in a design project, but because time is shorter there is no chance to carry out specific research. However, some examination boards tell candidates the general area of the design problems that will appear in the written papers, so background research can be carried out in advance. There are other examinations where no preparation is expected. However the design problems are usually associated with clear areas of a technology syllabus such as *structures*, *mechanisms*, *electronics*, *energy* and *hydraulics*. Be sure that you know what sort of design examination you will be faced with. Your teacher will have the details.

Nearly all design examination questions require the following parts in the answer:

1. An analysis of the design brief which reveals the critical factors. It is important to state even the most obvious points as they will be important in avoiding silly design errors.
2. An exploration of ideas in which two or three possible solutions are presented as brief sketches with notes to show how they take the critical factors into account.
3. A choice of final solution; perhaps one of those already presented or a further development. It is essential to state the reasons for your choice clearly.
4. (a) A more detailed description of the final solution. In the shorter examination papers (2 hours), high quality working drawings are not required, but a clear sketch in which dimensions and materials are noted is essential. The details of the solution can be filled in with supporting notes and sketches.
(b) In longer examinations (5 hours) where at a later stage, you have to actually make the solution you design, a scale working drawing *is* needed, complete with parts list and material specification.

As you can see, there is a lot to complete in a short time so it is important that you plan your use of time. In this way you will not spend too long on the beginning parts and then have to rush the later stages. On the other hand, it is important to spend sufficient time at the beginning, otherwise the solution you arrive at will be a poor one.

▼Fig. 1 Instructions to candidates for a 2 hour design paper of a technology examination

7878/2   **Wednesday, 22 June**

TECHNOLOGY, PAPER 2

Time allowed: 2 hours
Maximum mark **60**

Each candidate must be given:
(1) one copy of this question paper, 7878/2;
(2) two sheets of drawing paper (DP/TECH).

Item (2) is sent with the stationery parcel.

Instructions to candidates

Answer one *question.*

Write your name, index number, centre name, and number of this paper, **7878/2,** *on each sheet of paper in the space provided.*

Answers may be provided in any visual form, for example: working drawings, orthographic projection, sketches, pictorial isometric, circuit diagrams, block diagrams, flow diagrams and graphs.

Evidence should be presented of several solutions to a problem. **Credit will be given for sketches of alternative designs.**

Final solutions should be as detailed as possible, giving specifications and listing components, materials and fixings needed to solve the problem.

▶Fig. 2 A possible marking scheme for a 2 hour text design paper of a technology examination

ALLOCATION OF MARKS

For each question, marks should be awarded in the following areas:

Preliminary ideas showing appreciation of the problem with sketch solutions	15 marks
Quality and clarity	5 marks
Main solution	30 marks
Quality	10 marks

Figure 1 shows the instructions to candidates for the 2 hour design paper of a technology examination. Figure 2 shows the marking scheme. Notice how *one third* of the marks go towards the development of alternative solutions. Figure 3 shows the instructions to candidates for a 5 hour craft, design and technology examination. Figure 4 shows the marking scheme for this examination. In this case *half* the marks go towards the development of alternative solutions. Also notice how in both cases marks are awarded for high-quality visual communication. Note that marking schemes in actual examinations may differ from those suggested here.

On the following pages are some examples of students' examination answers. Answers along these lines all obtained high marks in the O level examination. Read them carefully and note the comments and queries.

At the end of the chapter are questions from past papers. Discuss them with your teacher and use them for practice.

▼Fig. 3 Instructions to candidates for a 5 hour craft, design and technology examination

7879/2

CRAFT, DESIGN AND TECHNOLOGY
PAPER 2

Time allowed: 5 hours
Two sessions, each of 2½ hours

Each candidate must be given:
(1) one copy of this question paper, 7879/2;
(2) drawing paper *DP/TECH*
2 sheets for the first session;
1 sheet for the second session.

NOTE : For the first examination session on Friday, 27 November, you may refer to the work you have prepared previously.

For the examination period on Friday, 4 December, you will only be allowed to have the designs you have prepared in the first examination session.

Candidates who choose to colour their work should not use red.

7879/2 (Preliminary sheet)

CRAFT, DESIGN AND TECHNOLOGY
PAPER 2 (P)

Each candidate must be issued with one copy of this preliminary information as soon as this packet is received at the school.

The area for study is design in relation to one-room accommodation with particular reference to the single person.

Candidates are to study the design problems associated with storage, working, relaxing, and sleeping in defined, restricted space. In addition, candidates are to study the general design problems implicit in the area of study. Some of these are given in a study guide which is printed on page 2.

This preparatory work may be taken into the examination room for the first examination session on Friday, 27 November, but must not be taken into the second examination session on Friday, 4 December.

The work must be available for the external examiner when he visits the school.

MARKING TEMPLATE		SECOND PAPER	
FIRST PAPER		Outline drawing	20
Design requirements	8	details	8
Ideas (3 × 6)	18	Parts list	6
Ideas, development	6	Dimensioning	4
Visual communication	8	Scale	2
Maximum total	40	Maximum total	40

◀Fig. 4 A possible marking scheme for a 5 hour craft, design and technology examination

EXAMPLE 1

During the course of maintenance and repair of machinery, an engineer may inadvertently drop a small component into an inaccessible position. Design a tool which could be used to retrieve such a small component which would not exceed 30 mm in length, 20 mm in diameter and 200 g in mass.

Oxford Local Examinations Summer 1983 Technology Paper 2
Time allowed 2 hours

---

6. Design of tool to retrieve small components dropped by an engineer during the course of repair on machinery.

SPECIFICATION:
Retrieve object of : 30mm long, 20mm diameter, 200g mass

1. The tool must be corrosion resistant.
2. It must be easily handled.
3. Lightweight
4. Strong
5. It must be able to be used in small confined spaces.
6. It must be capable of reaching a fair distance - 2m.
7. It must be able to pick up or deposit small components easily.
8. These components must not be damaged in any way.
9. The tool must need no maintenance and be long lasting.

The third solution was chosen because it is the most efficient and meets the specification better than the rest.
It is a better construction

MATERIALS USED AND PROPERTIES OF EACH

TUBE - The tube is round and has a diameter of 38mm externally and 30mm internally. It is 2m long. It is made of aluminium which can be extruded into this shape easily. Aluminium is corrosion resistant and lightweight. It is also strong enough for the job. It has a nice rich dull silver coloured finish.

HANDLE - The handle is 100cm long 20mm wide and 10mm thick. It is attached to the tube by a steel bolt. The handle is made out of aluminium which is lightweight, strong and corrosion resistant.

TRIGGER - This is the device which pulls the wire. The first finger fits the hole and pulls. The hole is 30mm diameter internally and 43mm diameter externally. On top of the hole is a tube which runs along a guide rail, this tube has the wire attached to it. The guide rail is 90mm and 5mm in diameter. It is attached to the tube at both ends by bolts. It is made of aluminium the same as the trigger.
A spring will return the trigger so the wire is kept taut and the operator knows when the grippers are open or closed.

GRIPPER - These are hinged. One is attached to the tube with bolts and is 195mm long with a pad made of soft rubber on one end. The pad is the same thickness as the gripper arm. This arm has a hinge - consisting of a rivet at 170mm from its end.
The second gripper arm is the same at the pad end but it is a differently shaped arm.
It is bent by 20° 45mm from the end pad. Here it has the hinge through it and this part is 115mm long, ending in a second hinge.
Attached to the second hinge is a small piece of metal with the wire attached.
A piece of spring steel holds open the gripper arms. They are made out of aluminium for its lightness, strength and resistance to corrosion. The hinge is steel, the pads are rubber pads. If they wear away they can be replaced easily. They are glued in place.

WIRE - this is steel wire of 3mm in diameter attached at both ends by a bolt.

EXAMPLE 1

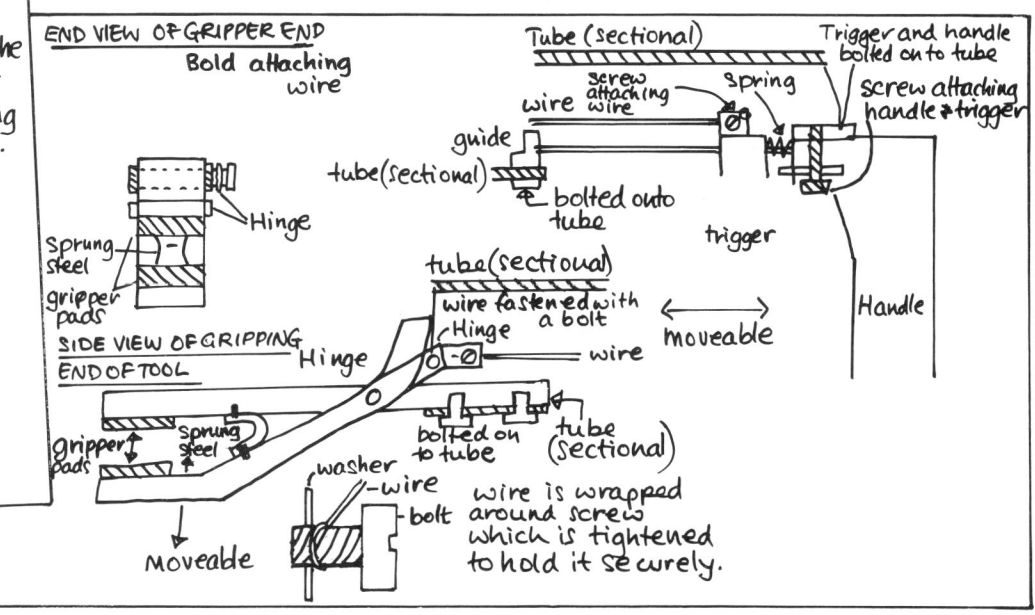

METHOD OF OPERATION

The tool is held with one hand on the trigger and handle while the other hand can steady or guide it.
The tool can be positioned above the object to be retrieved. When the trigger is pulled the wire pulls the moveable gripper arm against its opposing spring steel. The grippers close on the object gripping it with its soft rubber pads. The object can then be removed easily.

DISADVANTAGES

Unfortunately the tube cannot bend around corners and so this device cannot retrieve objects which have fallen out of sight. However objects which have fallen out of sight are very difficult to retrieve.

SKETCHES OF ALTERNATIVE DESIGNS

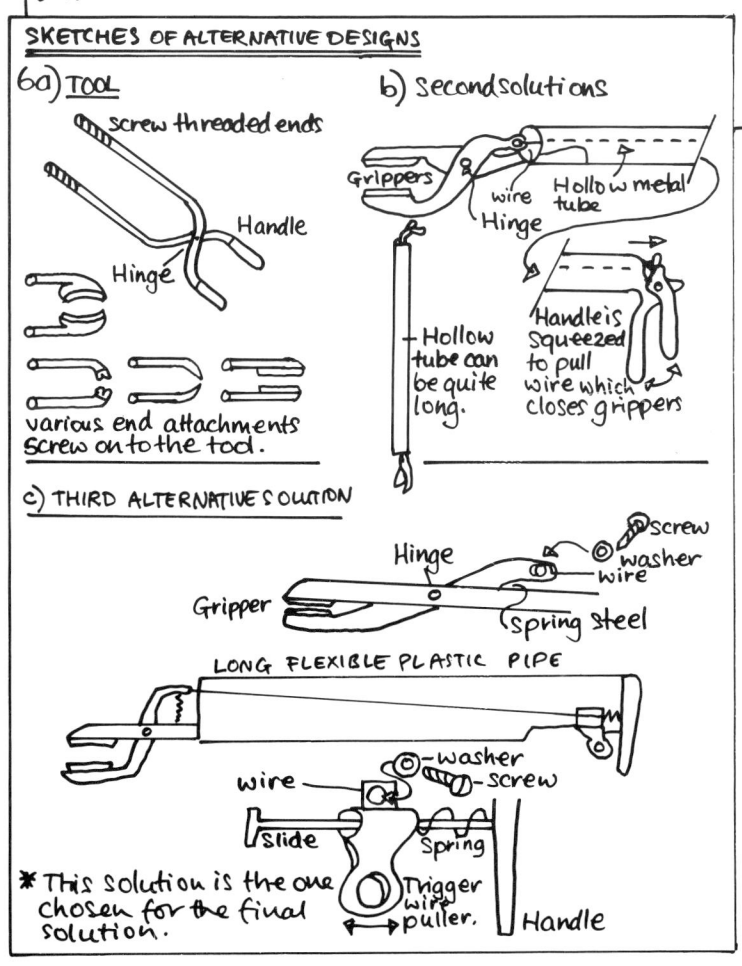

6 a) TOOL
screw threaded ends
Handle
Hinge
various end attachments screw onto the tool.

b) second solutions
Grippers
wire
Hinge
Hollow metal tube
Hollow tube can be quite long.
Handle is squeezed to pull wire which closes grippers

c) THIRD ALTERNATIVE SOLUTION
Hinge
Gripper
screw
washer
wire
spring steel
LONG FLEXIBLE PLASTIC PIPE
wire
slide
washer
screw
spring
Trigger wire puller.
Handle
✱ This solution is the one chosen for the final solution.

Comments

1. The student has presented a clear analysis of the requirements the tool must meet.
2. He has presented three alternative solutions with explanatory notes.
3. He has stated the chosen solution with reasons.
4. The sketches of the final solution are more detailed than the preliminary sketches.
5. The student has explained his choice of materials.
6. He has given size details.
7. He has shown that he understands how the tool will be used.

Questions

1 How could the shape of the movable gripping arm be improved to give more grip? c

2 What materials other than aluminium could be used for (a) the tube (b) the trigger (c) the gripper? c

3 Can you think of any other ways in which the final design could be improved?

EXAMPLE 2

At an athletics meeting, a race organiser needs to know which runners in sprint races cause false starts by leaving their starting blocks before the starting pistol is fired. Design a device to be fitted to the starting block, together with additional circuitry, which will allow the organiser to monitor from a central console which runners have started too soon. Assume that the firing of a starting pistol provides a suitable electrical switching signal.

Oxford Local Examinations Summer 1983 Technology
Paper 2 Time allowed 2 hours

Question 5

BASIC REQUIREMENTS

① A device to sense the presence of a foot on a starting block.
② This device must not be too bulky.
③ The starting blocks will need to be adjusted.
④ The sensor, if placed under the foot, would need to be able to withstand the pressure of the runner pushing off the block without breaking.
⑤ The device must be hard to fool, i.e. make it hard to cheat.
⑥ The device must be sensitive enough and quick enough to judge if a person has left the blocks too quickly, as the time gap may be very small.

CONSOLE

① To tell quickly when there has been a false start.
② Include an audible device.
③ Tell the organiser which lane was being naughty.
④ Easily reset.
⑤ Ignore signals from the blocks after the gun has been fired.

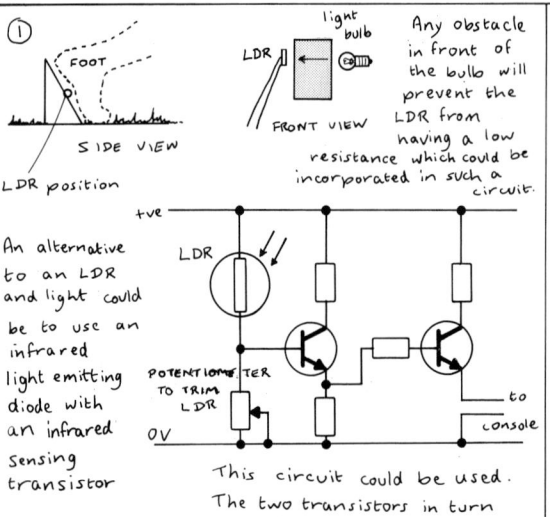

① An alternative to an LDR and light could be to use an infrared light emitting diode with an infrared sensing transistor

Any obstacle in front of the bulb will prevent the LDR from having a low resistance which could be incorporated in such a circuit.

This circuit could be used. The two transistors in turn amplify the sensitivity of the sensor.

AGAINSTS – The LDR takes a long time to react to the light changes
– Easily fooled with a piece of mud etc. over the LDR.

SENSORS

Candidates:
① Light and LDR
② Switch
③ Pressure pad

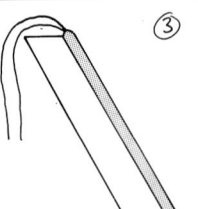

③ The pressure pad design would include a kind of mat, similar to those for security systems, to be placed over the block. This design would give the runner the full area of the block, although the pad might feel a bit spongy, and 'give' too much when pushing off from the block.

These types of pad are not very reliable or sensitive to pressure changes quickly enough. They may work all right for someone standing on them with all their weight, but may not work so well for someone getting off. The pad would not stop block being adjusted to different people's sizes.

② a rubber layer over the metal, not only improving friction but also covering switch. Note the bulb over the switch. This is so that the rubber does not hold the switch down.

The inclusion of a switch inside the block could also be used, but not so strong as to inhibit the athlete.

switch mounted inside the block. The switch must be small enough so that the pressure on the block is reasonably equal.

POSSIBLE SWITCH DESIGNS

i) microswitch – very sensitive; fragile; expensive; good quality

2) Normal push button – very sturdy and robust; not such good quality

Whichever type is used it would be a non-latching SPST switch. The switch would need to be high enough, and have a big enough movement so that 'twitches' of feet would not be noticed.

Advantages : very positive sensing; very simple; reliable; foolproof

NOTE
There would have to be a sensor for each foot on the blocks.

EXAMPLE 2

The main console will be made with electronic components. There are 2 possible ways of doing it.
① Using digital electronics e.g. CMOS or TTL series
② Using normal transistors and other discrete components.

The following design is going to use digital electronics, as
1) it is very simple to use
2) cheap
3) fast
4) available

METHODS OF TELLING ORGANISER
THE INFORMATION

① LEDs
② Lights
③ Sound

I am using LEDs as they are cheap, do not break easily and are very suitable for use with digital circuits

DIGITAL ELECTRONIC STATES

HI = 5V = a binary 1 — if uncorrected a digital input will assume a high state

LO = 0V = a binary 0

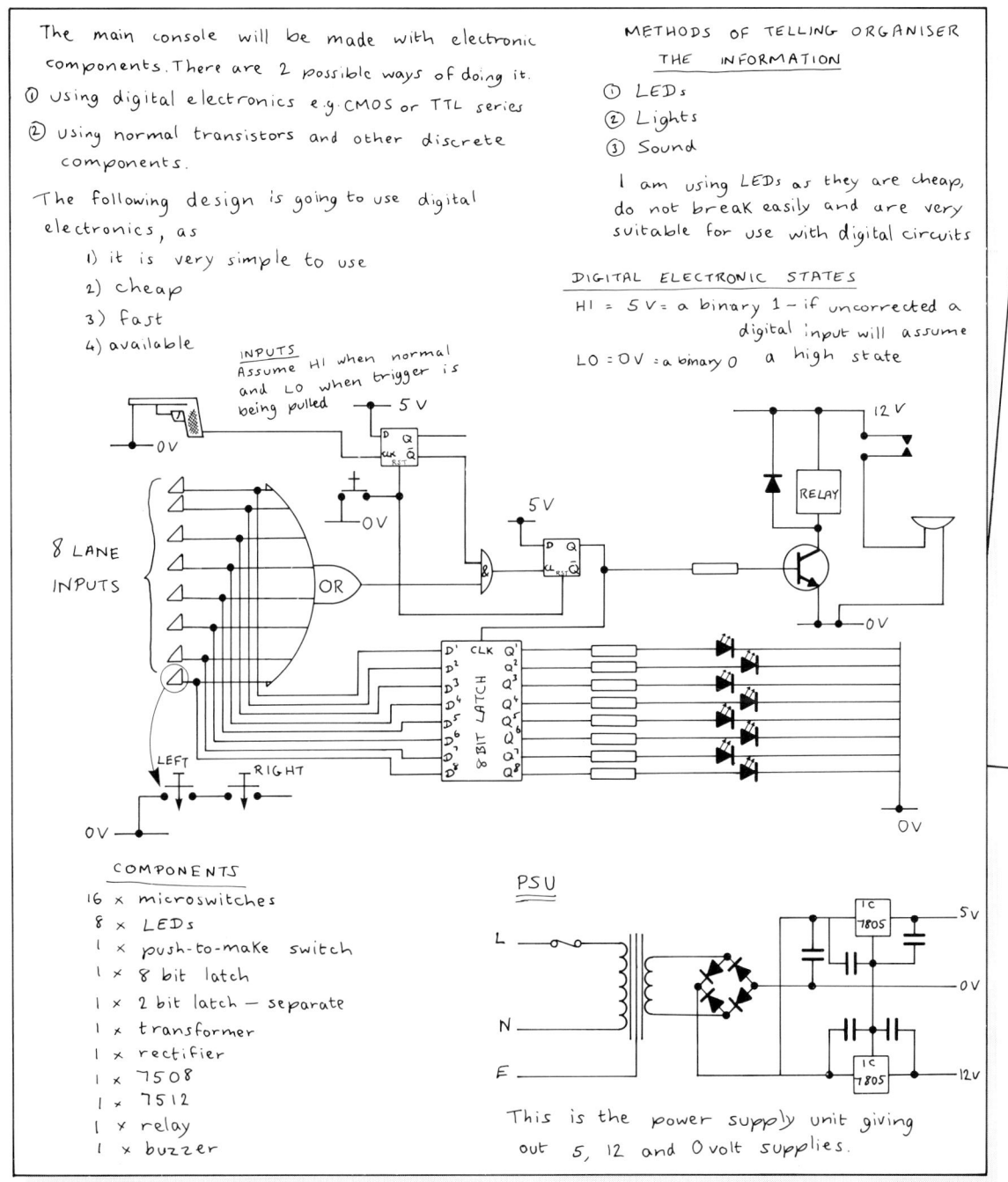

INPUTS
Assume HI when normal and LO when trigger is being pulled

8 LANE INPUTS

OR

D CLK Q

LEFT   RIGHT

0V

D¹ CLK Q¹
D² Q²
D³ Q³
D⁴ Q⁴
D⁵ Q⁵
D⁶ Q⁶
D⁷ Q⁷
D⁸ Q⁸
8 BIT LATCH

5V

D Q

RELAY

12V

0V

0V

COMPONENTS
16 × microswitches
8 × LEDs
1 × push-to-make switch
1 × 8 bit latch
1 × 2 bit latch — separate
1 × transformer
1 × rectifier
1 × 7508
1 × 7512
1 × relay
1 × buzzer

PSU

L

N

E

IC 7805 — 5V

0V

IC 7805 — 12V

This is the power supply unit giving out 5, 12 and 0 volt supplies.

THE FINAL DESIGN USES THE SWITCHES IN THE BLOCKS
These will give a high signal if there is no foot on them and a low signal if there is. The switches are the micro sort.

When the gun is fired, it clocks the first latch which gives an output of Ø at $\bar{Q}$: if at that instant or afterwords the system will not be activated because one of the inputs to the AND gate is a Ø.

IN₁	IN₂	OUT
0	0	0
0	1	0
1	0	0
1	1	1

AND gate truth table

If before the gun is triggered, and after the reset button has been pressed, one of the switches is released, the OR gate gives a high output because one of the inputs is high. The AND gate will go high, clocking the next latch. This will activate, via its output and a transistor, a relay which enables the audible warning device which could signal to the runners that there was a false start. The output from that latch also clocks the 8 bit latch, which latches all the inputs from the blocks at the instant someone moved, and the appropriate LED will light up, showing who moved. The system is reset with a simple push-to-make switch.

COMMENTS

1. The student has presented a clear account of the requirements.
2. He has presented three alternative solutions with the advantages and disadvantages clearly stated.
3. He has stated the chosen solution clearly and developed the circuitry to the point where it could be constructed.
4. He has shown that he understands how the device will work and how it will be used.

Questions

How might it be possible to 'fool' this false start alarm?

C

EXAMPLE 3

A manufacturer of hinges for kitchen cupboards needs to test new designs of hinge. It is planned that the types of hinges are fitted to a standard size cupboard which has an arrangement for opening the door (moving through an angle of 90°) and then closing after a short delay. This cycle is repeated regularly and the number of cycles recorded. Design such a test arrangement for the hinges.

Oxford Local Examinations Summer 1983 Technology Paper 2
Time allowed 2 hours

Question 2

Hinge Tester

a) Specification
   i) Must be able to accommodate different shapes and designs of hinge.
   ii) Must move the hinge through 90°
   iii) Between each movement of 90° a pause must be made
   iv) The motion has to be repeated uniformly
   v) The loading or stress put on the hinge must be similar to the real life situation of the door
   vi) The number of cycles needs to be recorded

b) For design purposes an arbitrary size hinge is taken for use in formulating ideas — the fact that the same size and type of hinge is used throughout does not mean that thought and facilities for smaller or different shaped hinges have not been made.

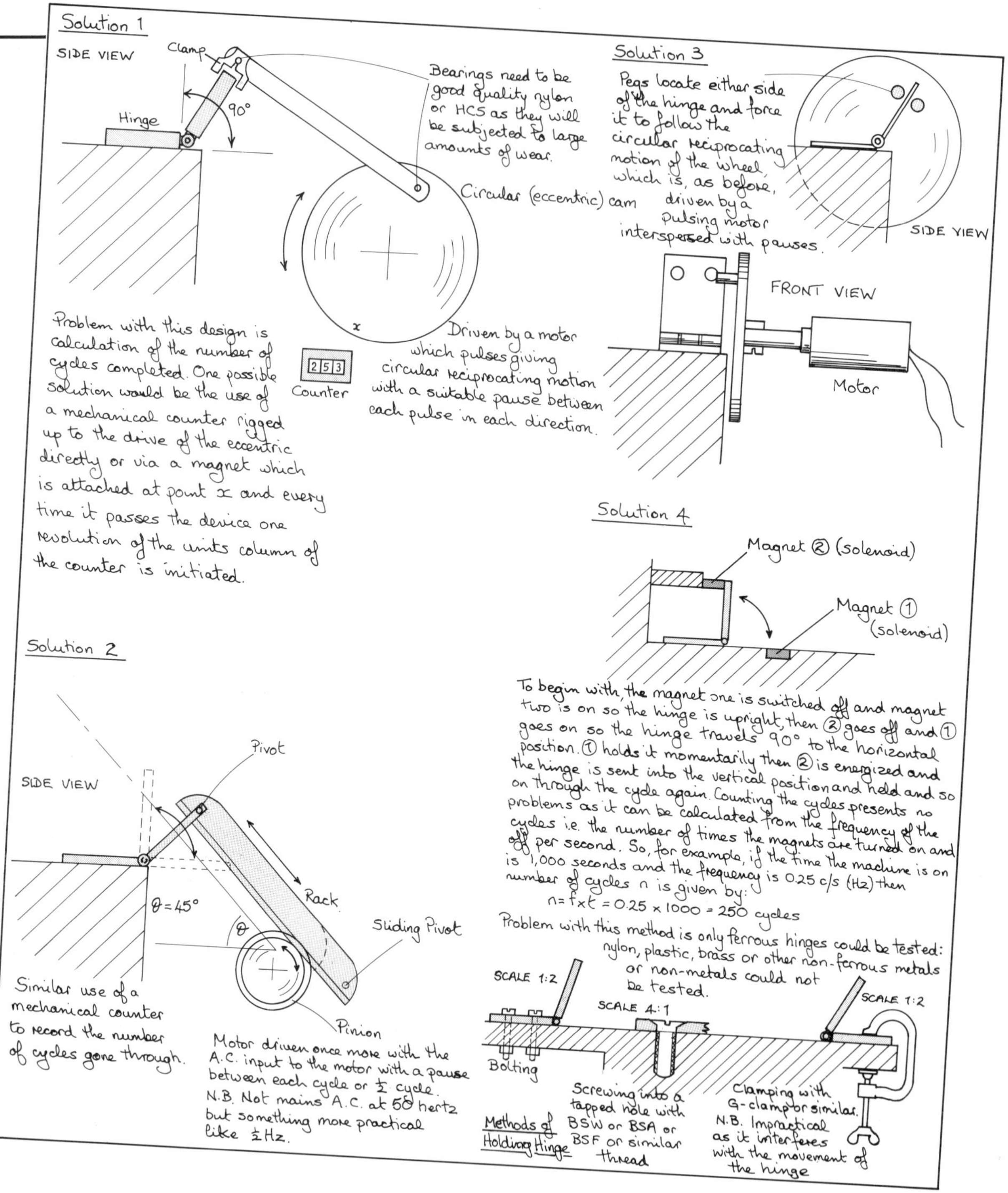

Solution 1

SIDE VIEW

Clamp

Hinge

90°

Bearings need to be good quality nylon or HCS as they will be subjected to large amounts of wear.

Circular (eccentric) cam

Problem with this design is calculation of the number of cycles completed. One possible solution would be the use of a mechanical counter rigged up to the drive of the eccentric directly or via a magnet which is attached at point x and every time it passes the device one revolution of the units column of the counter is initiated.

Counter

Driven by a motor which pulses giving circular reciprocating motion with a suitable pause between each pulse in each direction.

Solution 3

Pegs locate either side of the hinge and force it to follow the circular reciprocating motion of the wheel, which is, as before, driven by a pulsing motor interspersed with pauses.

SIDE VIEW

FRONT VIEW

Motor

Solution 2

SIDE VIEW

Pivot

Rack

θ = 45°

θ

Sliding Pivot

Pinion

Similar use of a mechanical counter to record the number of cycles gone through.

Motor driven once more with the A.C. input to the motor with a pause between each cycle or ½ cycle. N.B. Not mains A.C. at 50 hertz but something more practical like ½ Hz.

Solution 4

Magnet ② (solenoid)

Magnet ① (solenoid)

To begin with the magnet one is switched off and magnet two is on so the hinge is upright, then ② goes off and ① goes on so the hinge travels 90° to the horizontal position. ① holds it momentarily then ② is energized and the hinge is sent into the vertical position and held and so on through the cycle again. Counting the cycles presents no problems as it can be calculated from the frequency of the cycles ie. the number of times the magnets are turned on and off per second. So, for example, if the time the machine is on is 1,000 seconds and the frequency is 0.25 c/s (Hz) then number of cycles n is given by:

$$n = f \times t = 0.25 \times 1000 = 250 \text{ cycles}$$

Problem with this method is only ferrous hinges could be tested; nylon, plastic, brass or other non-ferrous metals or non-metals could not be tested.

SCALE 1:2

SCALE 4:1

SCALE 1:2

Bolting

Screwing into a tapped hole with BSW or BSA or BSF or similar thread

Clamping with G-clamp or similar. N.B. Impractical as it interferes with the movement of the hinge

Methods of Holding Hinge

EXAMPLE 3

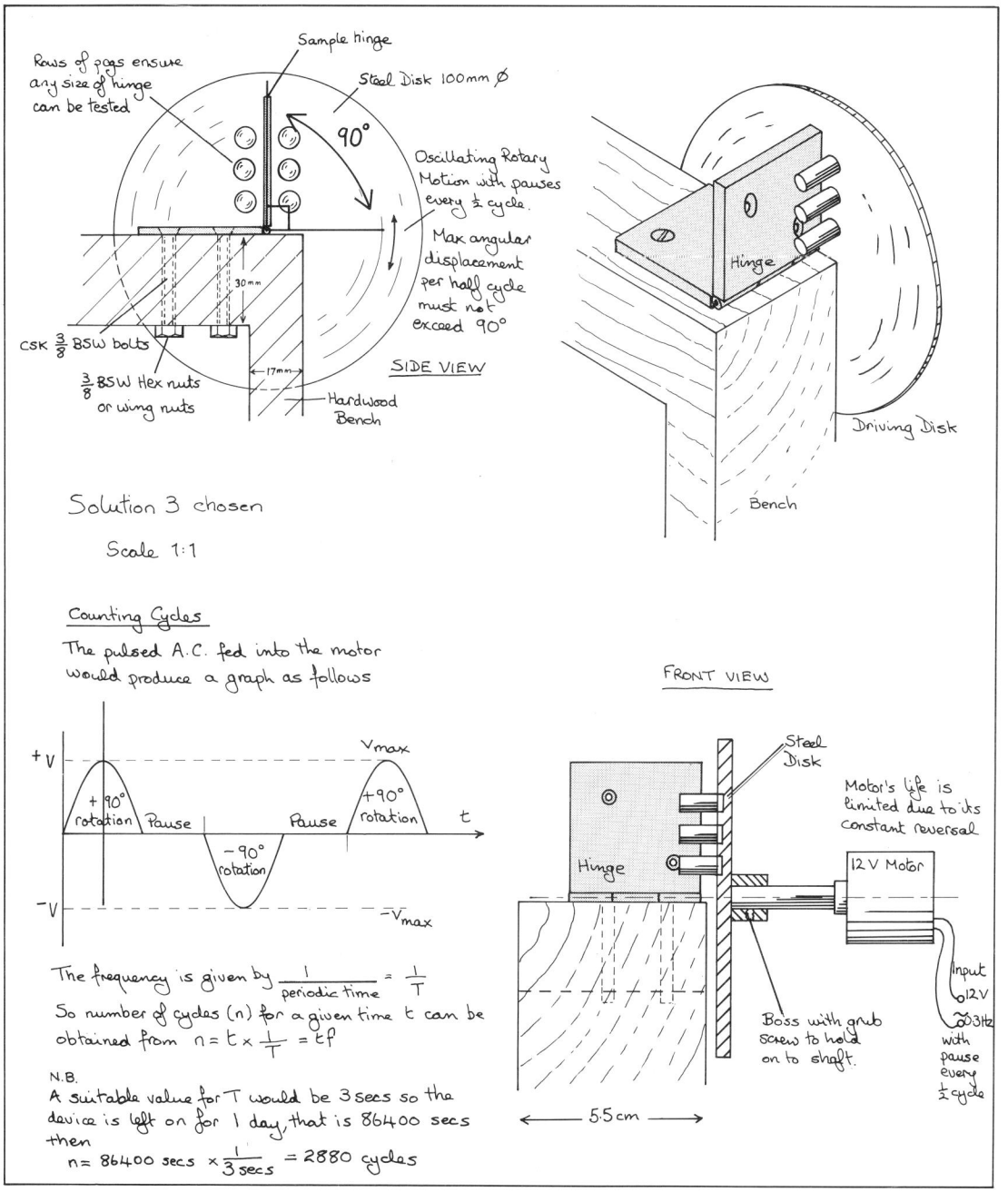

Rows of pegs ensure any size of hinge can be tested

Sample hinge

Steel Disk 100mm ∅

90°

Oscillating Rotary Motion with pauses every ½ cycle.

Max angular displacement per half cycle must not exceed 90°

30mm

CSK ⅜ BSW bolts

⅜ BSW Hex nuts or wing nuts

17mm

Hardwood Bench

SIDE VIEW

Hinge

Driving Disk

Bench

Solution 3 chosen

Scale 1:1

Counting Cycles

The pulsed A.C. fed into the motor would produce a graph as follows

FRONT VIEW

+V

Vmax

+90° rotation | Pause | Pause | +90° rotation

t

−90° rotation

−V

−Vmax

The frequency is given by $\dfrac{1}{\text{periodic time}} = \dfrac{1}{T}$

So number of cycles (n) for a given time t can be obtained from $n = t \times \dfrac{1}{T} = tf$

N.B.
A suitable value for T would be 3 secs so the device is left on for 1 day, that is 86400 secs then
$n = 86400 \text{ secs} \times \dfrac{1}{3 \text{ secs}} = 2880 \text{ cycles}$

Steel Disk

Hinge

Motor's life is limited due to its constant reversal

12 V Motor

Input 12V 0.3Hz with pause every ½ cycle

Boss with grub screw to hold on to shaft.

← 5.5cm →

COMMENTS

1. The student has stated the requirements clearly.
2. She has presented four alternative solutions with notes.
3. The chosen solution is clearly presented; dimensions, materials and fixings are noted.
4. The student has shown how the recording of cycles is linked to the total time the machine is running.

Questions

1 Has the student explained her choice of final solution? What reasons would you give?   C

2 Where does her solution depart from the requirements of the question?   C

3 Why would solution 4 be unlikely to work even for steel hinges?   C

4 How would you provide a 12 V 0.3 Hz a.c. current with a pause as required by the final solution? What advantage is there in having the frequency of the current adjustable?   C

5 What will happen when a hinge breaks?   C

EXAMPLE 4

Small pull-along toys are popular with pre-school age children. Design two toys of this type which would be suitable for use in a playgroup. One toy must have a visible oscillating-component and the other must incorporate a sound effect. Each toy must be related to an animal or an insect.

Oxford Local Examination Summer 1983
Craft Design and Technology Paper 2
Time allowed 2 × 2½ hours

DESIGN ANALYSIS

QUESTION TWO

THE TOY IS TO BE DESIGNED FOR PRE-SCHOOL AGE CHILDREN WHO WILL TEND TO BITE, CHEW, THROW AND BANG, AS WELL AS PULL THE TOY ALONG. THUS THE TOY NEEDS TO BE VERY DURABLE, AND THERE MUST BE NO SHARP EDGES OR TOXIC MATERIALS USED. ANY OSCILLATING PART MUST BE APPROACHED WITH SAFETY IN MIND AND SHOULD NOT BE MADE SO AS A CHILD COULD GET HIS/HER FINGER OR TONGUE CAUGHT THE SOUND-EFFECT, IF RELATED TO THE ANIMAL WILL HELP THE CHILD IN RECOGNITION ie SHEEP AND A 'BAA' NOISE. SO EVERY ATTEMPT SHOULD BE MADE TO OBTAIN THIS. THE TOY MUST ALSO BE MADE CLEANABLE, FOR HYGIENE REASONS AND IF BATTERIES ARE USED IN ANY WAY, THEY MUST BE PUT INTO A LOCKABLE COMPARTMENT. MEANS OF PULLING ALONG IS ALSO IMPORTANT AS CORD CAN BE EXTREMELY DANGEROUS.

SAFETY AND HYGIENE ARE ESSENTIAL

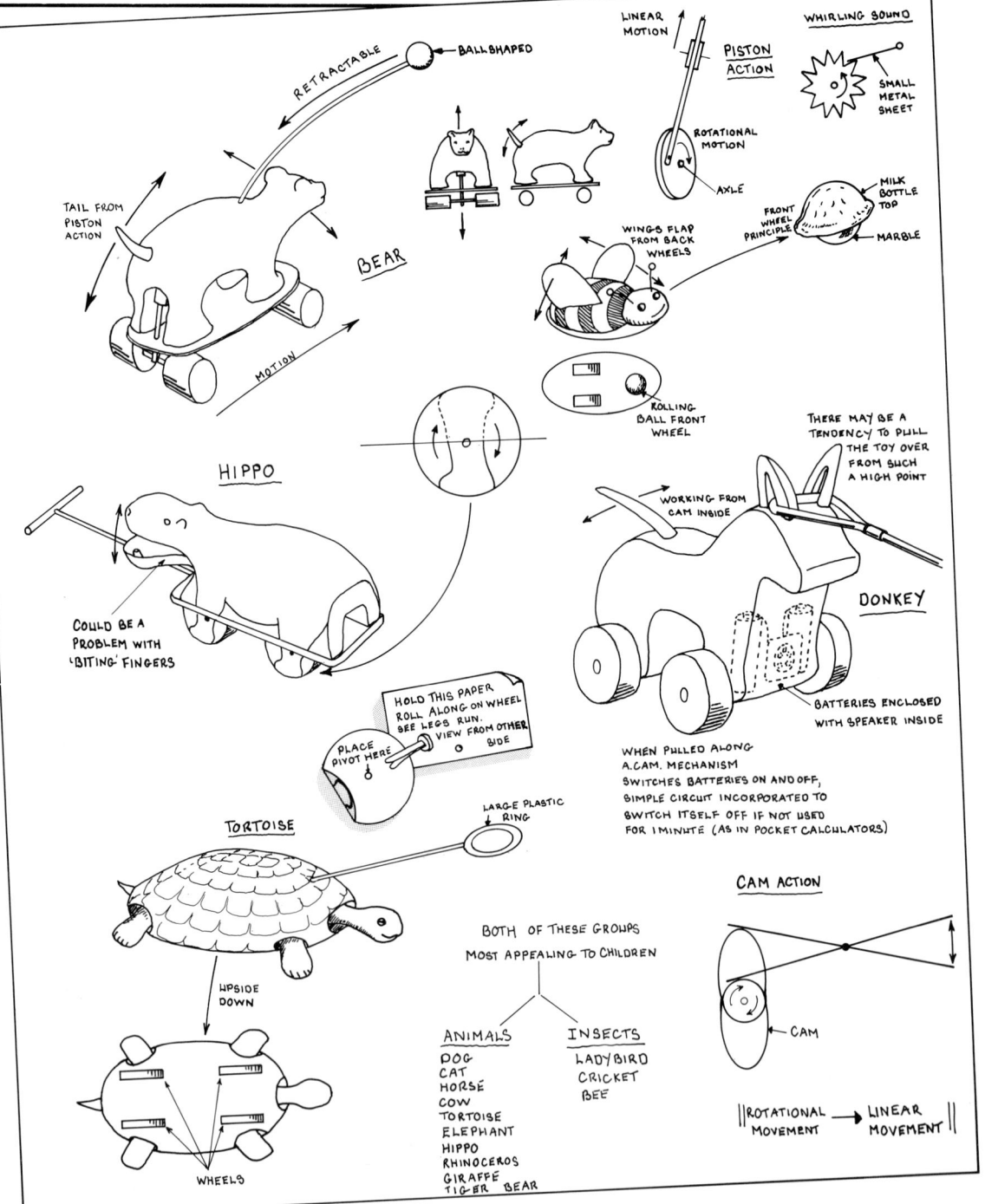

EXAMPLE 4

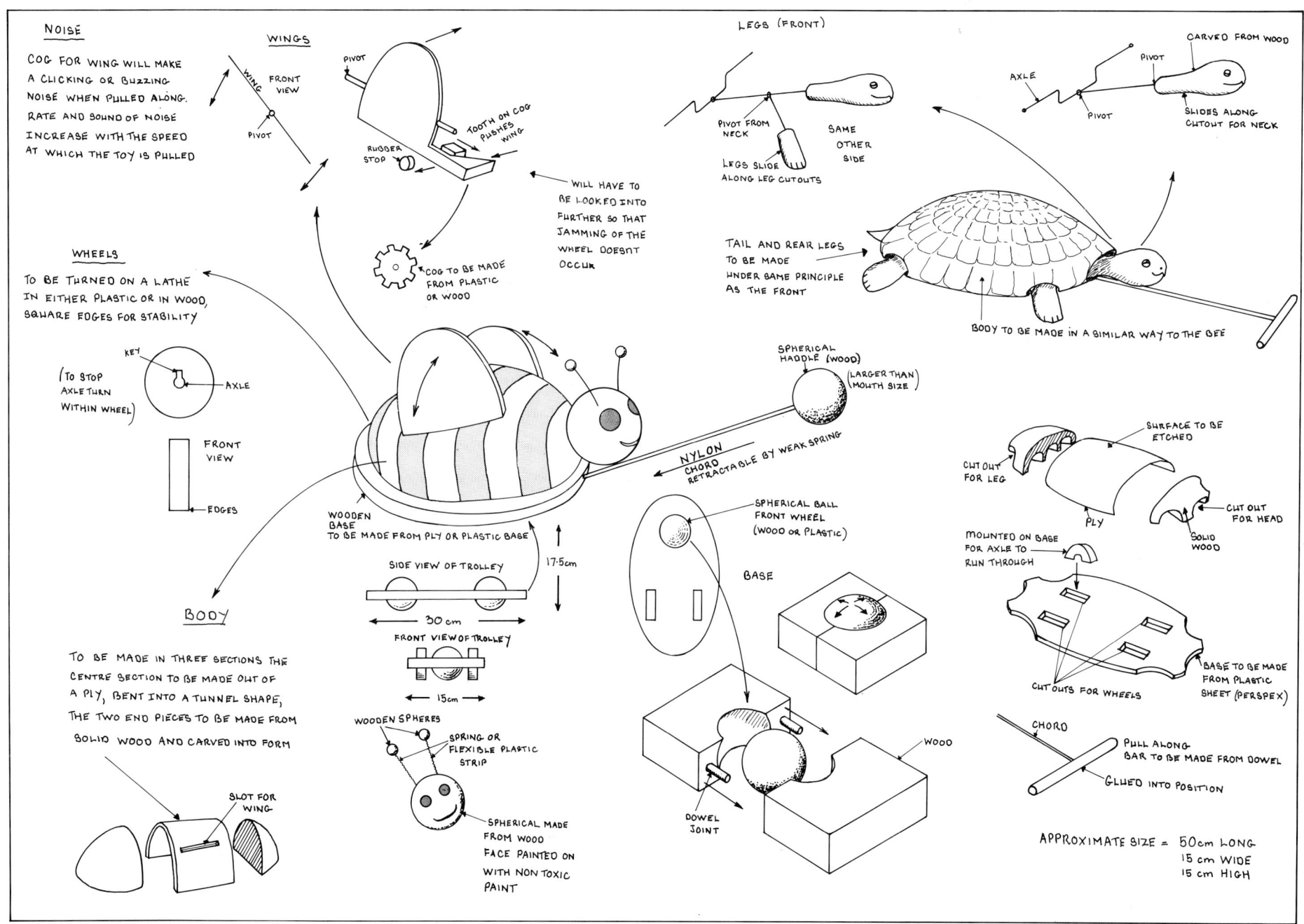

NOISE

COG FOR WING WILL MAKE A CLICKING OR BUZZING NOISE WHEN PULLED ALONG. RATE AND SOUND OF NOISE INCREASE WITH THE SPEED AT WHICH THE TOY IS PULLED

WINGS

FRONT VIEW

WING

PIVOT

PIVOT

RUBBER STOP

TOOTH ON COG PUSHES WING

WILL HAVE TO BE LOOKED INTO FURTHER SO THAT JAMMING OF THE WHEEL DOESN'T OCCUR

COG TO BE MADE FROM PLASTIC OR WOOD

LEGS (FRONT)

PIVOT

AXLE

CARVED FROM WOOD

PIVOT

SLIDES ALONG CUTOUT FOR NECK

PIVOT FROM NECK

SAME OTHER SIDE

LEGS SLIDE ALONG LEG CUTOUTS

TAIL AND REAR LEGS TO BE MADE UNDER SAME PRINCIPLE AS THE FRONT

BODY TO BE MADE IN A SIMILAR WAY TO THE BEE

WHEELS

TO BE TURNED ON A LATHE IN EITHER PLASTIC OR IN WOOD, SQUARE EDGES FOR STABILITY

KEY

AXLE

(TO STOP AXLE TURN WITHIN WHEEL)

FRONT VIEW

EDGES

BODY

TO BE MADE IN THREE SECTIONS THE CENTRE SECTION TO BE MADE OUT OF A PLY, BENT INTO A TUNNEL SHAPE, THE TWO END PIECES TO BE MADE FROM SOLID WOOD AND CARVED INTO FORM

SLOT FOR WING

WOODEN BASE TO BE MADE FROM PLY OR PLASTIC BASE

SIDE VIEW OF TROLLEY

30 cm

17.5 cm

FRONT VIEW OF TROLLEY

15 cm

WOODEN SPHERES

SPRING OR FLEXIBLE PLASTIC STRIP

SPHERICAL MADE FROM WOOD FACE PAINTED ON WITH NON TOXIC PAINT

SPHERICAL HADDLE (WOOD)

(LARGER THAN MOUTH SIZE)

NYLON CHORD RETRACTABLE BY WEAK SPRING

SPHERICAL BALL FRONT WHEEL (WOOD OR PLASTIC)

BASE

DOWEL JOINT

WOOD

SURFACE TO BE ETCHED

CUT OUT FOR LEG

PLY

CUT OUT FOR HEAD

SOLID WOOD

MOUNTED ON BASE FOR AXLE TO RUN THROUGH

CUT OUTS FOR WHEELS

BASE TO BE MADE FROM PLASTIC SHEET (PERSPEX)

CHORD

PULL ALONG BAR TO BE MADE FROM DOWEL

GLUED INTO POSITION

APPROXIMATE SIZE = 50 cm LONG
15 cm WIDE
15 cm HIGH

143

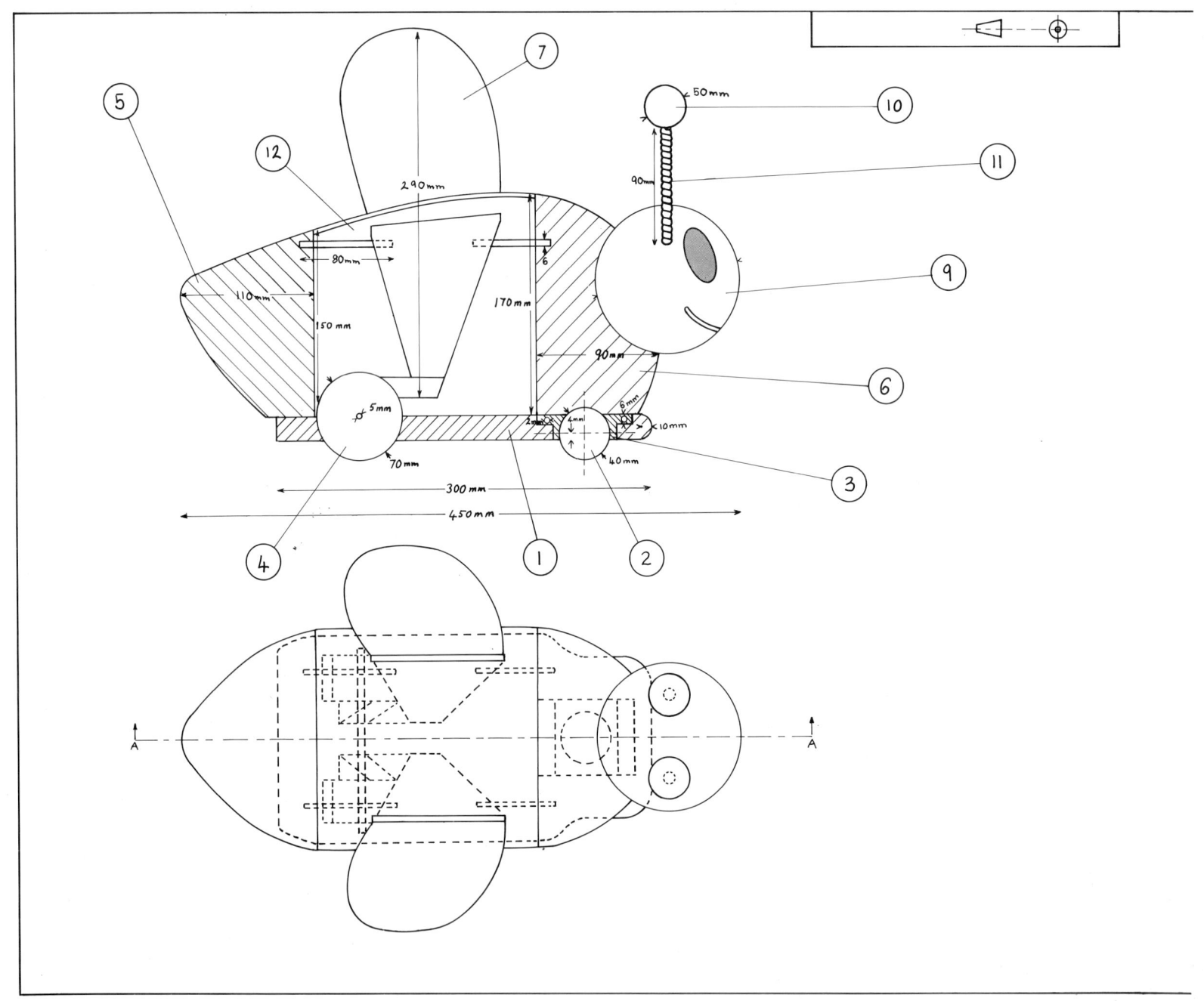

EXAMPLE 4

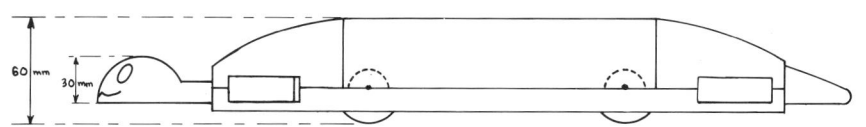

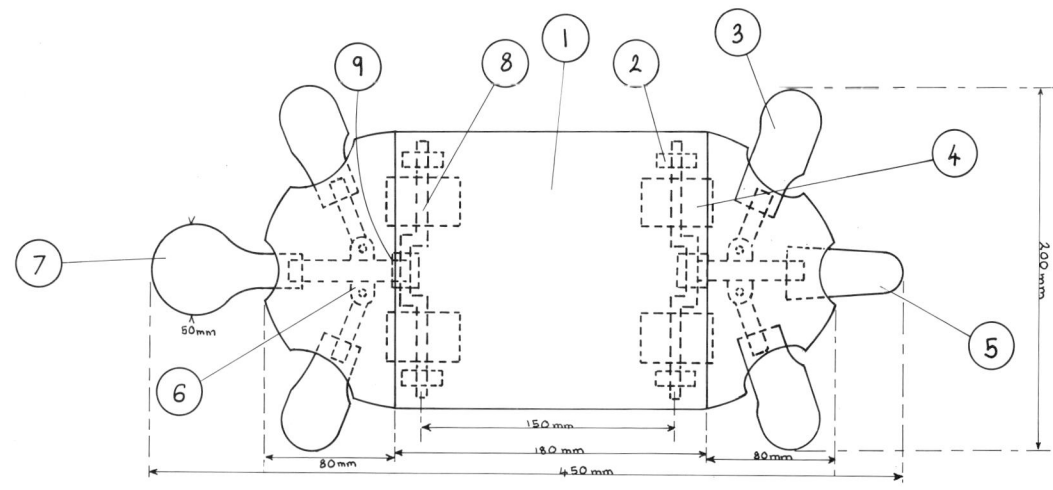

9	Pivot	Aluminium Alloy	2	Turned on a Lathe
8	Axle	Steel	2	Heated and Bent
7	Head	Ply Wood	1	Carved from Wood and Glued
6	Pivot	Aluminium Alloy	4	Made on a Lathe
5	Tail	Ply Wood	1	Hand Carved
4	Wheel	Hard Wood	4	Rounded Edges
3	Leg	Ply Wood	4	Hand Carved
2	Fixing for Axle	Hard Wood	4	Glued to Base
1	Main Body	Ply Wood	1	Same manufacture as 12
Bee	Bee	Bee	Bee	Bee
12	Main Body	Ply Wood	1	Same manufacture as one above
11	Antenna Spring	Plastic/Steel (90)	2	Close Compressed Spring
10	Antenna Top	Pine Wood (50mm³)	2	Carved from Square Block
9	Head	Pine Wood (120mm³)	1	Carved from Square Block
8	Pivot/Wing L/R	Dowel (80×6)	4	Glued into one end only
7	Wing L/R	Ply Wood (290×150)	2	Cut on Band Saw
6	Front Body	Solid Wood (90×170)	1	Carved by Hand
5	Rear Body	Solid Wood (110×150)	1	Carved by Hand
4	Rear Wheel	Plastic (35×10)	2	Turned on Lathe
3	Bearing Case	Wood (80²×20)	1	Bush may have to be inset
2	Front Bearing	Steel/Plastic (40)	1	Must be polished
1	Base	Wood/Plastic (300×20)	1	Flat Sheet
Part No.	Name of Part	Material l.w.d.	No. off	Comments

PARTS LIST

SCALE 1:2   Dimensions in mm.

COMMENTS

1. The student has given a careful analysis of the main requirements.

2. Several alternative forms and mechanisms are presented with supporting notes.

3. Two forms and their mechanisms are developed in greater detail.

4. Throughout, the diagrams are simple yet communicate clearly.

5. Neat working drawings with parts and materials lists are presented.

Questions

1 How robust is the mechanism in the tortoise? If it breaks, how easy will it be to repair?   c

2 Do the materials chosen for the tortoise meet the requirements for strength, safety and hygiene?   c

3 Is the wing beating mechanism on the bee clearly shown? Draw your own improved version.   c

4 How heavy do you think the bee is? What problems might this cause?   c

EXAMPLE 5

Table tennis is a popular club activity with many clubs entering local leagues. Design a device which will project table-tennis balls to give a player repetitive stroke practice. When in use the device is to be positioned at the end of the table opposite the player and operated by the coach.

Oxford Local Examinations Summer 1983
Craft, Design and Technology Paper 2
Time allowed $2 \times 2\frac{1}{2}$ hours

DESIGN BRIEF

QU. No 1

MATERIALS:- WOOD: HARD WOODS SAVE WEAR
BEECH, OAK, TEAK, MAHOGANY
METAL: ALUMINIUM — LIGHT, EASILY WORKED — DIFFICULT TO JOIN
E.G. BRAZING, WELDING — HOLDS FINISH WELL IN
INDOOR USE, NON-CORROSIVE.
BRASS — NON-CORROSIVE, GOOD FINISH, EASILY WORKED
AND JOINED — SILVER SOLDERING.
STEEL — STRONG, CORROSIVE, EASILY JOINED, HARDER TO
WORK THAN BRASS OR ALUMINIUM.
PLASTICS: ACRYLIC — GOOD FINISH, MODERATE STRENGTH, LIGHT,
NON-CORROSIVE, EASILY JOINED AND MOULDED.
FIBREGLASS: EASILY WORKED AND SHAPED, VERY VERSATILE IN
ALL ASPECTS.

BALLS MUST SHOOT OUT OF DEVICE .: GULLEY/CHUTE TO PROJECT BALLS IN
DESIRED DIRECTION SO MOVEMENT OF GULLEY IS NECESSARY. THIS COULD BE
RESTRICTED TO AREA OVER NET i.e. 45° ARC OF MOVEMENT.
MEANS OF PROJECTION:- SIMILAR TO TRIGGER OF GUN INCORPORATING SPRING
IN DEVICE.
:- SIMPLE HAND SLAPPING DEVICE WHEREBY BALL
PROJECTED ALONG CHUTE/GULLEY.
:- USE OF ELASTIC OR RUBBER BANDS TO SHOOT BALL OUT.
DEVICE MUST HOLD SEVERAL BALLS, SO NOT HAVING TO KEEP RELOADING EACH TIME,
BUT ALSO MUST BE EASILY RELOADED WHEN NECESSARY.
MUST HAVE CONTROL OF BALL, i.e. PROJECTION STRENGTH SO AS NOT TO OVERSHOOT
TABLE OTHER SIDE OF NET BUT MUST NOT HIT NET WHEN FIRED.
IN NORMAL SERVE BALL BOUNCES ON BOTH SIDES OF NET BEFORE IT CAN BE
RETURNED. TO ACHIEVE THIS IN A MECHANISED PROJECTION DEVICE WOULD BE
DIFFICULT AND HARD TO CONTROL DUE TO STRENGTH OF BALL PROJECTION.
THE WEIGHT OF THE BALL MAY CREATE A PROBLEM DUE TO ITS LIGHTNESS, AND
THE STRENGTH OF PROJECTION MUST BE SUITED ACCORDINGLY.
TO ACHIEVE THIS STRENGTH A SYSTEM OF MAXIMUM AND MINIMUM POINTS
MUST BE ESTABLISHED WHERE THE BALL WILL EITHER JUST DROP OVER
THE NET OR JUST BOUNCE ON THE FAR EDGE OF THE TABLE. THESE
POINTS WOULD PROBABLY BE FOUND BY TRIAL AND ERROR WHEN DEVICE
IS IN USE. DISTANCE OF PROJECTION ON A FULL SIZE 9' x 5' TABLE
WOULD VARY BETWEEN 5' AND 9' FROM ONE EDGE OF THE TABLE.

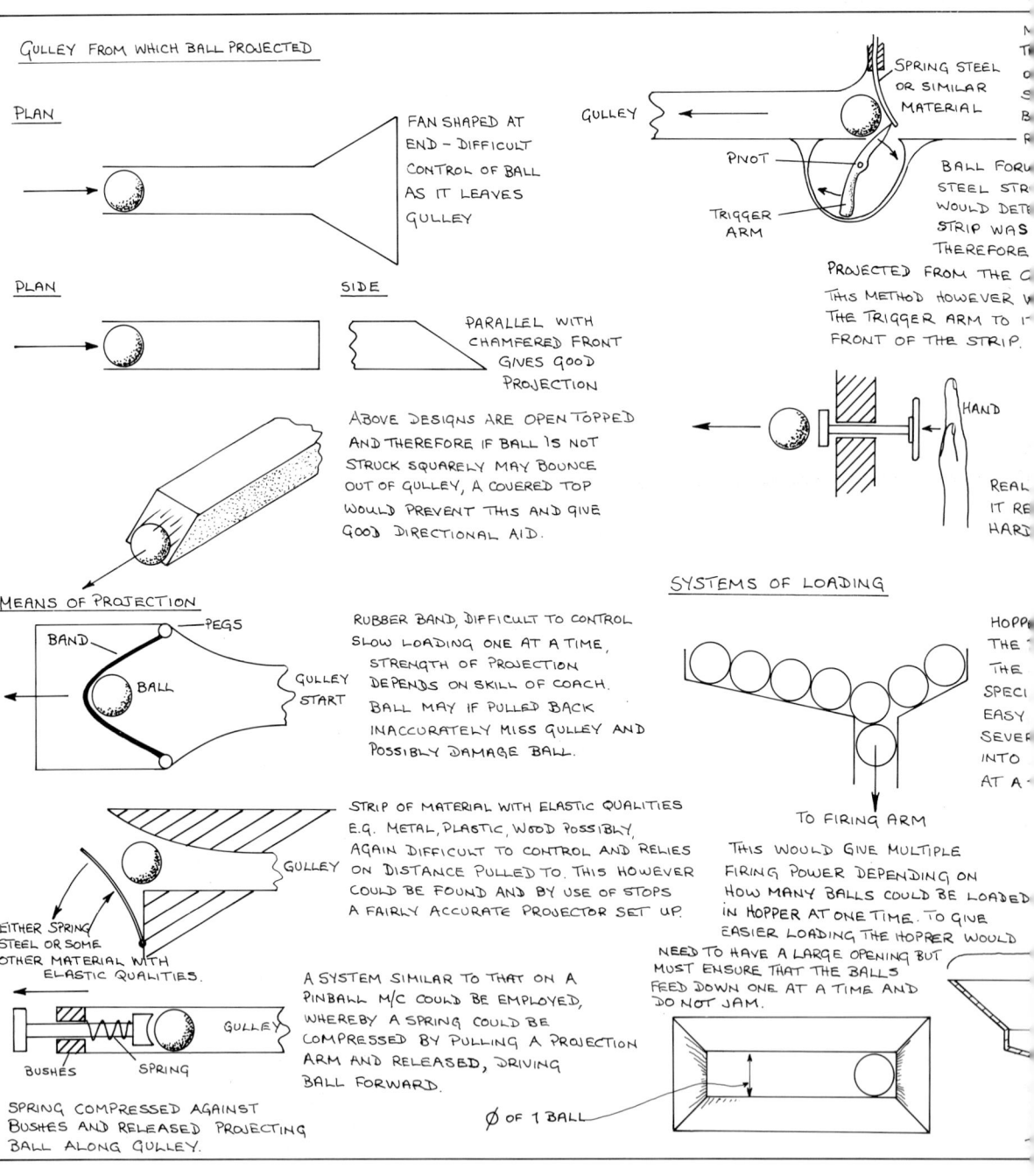

GULLEY FROM WHICH BALL PROJECTED

PLAN

FAN SHAPED AT
END — DIFFICULT
CONTROL OF BALL
AS IT LEAVES
GULLEY

PLAN   SIDE

PARALLEL WITH
CHAMFERED FRONT
GIVES GOOD
PROJECTION

ABOVE DESIGNS ARE OPEN TOPPED
AND THEREFORE IF BALL IS NOT
STRUCK SQUARELY MAY BOUNCE
OUT OF GULLEY, A COVERED TOP
WOULD PREVENT THIS AND GIVE
GOOD DIRECTIONAL AID.

MEANS OF PROJECTION

BAND   PEGS
BALL   GULLEY START

RUBBER BAND, DIFFICULT TO CONTROL
SLOW LOADING ONE AT A TIME,
STRENGTH OF PROJECTION
DEPENDS ON SKILL OF COACH.
BALL MAY IF PULLED BACK
INACCURATELY MISS GULLEY AND
POSSIBLY DAMAGE BALL.

GULLEY

EITHER SPRING
STEEL OR SOME
OTHER MATERIAL WITH
ELASTIC QUALITIES.

STRIP OF MATERIAL WITH ELASTIC QUALITIES
E.G. METAL, PLASTIC, WOOD POSSIBLY.
AGAIN DIFFICULT TO CONTROL AND RELIES
ON DISTANCE PULLED TO. THIS HOWEVER
COULD BE FOUND AND BY USE OF STOPS
A FAIRLY ACCURATE PROJECTOR SET UP.

BUSHES   SPRING   GULLEY

SPRING COMPRESSED AGAINST
BUSHES AND RELEASED PROJECTING
BALL ALONG GULLEY.

A SYSTEM SIMILAR TO THAT ON A
PINBALL M/C COULD BE EMPLOYED,
WHEREBY A SPRING COULD BE
COMPRESSED BY PULLING A PROJECTION
ARM AND RELEASED, DRIVING
BALL FORWARD.

Ø OF 1 BALL

SPRING STEEL
OR SIMILAR
MATERIAL

GULLEY
PINOT
TRIGGER ARM

BALL FOR[...]
STEEL STR[...]
WOULD DET[...]
STRIP WAS [...]
THEREFORE [...]
PROJECTED FROM THE [...]
THIS METHOD HOWEVER [...]
THE TRIGGER ARM TO I[...]
FRONT OF THE STRIP.

HAND

REAL[...]
IT RE[...]
HARD[...]

SYSTEMS OF LOADING

TO FIRING ARM

THIS WOULD GIVE MULTIPLE
FIRING POWER DEPENDING ON
HOW MANY BALLS COULD BE LOADED
IN HOPPER AT ONE TIME. TO GIVE
EASIER LOADING THE HOPPER WOULD

NEED TO HAVE A LARGE OPENING BUT
MUST ENSURE THAT THE BALLS
FEED DOWN ONE AT A TIME AND
DO NOT JAM.

HOPP[...]
THE [...]
THE [...]
SPECI[...]
EASY [...]
SEVER[...]
INTO [...]
AT A [...]

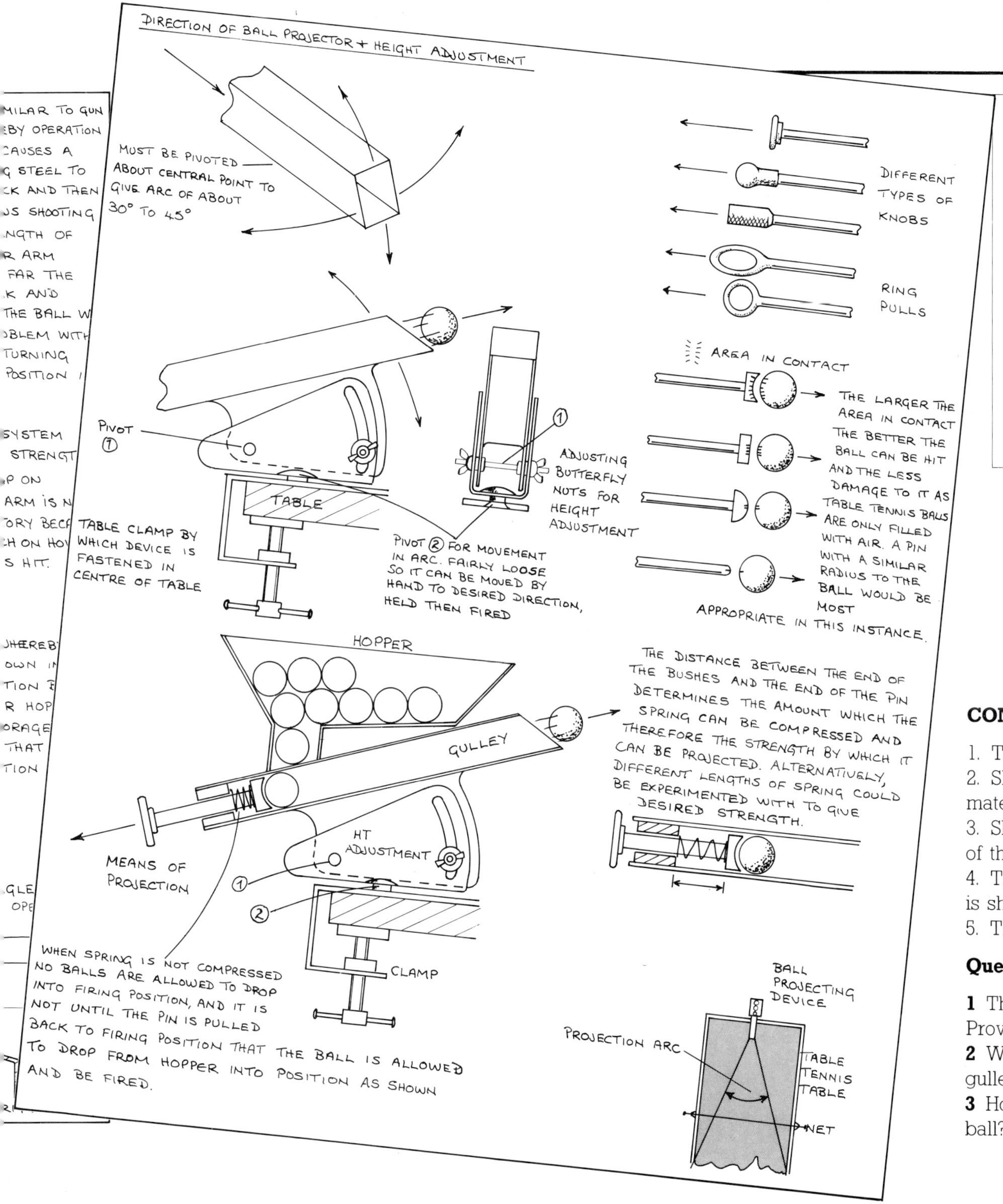

EXAMPLE 5

DIRECTION OF BALL PROJECTOR + HEIGHT ADJUSTMENT

MUST BE PIVOTED ABOUT CENTRAL POINT TO GIVE ARC OF ABOUT 30° TO 45°

PIVOT ①

TABLE

TABLE CLAMP BY WHICH DEVICE IS FASTENED IN CENTRE OF TABLE

ADJUSTING BUTTERFLY NUTS FOR HEIGHT ADJUSTMENT

PIVOT ② FOR MOVEMENT IN ARC. FAIRLY LOOSE SO IT CAN BE MOVED BY HAND TO DESIRED DIRECTION, HELD THEN FIRED

DIFFERENT TYPES OF KNOBS

RING PULLS

AREA IN CONTACT

THE LARGER THE AREA IN CONTACT THE BETTER THE BALL CAN BE HIT AND THE LESS DAMAGE TO IT AS TABLE TENNIS BALLS ARE ONLY FILLED WITH AIR. A PIN WITH A SIMILAR RADIUS TO THE BALL WOULD BE MOST APPROPRIATE IN THIS INSTANCE.

HOPPER

GULLEY

MEANS OF PROJECTION

HT ADJUSTMENT ① ②

CLAMP

THE DISTANCE BETWEEN THE END OF THE BUSHES AND THE END OF THE PIN DETERMINES THE AMOUNT WHICH THE SPRING CAN BE COMPRESSED AND THEREFORE THE STRENGTH BY WHICH IT CAN BE PROJECTED. ALTERNATIVELY, DIFFERENT LENGTHS OF SPRING COULD BE EXPERIMENTED WITH TO GIVE DESIRED STRENGTH.

WHEN SPRING IS NOT COMPRESSED NO BALLS ARE ALLOWED TO DROP INTO FIRING POSITION, AND IT IS NOT UNTIL THE PIN IS PULLED BACK TO FIRING POSITION THAT THE BALL IS ALLOWED TO DROP FROM HOPPER INTO POSITION AS SHOWN AND BE FIRED.

BALL PROJECTING DEVICE

PROJECTION ARC

TABLE TENNIS TABLE

NET

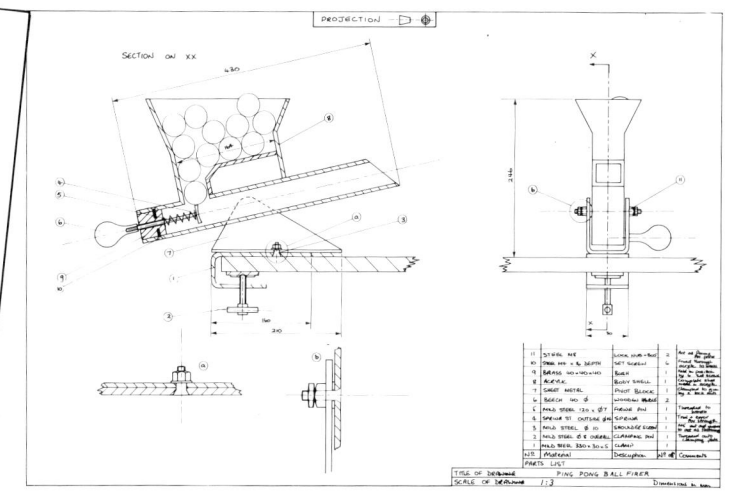

COMMENTS

1. The student has presented a clear analysis of the problem.
2. She has listed the advantages and disadvantages of a range of materials.
3. She has explored a range of alternatives for the different parts of the device.
4. The working drawing is neat and makes use of detail insets. (It is shown much larger on page 100.)
5. The parts list is clear; materials and dimensions are stated.

Questions

1 The construction to allow elevation of the device is not clear. Provide the missing details. **C**

2 What problems might arise in fabricating the entire hopper-gulley unit from acrylic sheet? **C**

3 How might the design be modified to produce top spin on the ball? Could this method be used to produce bottom spin? **C**

EXAMINATION QUESTIONS FOR PRACTICE

DESIGNING TOYS

1 You have been asked to design and make a puppet for use in a particular production being staged by the school's puppet theatre group. You have been given the following quotation from the script:

'This man-made monster shuffled towards me, bent and mis-shapen with arms like fins: it was as strange a thing as ever I saw.'

DESIGN A PUPPET WHICH PORTRAYS THIS DESCRIPTION. (The puppet should be designed for use in the puppet theatre shown in fig. 1. When realising your design, it may be scaled such that no overall dimension is greater than 300 mm.)

AEB Craftwork – Design, Communication and Application 1983

2 The fascination of 'executive toys' is often achieved by some simple movement and an element of surprise.

DESIGN AN 'EXECUTIVE TOY' USING A SINGLE MARBLE (Dia. 15 mm) FOR THIS PURPOSE.

The overall dimensions of the 'executive toy' must not exceed 200 mm × 200 mm × 200 mm.

AEB Craftwork – Design, Communication and Application 1984

3 Until babies are about six months old and able to sit up unsupported and play with toys, they tend to become very bored without something to attract their attention.

DESIGN A TOY WHICH, BY VIRTUE OF ITS MOVEMENT AND SHAPE, WILL INTEREST A BABY UNDER SIX MONTHS OF AGE. SAFETY IS AN ESSENTIAL CONSIDERATION.

AEB Craftwork – Design, Communication and Application 1984

4 Road safety is an important element in a child's education. Design a unit which will demonstrate the sequence of the traffic lights to young children.

NOTE: If an electrical solution is anticipated, mains electricity **must not** be used.

Oxford Local Examination Board: Craft, Design & Technology 1983

DESIGNING CONTROL DEVICES

5 In the manufacture of computer components, it is necessary to count small circuit boards as they pass down a production line. It

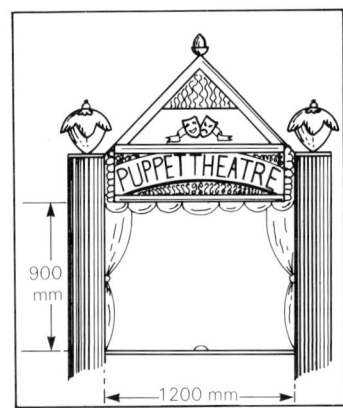

▲Fig. 1

is important that the components are not subjected to electric or magnetic fields at this stage of their construction. Design a system that will both count the components as they pass down the production line and also sound a short audible alarm when 1000 components have passed by.

Oxford Local Examination Board: Technology 1980

6 In a game of lightning chess the moves are made by each player in turn when a buzzer is sounded at regular time intervals. White makes the opening move when the buzzer sounds to start the game, a 10-second interval elapses and the buzzer sounds again whereupon Black replies; a further 10-second interval elapses before the buzzer sounds again and White makes a second move. Failure to move on the sound of the buzzer results in loss of the game.

Signal lamps to indicate which player is due to make the next move when the buzzer sounds and a display showing the number of moves made by each player are required.

Produce a complete design of a unit to be used with a chess set for playing lightning chess.

Oxford Local Examination Board: Technology 1982

7 The owner of an industrial engine used for emergency electricity production has to service the engine after every 200 hours running. There is a need for some means by which an accurate total of the number of hours run can be automatically recorded and displayed. Additionally, a warning of some sort should be given to the owner 10 hours before servicing is due. The engine has a 12 volt battery supply for starting purposes. Industrial fire regulations require the battery to be disconnected when the engine is left unattended. Design a solution to the owner's problems.

Oxford Local Examination Board: Technology 1983

8 Most types of plants normally kept in an unheated greenhouse can suffer damage by excessive heat and/or excessive cold. The greenhouse is often some distance from the home. A gardener requires some kind of warning in the home when the plants in the greenhouse are in danger.

DESIGN A WARNING DEVICE WHICH WILL OPERATE IN THE HOME WHEN THE GREENHOUSE TEMPERATURE FALLS BELOW 4°C OR RISES ABOVE 25°C.

AEB Craftwork – Design, Communication and Application 1984

DESIGNING DISPLAYS

9 A police station communications room needs a visual display to show the location of each of its patrol cars, senior officers, foot patrolmen, reported accidents and other reported incidents. The communications room has two operators and a supervisor who also have to receive and transmit messages for their patrols and take emergency calls from the general public. The supervisor has to make decisions based on the information available.

A display panel is needed to present clearly all this information.

(a) Fully analyse this problem.

(b) Sketch and explain a suitable design.

SUJB Technology 1983

10 A group of 100 adults is due to attend a conference about the protection of wild animals throughout the world. The conference organisers plan to print the name of each person attending on a card such as that shown in fig. 2.

DESIGN A HOLDER FOR THE NAME CARDS WHICH IS EASILY FASTENED TO THE CLOTHING AND MAY BE RE-USED BY OTHERS ATTENDING FUTURE CONFERENCES ON THE SAME SUBJECT. THE HOLDER SHOULD ALSO INCORPORATE A LOGO WHICH DEPICTS THE CONFERENCE THEME.

AEB Craftwork – Design, Communication and Application 1984

DESIGNING MECHANISMS AND MACHINES

11 Design a machine that could be used to exercise the leg muscles of a hospital patient who has to be in bed for many months. The machine should automatically count the number of movements or revolutions made and allow for the pushing force made by the patient to be varied.

Oxford Local Examination Board: Technology 1980

12 A school collects waste aluminium foil in order to recycle it for castings made in the school workshop. In order to keep oxidation to a minimum, it has been found necessary to compress the foil into suitable small blocks. Design a device that will make such blocks of uniform shape with ease and rapidity.

Oxford Local Examination Board: Technology 1980

13 On a golf course the holes on the greens are renewed in different positions each day to avoid uneven wear. The preparation of a hole involves the careful removal of a cylindrical piece of turf 108 mm in diameter and 150 mm deep. This must be done in such a way that no damage is caused to the grass surrounding the hole.

Design an implement for making such holes conveniently and quickly.

Oxford Local Examination Board: Technology 1982

14 In the diagram (fig. 3) of the trailer chassis a hand-operated braking system is required for safe parking when the load (not shown) is being loaded or unloaded, with the trailer not attached to any vehicle.

The two wheel hubs contain drum brakes which are operated when the two M12 studs are pulled in the direction of the arrows (inwards). The lever at Y is to be used as the initiator of this pulling force.

(i) Design a system which will activate the drum brakes by movement on the lever at Y.

(ii) Incorporate a method of restraining the handle/lever when the brakes are in the 'on' position.

(iii) Design a suitable body which will serve the needs of a jobbing builder.

Cambridge University Examination Board: Technology 1983

15 A simple machine is required to load lorries 2 metres high with loads up to a maximum weight of 20 000 newtons, and with a maximum efficiency of 50% so that the loads do not slip.

Design and explain a machine that meets this specification. Show all necessary calculations. *SUJB: Technology 1983*

16 Figure 4 shows a circular saw with an automatic feed table. It is required that saw speeds of 500, 1000 and 2000 rpm (revs/min) are available and that the table moves at 10 mm s^{-1}. Both will be driven by the same electric motor making 500 rpm.

Design, sketch and explain a solution to this problem showing all necessary calculations. *SUJB: Technology 1983*

17 A game of skittles is to be designed using a ping-pong ball as a projectile and skittles based on any oddments of suitable tubing available.

DESIGN (i) A DEVICE FOR PROJECTING A PING-PONG BALL (DIAMETER 35 mm) OVER A DISTANCE OF 2500 mm TO HIT THE SKITTLES AND KNOCK THEM OVER. THE DEVICE MUST BE CAPABLE OF BEING LOADED, COCKED, AIMED AND FIRED IN SEPARATE STAGES.

(ii) A SET OF NINE SKITTLES MADE FROM ODDMENTS OF TUBING.

AEB Craftwork – Design, Communication and Application 1983

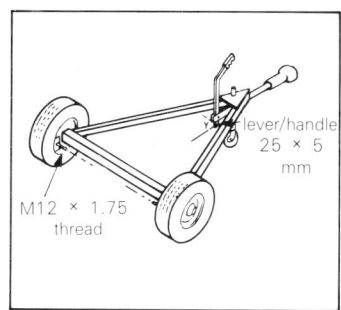

▲Fig. 3

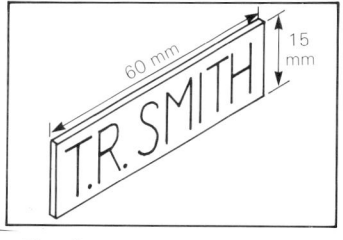

▲Fig. 2

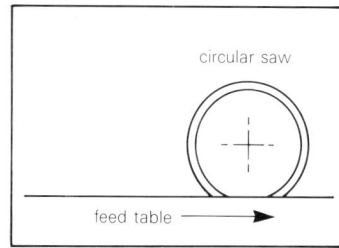

▲Fig. 4

18 Figure 5 shows the layout of a model car driven by an electric motor that makes 480 rev/min. The rear wheels of the car have a diameter of 20 mm. The motor is to drive the rear wheels and the car is to have a speed of about 20 mm/s. Design and sketch a method to do this, showing all necessary calculations. (Take π = 3.14)

SUJB: Technology 1984

▼Fig. 5

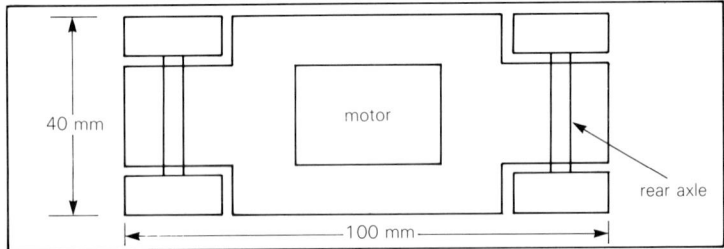

19 A telephone cable is to be pulled through an existing underground pipe, 100 m long, by means of a wire rope passed through the pipe. The greatest force required is 1000 N and is to be applied by a hand-operated machine at the end of the pipe. The operator can comfortably apply an effort of 100 N. Make a sketch showing the essential parts of a machine suitable for this purpose. Show all necessary calculations.

SUJB: Technology 1984

DESIGNING STRUCTURES

20 A young person who uses a bicycle for a newspaper delivery round finds it difficult to carry the newspapers with safety.

Design a lightweight bicycle-trailer to overcome this problem. The trailer should have a volume capacity of approximately 0.2 m^3 and be suitable for loads up to 40 kg. Show clearly in your design the method of attachment of the trailer to the bicycle.

Oxford Local Examination Board: Technology 1981

21 When camping, washing up presents problems. Design a unit which will hold a washing-up bowl. The unit should be adjustable in height and weigh as little as possible.

[Before the next examination session you must determine the dimensions of the washing-up bowl which is to form the basis of your design.]

Oxford Local Examination Board: Craft, Design and Technology 1983

22 A pupil wishes to make a number of basketball hoops from 15 mm diameter steel tube. The hoops are to be 450 mm in diameter. Design a suitable jig and other necessary apparatus that will allow a number of these items to be produced. In your analysis consider some of the problems which you would expect to encounter in making these items. Explain how the ends of the hoops could be joined together with strength and accuracy.

Cambridge University Examination Board: Technology 1983

23 You wish to convert a small bedroom at home into a workroom and office. You require a worktop that can be used as a desk, drawing board at various angles, and a sewing machine table, and be folded away when not in use.

Design, sketch and explain a solution to this problem taking account of:

(i) all forces in the structure   (ii) the materials use;
(iii) methods of joining;   (iv) safety and costs.

The maximum load required is 200 N.

SUJB: Technology 1983

24 Design a unit or fitment which can be fixed to the back of your bedroom door. It must include at least **five** storage compartments or shelves or hooks or a combination of these features.

NREB: Craft, Design and Technology 1984

25 Design a shelf which is strong enough to be used as a writing surface, and which can fold against the wall when not in use.

This item must be able to be fixed to a wall.

NREB: Craft, Design and Technology 1984

26 A painting contractor has obtained the contract for repainting the inside roof of a swimming pool, a cross section of which is shown in fig. 7.

Design, sketch and explain a suitable structure from which three men can carry out the work, paying particular attention to:

(i) all forces in the structure;
(ii) the materials use;
(iii) methods of joining;
(iv) safety and costs.

SUJB: Technology 1984

▼Fig. 6

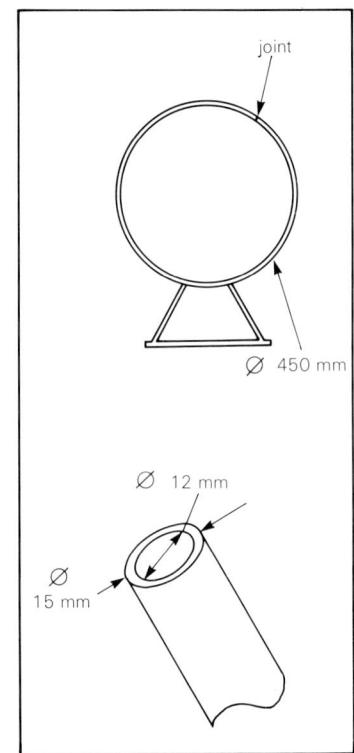

▼Fig. 7

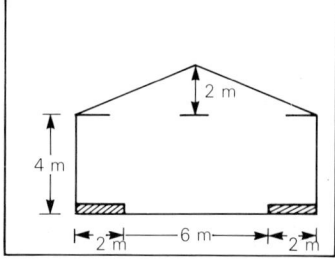

27 A footbridge is required to cross a busy dual-carriageway. The width of the road is 20 m and it is used by all types of vehicles, including large lorries.
(a) State fully the design factors to be considered when designing a bridge for this purpose.
(b) Sketch a solution to the problem paying attention to:
 (i) forces in the bridge;
 (ii) materials to be used;
 (iii) safety;
 (iv) dimensions;
 (v) costs.

SUJB: Technology 1984

DESIGNING CONTAINERS

28 A small vehicle, designed for use by children, is to be driven by an electric motor. The electricity will be supplied by two rechargeable accumulators containing acid. A method of mounting these accumulators safely is required, so that the acid would not be released in the event of an accident.
(a) Fully analyse this problem.
(b) Sketch and fully describe a solution to the problem, including the materials to be used.

SUJB: Technology 1983

29 DESIGN A COMPACT UNIT WHICH MAY BE USED FOR STORING AND CARRYING AROUND THE HOME A BASIC D.I.Y. TOOL KIT.

Provision must be made for all tools listed below, together with any other small items which you consider appropriate.

Tools	Maximum Dimensions (length, width and depth in mm)
Portable power drill	280 × 180 × 70
Hammer	300 × 120 × 30
Screwdriver	210 × 35 × 35
Bradawl	125 × 30 × 30
Combination pliers	150 × 45 × 10
Modelling knife	140 × 30 × 25
Tape measure	55 × 55 × 18

AEB Craft – Design, Communication and Application 1984

▼Fig. 9

▼Fig. 8

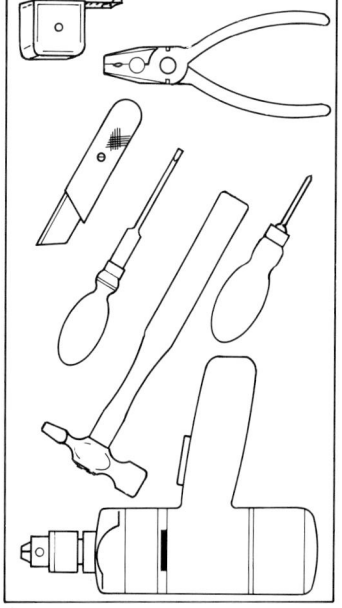

30 When wrapping a parcel it is often difficult to hold the paper in place whilst securing it with self-adhesive tape or string.
DESIGN A DISPENSER FOR THE SELF-ADHESIVE TAPE *AND* STRING, SHOWN IN FIG. 9, WHICH CAN BE OPERATED USING ONE HAND ONLY.

STRING
Height of ball = 40 mm
Maximum Diameter of ball = 50 mm
TAPE
Maximum Diameter of roll = 55 mm
Width of tape = 20 mm
Diameter of hole = 25 mm

AEB Craft – Design, Communication and Application 1983

DESIGNING TESTING DEVICES

31 Design a simple bench-mounted impact test device to measure the degree of hardness of case-hardened components. The impact load delivered should be constant and the indentation produced should be easily measurable.

Oxford Local Examination Board: Technology 1981

32 An audio service engineer needs to check the accuracy of the rotational speed of record playing decks. You are asked to design a device that will enable the engineer to accurately check the speed of the decks for two operational speeds: $33\frac{1}{3}$ and 45 r.p.m. It should be noted that different makes of deck vary slightly in size and constructional material.

Cambridge University Examinations Board: Technology 1983

33 A consumer research group are investigating the quality of ball-point pens. They are intending to test the pens in two ways: (a) by a continuous writing test and (b) to test the retractable types by a repeated press/depress cycle. In test (a) it is important to find out how long the ink/ball point lasts. In (b) the repeated operation of the spring-loaded mechanism must be counted until failure occurs. Design suitable devices that will effectively carry out each test for the group.

Cambridge University Examinations Board: Technology 1983

INDEX